KOREAN

AT A GLANCE

PHRASE BOOK AND DICTIONARY FOR TRAVELERS

Second Edition

by

DANIEL D. HOLT, M.A.
Education Consultant
Sacramento, California

GRACE MASSEY HOLT, M.A.
Education Consultant
Sacramento, California

WITH TRANSLATION ASSISTANCE BY
Wonkyung Hahm, M.A.
Busan, Korea

Chang-Ho Kim, Ph.D.
Busan University of Foreign Studies
Busan, Korea

D0125272

All inquiries should be addressed to:
Barron's Educational Series, Inc.
250 Wireless Boulevard
Hauppauge, NY 11788
www.barronseduc.com

ISBN-13: 978-0-7641-4212-3
ISBN-10: 0-7641-4212-7
Library of Congress Control Number 2009924486

Printed in China
9 8 7 6

CONTENTS

PREFACE

So you're taking a trip to one of the many fascinating countries of the world. That's exciting! This phrase book will prove an invaluable companion that will make your stay far more interesting.

This book is part of a series published by Barron's Educational Series, Inc. In these books we present the phrases and words that a traveler most often needs for a brief visit to a foreign country, where the customs and language are often different. Each of the phrase books highlights the terms particular to that country, in situations that the tourist is most likely to encounter. With a specially developed key to pronunciation, this book will enable you to communicate quickly and confidently in colloquial terms. It is intended not only for beginners with no knowledge of the language, but also for those who have already studied it and have some familiarity with it.

Some of the unique features and highlights of the Barron's series are:

■ Easy-to-follow *pronunciation keys* and complete phonetic transcriptions of all words and phrases in the book.

■ Compact *dictionary* of commonly used words and phrases—built right into the phrase book so there's no need to carry a separate dictionary.

■ Useful phrases for the *tourist*, grouped together by subject matter in a logical way so that the appropriate phrase is easy to locate when you need it.

■ Special phrases for the *business traveler*, including banking terms.

■ Comprehensive section on *food and drink*, with comprehensive food terms you will find on menus; these terms are often difficult or impossible to locate in dictionaries, but our section gives you a description of the preparation as well as a definition of what it is.

■ *Emergency phrases* and terms you hope you won't need: medical problems, theft or loss of valuables, replacement or repair of watches, cameras, and the like.

■ *Sightseeing itineraries*, shopping tips, practical travel tips to help you get off the beaten path and into the countryside, to the small towns and cities, and to the neighboring areas.

■ A *reference section* providing important signs, conversion tables, holidays, telling time, days of the week and months of the year.

■ A brief *grammar section*, with the basic elements of the language briefly explained.

Enjoy your vacation and travel with confidence. You have a friend by your side.

ACKNOWLEDGMENTS

We could not have written this book without the help of many people. Wonkyung Hahm and Chang-Ho Kim provided steadfast and reliable assistance by creating the Korean expressions and critiquing our descriptions of Korean culture. Their enduring kindness and generosity are deeply appreciated.

We are also grateful to the following individuals for their help: Song Que Hahn, Lecturer, Sacramento, California; Sang-Ho Lee, Professor, Chonnam National University, Korea; and staff of the Korea Tourism Organization, Los Angeles, California.

We greatly appreciate the support and direction that we received from Barron's staff. In particular, we wish to thank our editor, Dimitry Popow, for his clear-minded review of every detail of our work. Also, we owe a special debt of gratitude to Carol Akiyama and Nobuo Akiyama, authors of *Japanese at a Glance*. Their splendid work was a valuable model to consult as we wrote.

Finally, a word about Peace Corps and the Korean people. It was as Peace Corps volunteers that we first went to Korea to work as English teachers. We will be forever indebted to the people of Korea, whose patience and encouragement have helped us to develop our life-long interest in the Korean language and culture.

INTRODUCTION TO THE KOREAN LANGUAGE

Using Korean whenever possible will make your visit to Korea more enjoyable, and trying a few expressions indicates your willingness to get to know the people. Any use of the language is greatly appreciated by Koreans and warmly returned.

Korean is probably different from any other language you know. It is believed to belong to the Ural-Altaic language family along with Turkish, Mongolian, and Tungustic. It is the official language of North Korea and South Korea. Originally, Chinese characters were used for writing Korean. They are still used in combination with the Korean alphabet. Pronunciation of the characters, however, differs considerably from any of the Chinese dialects. During the reign of King Sejong (1418–1450), a phonetic alphabet called *Hangeul* was developed. Its invention was such a historical event in Korean culture that there is a special day, Hangeul Day, on October 9 celebrating the anniversary of its creation. The use of *Hangeul* has resulted in a dramatic increase in the number of people who can read and write Korean.

The culture of Korea is woven throughout its language. Korean reflects the thinking patterns of the Korean people, and using the language will help you better understand Koreans and their view of life.

QUICK PRONUNCIATION GUIDE

In 2000 the Korean Government established the Revised Romanization of Korean, an official system for using Roman letters to transcribe Korean. In Korea you will see this system used in such places as English newspapers and on buildings, street signs, and subway maps. In this book we use Korea's official system for all proper nouns and place names. However, to help you pronounce the words and phrases in this book, we use a phonetic transcription adapted from McCune-Reischauer, an international romanization system. Remember that romanization provides only approximations of the way Korean is actually spoken. There is no substitute for listening to and imitating Koreans as they use their language.

For each entry in this book, the English expression is followed by the Korean, and then the romanization.

Thank you.   감사합니다.   *Kam-sa-ham-ni-da.*

Spelling Conventions

Listed below are the vowels and consonants of *Hangeul*, the corresponding romanization used in this book, and examples of the sounds in English. Since corresponding sounds cannot always be found in English, some of these are approximations. Although your pronunciation may not be native-like at first, you will find that you will be understood by most Koreans.

VOWELS

Unlike English, Korean vowels are pure and distinct. When pronouncing them, you should take care to avoid running them together to form diphthongs.

Hangeul	Romanization	Pronunciation
아	a	father
야	ya	*Yom* Kippur
어	eo	Between the *u* in *u*gly and the *aw* in *aw*ful
여	yeo	be*yo*nd
오	o	*go*
요	yo	*yo*lk
우	u	*sue*
유	yu	*you*
으	eu	p*u*t
이	i	s*ee*n
애	ae	p*a*n
얘	yae	*ya*m
에	e	t*e*n
예	ye	*yes*
외	oe	*we*t
위	wi	*we*
의	eui	the reduced schwa sound produced by slurring the vowel sounds in "to eat" (t*a eat*)
와	wa	*wa*tt
왜	wae	*wea*r
워	weo	*wa*ll
웨	we	*we*t

CONSONANTS

Each of the Korean letters ㄱ, ㄷ, ㅂ, and ㅈ, is pronounced with the expulsion of more or less breath. At the beginning of a word, they require the greatest degree of aspiration (e.g., the *k* romanization of ㄱ below). In the middle of a word, less aspiration is required (e.g., the *g* romanization of ㄱ). When they occur in final position, pronounce them with their more aspirated sound, but as a stop, without releasing any air (e.g., boo*k*). These letters have counterparts which are intensely aspirated—indicated with an apostrophe (e.g., *k'*) and which are glottalized—represented with double letters (e.g., *kk*).

ㄱ	*k*	Between the *k* in *k*iss and the *g* in *g*uide.
	g	*g*uide
ㄴ	*n*	*n*o
ㄷ	*t*	Between the *t* in *t*o and the *d* in *d*o.
	d	*d*o
ㄹ	*r*	Close to the sound of *t* in the American English pronunciation of wa*t*er, a soft *d*.
	l	i*ll*
ㅁ	*m*	*m*oney
ㅂ	*p*	Between the *p* in *p*uff and the *b* in *b*oon.
	b	*b*oon
ㅅ	*s*	Like the *s* in *s*igh, but with a very light tongue.
ㅇ	—	In an initial position, this letter is silent. In final position, it sounds like the *ng* in ri*ng*.
	ng	
ㅈ	*ch*	Between the *ch* in *ch*urch and the *j* in *j*ump.

	j	*j*ump
ㅊ	*ch'*	*ch*urch
ㅋ	*k'*	*k*ite
ㅌ	*t'*	*t*o
ㅍ	*p'*	*p*uff
ㅎ	*h*	*h*ot
ㄲ	*kk*	s*ch*ool
ㄸ	*tt*	s*t*eep
ㅃ	*pp*	s*p*ort
ㅆ	*ss*	*s*eed
ㅉ	*jj*	Like the *j* in *j*eep, but more tense.

STRESS AND INTONATION

Intonation patterns in Korean are quite similar to English. Statements and information questions (e.g., "What's your name?" and "Where are you from?") have falling intonation; questions with a yes/no answer (e.g., "Is this your bag?") require rising intonation.

Stress (i.e., voice volume or emphasis) is primarily found on glottalized and aspirated consonants, rather than on vowels or whole syllables. You should be careful to give words and syllables equal stress when speaking Korean.

ROMANIZATION PRINCIPLES

The following principles should help you understand some further details about the romanization system used in this book.

1. Hyphens have been used between syllables of words in order to help with pronunciation.

travel   여행   *yeo-haeng*

2. Consistent with the system of romanization used by the Korean Government, hyphens are not generally used in proper nouns. This principle is used in this book when

proper nouns appear in the narrative. When they are written next to their *Hangeul* equivalent, hyphens are added and the romanization follows the system used throughout the book.

Bulguksa   불국사   *Pul-guk-sa*

3. Spaces are used to separate words and phrases.

Let's go to Seoul.   서울에 갑시다.   *Seo-u-re kap-shi-da.*

4. In those cases where there is a conflict between spelling and pronunciation, romanization is based on the way the language is pronounced, not on the way it is spelled.

It's finished.   끝났어요   *Kkeun-na-sseo-yo.*

5. Different romanizations of the same consonant illustrate variations in aspiration. Note in the example that the initial ㅈ is romanized differently than the two less-aspirated ㅈ's which appear within the word.

kettle   주전자   *chu-jeon-ja*

6. The Korean consonant, ㄹ, is romanized either *r* or *l*, depending on its placement in the word. *R* is used at the beginning of a word or between two vowels.

Rome   로마   *Ro-ma*

country   나라   *na-ra*

L is used before a consonant or at the end of a word.

thing   물건   *mul-geon*

liquor   술   *sul*

Two *l*'s are used when one ㄹ follows another.

discourtesy   실례   *shil-lye*

THE BASICS FOR GETTING BY

MOST FREQUENTLY USED EXPRESSIONS

The expressions in this section are the ones you will use again and again—the fundamental building blocks of conversation, the way to express your wants or needs, and some simple forms you can use to construct questions. It is a good idea to practice these phrases until you know them by heart.

GREETINGS

Good morning.	안녕하세요 ?	*An-nyeong-ha-se-yo?*
Good afternoon.		
Good evening.		
How are you?		

The reply to all of these greetings is the same in Korean:

네, 안녕하세요 ?   *Ne, an-nyeong-ha-se-yo?*

The expression, 안녕하세요 ? (*an-nyeong-ha-se-yo*), is given as the appropriate greeting for any time of day. It means literally, "Are you at peace?" The alternative, 안녕하십니까 ? (*an-nyeong-ha-shim-ni-kka*), has the same meaning but is the more formal form.

Pleased to meet you.	반갑습니다.	*Pan-gap-sseum-ni-da.*
See you again.	또 뵙겠어요.	*Tto poep-kke-sseo-yo.*
Good-bye. (Said to the person leaving.)	안녕히 가세요.	*An-nyeong-hi ka-se-yo.*
Good-bye. (Said to the person staying as you leave.)	안녕히 계세요.	*An-nyeong-hi kye-se-yo.*

TITLES

When speaking with Koreans, you will notice that given names are rarely used except between close friends and family members. Instead of given names, Koreans use titles, sometimes along with the person's family name. The title is chosen according to the social status and the relationship between the two people talking. The higher the level of the person, or the less familiar you are with the person, the more likely you will address that person by title. When deciding how to address someone, it is often useful to ask the person to indicate the most appropriate title.

A person with a formal position is addressed using the name of the position, such as director, manager, or teacher, followed by the honorific suffix *nim*; e.g., Director Kim (*Kim sa-jang-nim*), Teacher Park (*Park seon-saeng-nim*), or Dr. (Ph.D) Min (*Min pak-sa-nim*). Adding the person's given name is optional. In the workplace, colleagues at the same level attach "sshi" to a person's full name; e.g., *Kim Hee-won sshi*.

A simple way to get someone's attention in a restaurant and other public places is to use *Yeo-gi-yo* ("Here"), *Shil-lye-ham-ni-da* ("Excuse me"), or *Yeo-bo-se-yo* ("Please look here").

COMMON EXPRESSIONS

Yes.	네/에.	*Ne/Ye.*
No.	아니오.	*A-ni-o.*
Thank you. (Said in general to express appreciation.)	감사합니다.	*Kam-sa-ham-ni-da.*

An alternative expression for "Thank you" that you will hear is:

고맙습니다.	*Ko-map-sseum-ni-da.*
Thank you. (Said to those who have helped you as part of their job.)	수고하셨어요. *Su-go-ha-shyeo-sseo-yo.*

You're welcome.	천만에요.	*Ch'eon-man-e-yo.*
I'm sorry./Excuse me.	미안합니다.	*Mi-an-ham-ni-da.*
I'm sorry. (Used when being more formal than *Mi-an-ham-ni-da*.)	죄송합니다.	*Choe-song-ham-ni-da.*
Excuse me. (Asking forgiveness for an impolite act that is about to happen, such as leaving the table or asking someone a question.)	실례합니다.	*Shil-lye-ham-ni-da.*
That's all right.	괜찮아요.	*Kwaen-ch'an-a-yo.*
Hello. (Used for the telephone.)	여보세요.	*Yeo-bo-se-yo.*
Really?	그래요 ?	*Keu-rae-yo?*
That's right. (response)	네, 그래요.	*Ne, keu-rae-yo.*
It's interesting/fun.	재미 있어요.	*Chae-mi i-sseo-yo.*
It's over/finished.	끝났어요.	*Kkeun-na-sseo-yo.*
Just a moment, please.	잠깐만요.	*Cham-kkan-man-yo.*
Now.	지금.	*Chi-geum.*
Later.	나중에.	*Na-jung-e.*
Good night. (before sleeping)	안녕히 주무세요.	*An-nyeong-hi chu-mu-se-yo.*

SOME QUESTIONS AND QUESTION WORDS

What's the matter?	웬일이세요 ?	*Wen-i-ri-se-yo?*
What's this?	이것이 뭐예요 ?	*I-geo-shi mweo-ye-yo?*
Where's the bathroom?	화장실이 어디 있어요 ?	*Hwa-jang-shil-i eo-di i-sseo-yo?*
▧ entrance	입구(가)	*ip-kku(ga)*
▧ exit	출구(가)	*ch'ul-gu(ga)*
▧ telephone	전화(가)	*cheon-hwa(ga)*

The particles, 이 (*i*) and 가 (*ga*), are attached to words to indicate that they are the subjects of a sentence. 이 is attached to *hwa-jang-shil* since *shil* ends with a consonant; 가 is attached to *cheon-hwa* since *hwa* ends with a vowel.

When?	언제요 ?	*Eon-je-yo?*
Where?	어디에요 ?	*Eo-di-e-yo?*
How much?	얼마예요 ?	*Eol-ma-ye-yo?*
Who?	누구예요 ?	*Nu-gu-ye-yo?*
Why?	왜요 ?	*Wae-yo?*
How?	어떻게요 ?	*Eo-tteo-k'e-yo?*
What?	뭐예요 ?	*Mweo-ye-yo?*
Which?	어느 것이에요 ?	*Eo-neu geo-shi-e-yo?*

NEEDS

Please give me a map. 지도를 좀 주세요. *Chi-do-reul chom chu-se-yo.*

The particles, 을 (*eul*) and 를 (*reul*) are attached to words to indicate they are the objects of a sentence. 를 is attached to *chi-do* (above) since *do* ends with a vowel; 을 is attached to *ch'aek* (below) since it ends with a consonant.

I want to buy a book. 책을 사고 싶어요. *Ch'aek-eul sa-go shi-p'eo-yo.*

I want to go to Seoul. 서울에 가고 싶어요. *Seo-u-re ka-go shi-p'eo-yo.*

I want to see a movie. 영화를 보고 싶어요. *Yeong-hwa-reul po-go shi-p'eo-yo.*

I want to eat rice. 밥을 먹고 싶어요. *Pap-eul meok-kko shi-p'eo-yo.*

I want to drink beer. 맥주를 마시고 싶어요. *Maek-jju-reul ma-shi-go shi-p'eo-yo.*

I'm thirsty. 목이 말라요. *Mok-i mal-la-yo.*

I'm hungry. 배가 고파요. *Pae-ga ko-p'a-yo.*

I'm full. 배가 불러요. *Pae-ga pul-leo-yo.*

I'm tired. 피곤해요. *P'i-gon-hae-yo.*

I'm sleepy. 졸려요. *Chol-lyeo-yo.*

I'm sick. 병이 났어요. *Pyeong-i na-sseo-yo.*

I'm fine. 기분이 좋아요. *Ki-bun-i cho-a-yo.*

I'm all right. 괜찮아요. *Kwaen-ch'an-a-yo.*

SOME ADJECTIVES

It's cold.	추워요. *Ch'u-weo-yo.*
It's hot.	더워요. *Teo-weo-yo.*
It's humid.	습기가 있어요. *Seup-kki-ga i-sseo-yo.*

▦ pretty/ugly	예뻐요/미워요. *Ye-ppeo-yo/Mi-woe-yo.*
▦ delicious/awful-tasting or bland	맛이 있어요/맛이 없어요. *Ma-shi i-sseo-yo/Ma-shi eop-sseo-yo.*
▦ good/bad	좋아요/나빠요. *Cho-a-yo/Na-ppa-yo.*
▦ fast/slow	빨라요/느려요. *Ppal-la-yo/Neu-ryeo-yo.*
▦ high/low	높아요/낮아요. *No-p'a-yo/Na-ja-yo.*
▦ expensive/cheap	비싸요/싸요. *Pi-ssa-yo/Ssa-yo.*
▦ hot/cold (to the touch)	뜨거워요/차가워요. *Tteu-geo-weo-yo/Ch'a-ga-weo-yo.*
▦ same/different	같아요/달라요. *Ka-t'a-yo/Tal-la-yo.*
▦ big/small	커요/작아요. *K'eo-yo/Cha-ga-yo.*
▦ long/short	길어요/짧아요. *Ki-reo-yo/Jjal-ba-yo.*
▦ far/near	멀어요/가까워요. *Meo-reo-yo/Ka-kka-weo-yo.*
▦ wide/narrow	넓어요/좁아요. *Neol-beo-yo/Cho-ba-yo.*
▦ heavy/light	무거워요/가벼워요. *Mu-geo-weo-yo/Ka-byeo-weo-yo.*
▦ new/old	새로워요/낡았어요. *Sae-ro-weo-yo/Nal-ga-sseo-yo.*
▦ young/old	젊어요/늙었어요. *Cheol-meo-yo/Neul-geo-sseo-yo.*
▦ quiet/noisy	조용해요/시끄러워요. *Cho-yong-hae-yo/Shi-kkeu-reo-weo-yo.*

■ a lot, many/ a little, few	많아요/거의 없어요.	*Man-a-yo/ Keo-eui eop-sseo-yo.*
■ right/wrong	맞아요/틀려요.	*Ma-ja-yo/T'eul-lyeo-yo.*
■ easy/difficult	쉬워요/어려워요.	*Shwi-weo-yo/ Eo-ryeo-weo-yo.*
■ early/late	빨라요/늦어요.	*Ppal-la-yo/Neu-jeo-yo.*

DIRECTION WORDS

here	여기	*yeo-gi*
there	저기	*cheo-gi*
up	위로	*wi-ro*
down	아래로	*a-rae-ro*
from	(에)서	*(e)-seo*
to	에/(으)로	*e/(eu)-ro*
at	(에)서	*(e)-seo*
in	안에	*an-e*
left	왼쪽으로	*woen-jjok-eu-ro*
right	오른쪽으로	*o-reun-jjok-eu-ro*
on	위에	*wi-e*
in front of	앞에	*a-p'e*
behind	뒤에	*twi-e*
between	사이에	*sa-i-e*

beside	옆에	*yeo-p'e*
outside	밖에	*pa-kke*

COMMUNICATING

Do you understand?	아시겠어요 ?	*A-shi-ge-sseo-yo?*
Yes, I understand.	네, 알겠어요.	*Ne, al-ge-sseo-yo.*
No, I don't understand.	아니오, 모르겠어요.	*A-ni-o, mo-reu-ge-sseo-yo.*
Do you speak English?	영어를 할 줄 아세요 ?	*Yeong-eo-reul hal jjul a-se-yo?*
I speak a little Korean.	한국말을 좀 해요.	*Han-gung-ma-reul chom hae-yo.*
I don't understand Korean.	한국말을 몰라요.	*Han-gung-ma-reul mol-la-yo.*
Could you repeat it, please?	다시 말씀해 주시겠어요 ?	*Ta-shi mal-sseum-hae chu-shi-ge-sseo-yo?*
Please speak slowly.	천천히 말씀하세요.	*Ch'eon-ch'eon-hi mal-sseum-ha-se-yo.*
Write it down on the paper, please.	이 종이에 써 주세요.	*I chong-i-e sseo chu-se-yo.*
What's this called in Korean?	한국말로 뭐라고 해요 ?	*Han-gung-mal-lo meo-ra-go hae-yo?*
Excuse me, could you help me, please?	미안하지만 좀 도와주시겠어요 ?	*Mi-an-ha-ji-man chom to-wa-ju-shi-ge-sseo-yo?*
Please point to the phrase in this book.	이 책에서 그 말을 찾아 주세요.	*I ch'aek-e-seo keu ma-reul ch'a-ja chu-se-yo.*

POLICE

For police emergencies, dial 112; for fire, 119.

Would you call the police for me, please?	경찰서에 전화 좀 해주시겠어요 ? *Kyeong-ch'al-seo-e cheon-hwa chom hae-ju-shi-ge-sseo-yo?*
I've lost my <u>wallet</u>.	지갑을 잃어버렸어요. *Chi-gap-eul i-reo-beo-ryeo-sseo-yo.*
▓ hand bag	가방(을) *ka-bang(eul)*
▓ passport	여권(을) *yeo-kkweon(eul)*
▓ plane tickets	비행기표(를) *pi-haeng-gi-p'yo(reul)*
▓ money	돈(을) *ton(eul)*
▓ camera	카메라(를) *k'a-me-ra(reul)*
What shall I do?	어떻게 할까요 ? *Eo-tteo-k'e hal-kka-yo?*
Someone stole my _____.	누가 제 _____(을/를) 훔쳐 갔어요. *Nu-ga che _____ (eul/reul) hum-ch'yeo ka-sseo-yo.*
My name is _____.	제 이름은 _____이에요. *Che i-reum-eun _____ -i-e-yo.*
I'm an <u>American</u> citizen.	저는 미국 사람이에요. *Cheo-neun Mi-guk sa-ram-i-e-yo.*
▓ a British	영국 사람 *Yeong-guk sa-ram*
▓ a Canadian	캐나다 사람 *K'ae-na-da sa-ram*
I'm in Korea <u>on business</u>.	한국에는 사업차 왔어요. *Han-guk-e-neun sa-eop-ch'a wa-sseo-yo.*
▓ as a tourist	관광하러 *kwan-gwang-ha-reo*
I'm staying at _____.	_____에 묵고 있어요. *_____ -e muk-kko i-sseo-yo.*

My telephone number is _____.	제 전화 번호는 _____ 이에요. *Che cheon-hwa peon-ho-neun _____ - i-e-yo.*
I've lost my way.	길을 잃어버렸어요. *Ki-reul i-reo-beo-ryeo-sseo-yo.*
Can you direct me to _____?	_____ 가는 길을 가르쳐 주시겠어요? *_____ ka-neun ki-reul ka-reu-ch'yeo chu-shi-ge-sseo-yo?*

NUMBERS

There are two sets of cardinal numbers, one derived from Chinese and one native Korean. For the numerals 1–99 both sets are used, depending on what is being counted; for the numerals 100 and higher, only the Chinese-derived set is used.

CARDINAL NUMBERS (CHINESE-DERIVED)

0	공/영	*kong/yeong*
1	일	*il*
2	이	*i*
3	삼	*sam*
4	사	*sa*
5	오	*o*
6	육	*yuk*
7	칠	*ch'il*
8	팔	*p'al*
9	구	*ku*
10	십	*ship*

11	십일	*ship-il*
12	십이	*ship-i*
13	십삼	*ship-sam*
14	십사	*ship-sa*
15	십오	*ship-o*
16	십육	*shim-nyuk*
17	십칠	*ship-ch'il*
18	십팔	*ship-p'al*
19	십구	*ship-kku*
20	이십	*i-ship*
30	삼십	*sam-ship*
40	사십	*sa-ship*
50	오십	*o-ship*
60	육십	*yuk-ship*
70	칠십	*ch'il-ship*
80	팔십	*p'al-ship*
90	구십	*ku-ship*
100	백	*paek*
200	이백	*i-baek*
300	삼백	*sam-baek*
400	사백	*sa-baek*
500	오백	*o-baek*
600	육백	*yuk-ppaek*
700	칠백	*ch'il-baek*
800	팔백	*p'al-baek*
900	구백	*ku-baek*

1,000	천	*ch'eon*
2,000	이천	*i-ch'eon*
10,000	만	*man*
20,000	이만	*i-man*
100,000	십만	*shim-man*
200,000	이십만	*i-shim-man*
1,000,000	백만	*paeng-man*
2,000,000	이백만	*i-baeng-man*
10,000,000	천만	*ch'eon-man*
20,000,000	이천만	*i-ch'eon-man*
100,000,000	억	*eok*

CARDINAL NUMBERS (NATIVE KOREAN)

1	하나	*ha-na*
2	둘	*tul*
3	셋	*set*
4	넷	*net*
5	다섯	*ta-seot*
6	여섯	*yeo-seot*
7	일곱	*il-gop*
8	여덟	*yeo-deol*
9	아홉	*a-hop*
10	열	*yeol*
11	열하나	*yeol-ha-na*
12	열둘	*yeol-ttul*
13	열셋	*yeol-set*

14	열넷	*yeol-net*
15	열다섯	*yeol-tta-seot*
16	열여섯	*yeol-yeo-seot*
17	열일곱	*yeol-il-gop*
18	열여덟	*yeol-yeo-deol*
19	열아홉	*yeol-a-hop*
20	스물	*seu-mul*
30	서른	*seo-reun*
40	마흔	*ma-heun*
50	쉰	*shwin*
60	예순	*ye-sun*
70	일흔	*i-rheun*
80	여든	*yeo-deun*
90	아흔	*a-heun*

ORDINAL NUMBERS

first	첫째	*ch'eot-jjae*
second	둘째	*tul-jjae*
third	세째	*se-jjae*
fourth	네째	*ne-jjae*
fifth	다섯째	*ta-seot-jjae*
sixth	여섯째	*yeo-seot-jjae*
seventh	일곱째	*il-gop-jjae*
eighth	여덟째	*yeo-deol-jjae*
ninth	아홉째	*a-hop-jjae*
tenth	열째	*yeol-jjae*

THE LAND AND PEOPLE

GEOGRAPHY

Korea is a peninsula extending south into the Pacific Ocean from the Asian mainland. It borders Manchuria and Russia to the north, and faces China across the West Sea and Japan across the East Sea. North Korea, officially the Democratic People's Republic of Korea, occupies the northern portion of the peninsula. Pyongyang is its capital and largest city. To the south beyond the 38th parallel is South Korea, officially the Republic of Korea. South Korea is divided into nine provinces and several specially designated cities. Its capital, Seoul, has special government status, referred to as *t'euk-ppyeol-shi*. Six other cities have metropolitan government status, referred to as *kwang-yeok-sshi*: Busan, Incheon, Daegu, Ulsan, Daejeon, and Gwangju. The nine provinces and some major cities are listed below.

PROVINCES

Gyeonggi-do	경기도	*Kyeong-gi-do*
Gangwon-do	강원도	*Kang-weon-do*
Chungcheongbuk-do	충청북도	*Ch'ung-ch'eong-buk-tto*
Chungcheongnam-do	충청남도	*Ch'ung-ch'eong-nam-do*
Jeollabuk-do	전라북도	*Cheol-la-buk-tto*
Jeollanam-do	전라남도	*Cheol-la-nam-do*
Gyeongsangbuk-do	경상북도	*Kyeong-sang-buk-tto*
Gyeongsangnam-do	경상남도	*Kyeong-sang-nam-do*
Jeju-do	제주도	*Che-ju-do*

MAJOR CITIES

Seoul	서울	*Seo-ul*
Busan	부산	*Pu-san*
Daegu	대구	*Tae-gu*
Incheon	인천	*In-ch'eon*
Gwangju	광주	*Kwang-ju*
Daejeon	대전	*Tae-jeon*
Ulsan	울산	*Ul-san*
Gyeongju	경주	*Kyeong-ju*
Pohang	포항	*P'o-hang*
Chuncheon	춘천	*Ch'un-ch'eon*

TALKING ABOUT THE COUNTRY

Korea	한국	*Han-guk*
population	인구	*in-gu*
land area	지방	*chi-bang*
Pacific Ocean	태평양	*T'ae-p'yeong-yang*
East Sea	동해	*Tong-hae*
West Sea	서해 *Seo-hae* or 황해 *Hwang-hae*	
hot springs	온천	*on-ch'eon*

ocean	바다	*pa-da*
coast	해안	*hae-an*
island	섬	*seom*
mountain	산	*san*
hill	언덕	*eon-deok*
river	강	*kang*
lake	호수	*ho-su*
waterfall	폭포	*p'ok-p'o*
capital	수도	*su-do*
province	도	*to*
provincial capital	도청 소재지	*to-ch'eong so-jae-ji*
city	도시	*to-shi*
big city	대도시	*tae-do-shi*
town	소도시	*so-do-shi*
village	마을	*ma-eul*
countryside	시골	*shi-gol*
map	지도	*chi-do*
national park	국립 공원	*kung-nip kong-weon*

SEASONS AND WEATHER

season	계절	*kye-jeol*
four seasons	사 계절	*sa kye-jeol*
spring	봄	*pom*
March/April/May	3월/4월/5월	*sam-weol/sa-weol/o-weol*
summer	여름	*yeo-reum*
June/July/August	6월/7월/8월	*yu-weol/ch'i-rweol/p'a-rweol*
fall	가을	*ka-eul*
September/October/November	9월/10월/11월	*ku-weol/shi-weol/ship-i-rweol*
winter	겨울	*kyeo-ul*
December/January/February	12월/1월/2월	*ship-i-weol/i-rweol/i-weol*
climate	기후	*ki-hu*
weather	날씨	*nal-sshi*
cloud	구름	*ku-reum*
wind	바람	*pa-ram*
rain	비	*pi*
rainy season	장마철	*chang-ma-ch'eol*
snow	눈	*nun*

typhoon	태풍	*t'ae-p'ung*
flood	홍수	*hong-su*

It's <u>hot</u> today, isn't it? 오늘은 날씨가 <u>덥지요</u> ? *O-neu-reun nal-sshi-ga <u>teop-ji-yo</u>?*

▨ cool 쌀쌀하지요 *ssal-ssal-ha-ji-yo*

▨ cold 춥지요 *ch'up-ji-yo*

▨ warm 따뜻하지요 *tta-tteut-t'a-ji-yo*

It's fine. 날씨가 좋아요. *Nal-sshi-ga cho-a-yo.*

It's cloudy. 날씨가 흐려요. *Nal-sshi-ga heu-ryeo-yo.*

It's raining. 비가 와요. *Pi-ga wa-yo.*

It's snowing. 눈이 와요. *Nun-i wa-yo.*

Will it stop <u>raining</u> soon? 비가 곧 그칠까요 ? *<u>Pi-ga</u> kot keu-ch'il-kka-yo?*

▨ snowing 눈이 *nun-i*

I hope it will clear up. 날씨가 맑으면 좋겠어요. *Nal-sshi-ga mal-geu-myeon cho-k'e-sseo-yo.*

What's tomorrow's weather forecast? 내일 일기예보가 어때요 ? *Nae-il il-gi-ye-bo-ga eo-ttae-yo?*

GETTING TO KNOW THE KOREANS

Korea is a rich blend of old and new. Changes have occurred rapidly within the country, but beneath the economic and social transformation remains a culture steeped in centuries of customs and values. Although Koreans do not view themselves as Confucian, much of their society is based on Confucian philosophy and reflected in the way Koreans deal with each other. This is apparent in social life as well as family relations. Knowing something about Korean customs will aid you in better understanding and speaking the language.

INTRODUCTIONS

Introductions are usually made through third parties in formal settings. It is not uncommon, however, for a Korean to initiate meeting a stranger, especially a foreigner, in a less formal situation. Should there be occasions when you wish to talk with someone and there is no one to introduce you, it is appropriate for you to introduce yourself.

Upon meeting someone for the first time or when greeting friends, Koreans ordinarily bow. The degree of the bow depends on the relative status, age, and respect of the individuals. A Westerner is not expected to bow, but Koreans would appreciate your doing so. The best way to learn to do a Korean-style bow is through observation and practice.

Koreans have been influenced by Western customs, and men in general will shake hands when greeting each other. Shaking hands is usually done along with a slight bow. The handshake is generally not as vigorous as one by a Westerner. A greeting hug or kiss, however, could be awkward for Koreans unless they are "Westernized" and are extremely close to you.

Who is that? (referring to an adult)	저 분이 누구세요 ?	*Cheo pun-i nu-gu-se-yo?*
Would you introduce me to him/her (literally, that person)?	저 분을 좀 소개해 주시겠어요 ?	*Cheo pun-eul chom so-gae-hae chu-shi-ge-sseo-yo?*
Please introduce yourself.	인사하세요.	*In-sa-ha-se-yo.*
I will introduce myself.	인사드리겠어요.	*In-sa-deu-ri-ge-sseo-yo.*

This is my <u>friend</u>.	제 친구예요. *Che ch'in-gu-ye-yo.*
husband	남편 *nam-p'yeon*
wife	아내 *a-nae*
son	아들 *a-deul*
daughter	딸 *ttal*
father	아버지 *a-beo-ji*
mother	어머니 *eo-meo-ni*

How do you do? (Literally, I am seeing you for the first time.)	처음 뵙겠어요. *Ch'eo-eum poep-kke-sseo-yo.*
How do you do? (reply)	처음 뵙겠어요. *Ch'eo-eum poep-kke-sseo-yo.*
I am pleased to meet you.	반갑습니다. *Pan-gap-sseum-ni-da.*
My name is _____.	제 이름은 _____이에요. *Che i-reum-eun _____-i-e-yo.*
I look forward to working with you.	함께 일하게 되어서 기쁩니다. *Ham-kke il-ha-ge toe-eo-seo ki-ppeum-ni-da.*

CARDS

Koreans often exchange business cards when meeting for the first time. Information on the card such as job, title, and position helps each person to know the correct level of formality as well as other linguistic nuances to use with each other. Having your own cards for Korea will be very useful.

card	명함 *myeong-ham*
Here's my card.	제 명함이에요. *Che myeong-ham-i-e-yo.*
Thank you.	감사합니다. *Kam-sa-ham-ni-da.*

May I have your card?	명함 한 장 주시겠어요 ?	*Myeong-ham han chang chu-shi-ge-sseo-yo?*

NAMES

Korean names are composed of three syllables, which are derived from the three Chinese characters used for writing the names. The first syllable stands for the family name while the last two syllables indicate the given name. The given name is never separated. When Korean names are used, the family name always comes first, followed by the given name; for example, Hong (family name), Dae-shik (given name).

What's your name? (Said to people older than you.)	성함이 어떻게 되세요 ?	*Seong-ham-i eo-tteo-k'e toe-se-yo?*
What's your name? (Said to people younger than you.)	이름이 어떻게 되세요 ?	*I-reum-i eo-tteo-k'e toe-se-yo?*
What's your name? (Said to people much younger than you.)	이름이 뭐예요 ?	*I-reum-i mweo-ye-yo?*
My name is _____.	제 이름은 _____이에요.	*Che i-reum-eun _____-i-e-yo.*

PERSONAL INFORMATION

Where are you from?	어디에서 오셨어요 ?	*Eo-di-e-seo o-shyeo-sseo-yo?*
I'm from <u>the United States</u>.	미국에서 왔어요.	*Mi-guk-e-seo wa-sseo-yo.*
▓ England	영국	*Yeong-guk*
▓ Canada	캐나다	*K'ae-na-da*
▓ Australia	호주	*Ho-ju*
▓ New Zealand	뉴질랜드	*Nyu-jil-laen-deu*

Where were you born?	고향이 어디세요 ? *Ko-hyang-i eo-di-se-yo?*
I was born in _____. (reply)	고향이 _____이에요. *Ko-hyang-i _____-i-e-yo.*
Where do you live?	어디 사세요 ? *Eo-di sa-se-yo?*
I live in _____.	_____ 에 살아요. *_____ -e sa-ra-yo.*
Are you married?	결혼하셨어요 ? *Kyeo-ron-ha-shyeo-sseo-yo?*
I'm married.	결혼했어요. *Kyeo-ron-hae-sseo-yo.*
I'm single.	미혼이에요. *Mi-hon-i-e-yo.*
Do you have any children?	아이들이 있으세요 ? *A-i-deu-ri i-sseu-se-yo?*
How old are you? (for older people)	연세가 어떻게 되세요 ? *Yeon-se-ga eo-tteo-k'e toe-se-yo?*
How old are you? (for people younger than you)	나이가 어떻게 돼요 ? *Na-i-ga eo-tteo-k'e twae-yo?*
How old are you? (for children)	몇 살이에요 ? *Myeot ssal-i-e-yo?*
I'm 25 years old. (Native Korean numbers are used for one's age.)	스물 다섯 살이에요. *Seu-mul ta-seot ssal-i-e-yo.*
What do you do?	무슨 일을 하세요 ? *Mu-seun i-reul ha-se-yo?*

I'm <u>a student</u>.	학생이에요.	*Hak-ssaeng-i-e-yo.*
▨ a professor	교수	*kyo-su*
▨ an office worker	사무원	*sa-mu-weon*
▨ a secretary	비서	*pi-seo*
▨ an engineer	기술자	*ki-sul-jja*
▨ in the military	군인	*kun-in*
▨ a company executive	회사 간부	*hoe-sa kan-bu*
▨ a doctor	의사	*eui-sa*
▨ a dentist	치과 의사	*ch'i-kkwa eui-sa*
▨ a nurse	간호원	*kan-ho-weon*
▨ a lawyer	변호사	*pyeon-ho-sa*
▨ an architect	건축 기사	*keon-ch'uk ki-sa*
▨ a writer	작가	*chak-kka*
▨ a politician	정치가	*cheong-ch'i-ga*
▨ an athlete	운동 선수	*un-dong seon-su*

DAILY GREETINGS AND LEAVE-TAKINGS

When greeting someone, there are no specific Korean expressions for "Good morning," "Good afternoon," and "Good evening." The equivalent for "Hi" or "Hello" is useful for greeting someone at any time of the day.

Hi.	안녕하세요.	*An-nyeong-ha-se-yo.*
Hello.		

If you are a guest in a Korean home, you may use the following expressions for initial greetings in the morning and final leavetaking at night.

Did you sleep well?	안녕히 주무셨어요?	*An-nyeong-hi chu-mu-shyeo-sseo-yo?*
Sleep well.	안녕히 주무세요.	*An-nyeong-hi chu-mu-se-yo.*

Upon entering or leaving a store or an office, the following expressions are used.

Please come in. Welcome. (Said by an occupant of a store or an office.)	어서 오세요.	*Eo-seo o-se-yo.*
Good-bye. Work hard. (Said by a person leaving the store or the office.)	수고하세요.	*Su-go-ha-se-yo.*

When leaving a home or other place to which you are *not* likely to return soon, the following expressions are used.

Good-bye. (Literally, "Stay in peace"; said by guest.)	안녕히 계세요.	*An-nyeong-hi kye-se-yo.*
Good-bye. (Literally, "Go in peace"; said by host.)	안녕히 가세요.	*An-nyeong-hi ka-se-yo.*

When leaving a home or other place to which you will return, the following expressions are used.

See you later. (Literally, "I will return"; said by the person leaving.)	다녀오겠어요.	*Ta-nyeo-o-ge-sseo-yo.*
See you later. (Literally, "Please return"; said by the person staying.)	다녀오세요.	*Ta-nyeo-o-se-yo.*

Other common expressions for greeting and leave-taking follow.

It's been a long time.	오래간만이에요.	*O-rae-gan-man-i-e-yo.*
How have you been lately?	요새 어떻게 지내세요?	*Yo-sae eo-tteo-k'e chi-nae-se-yo?*
See you again.	또 뵙겠어요.	*Tto poep-kke-sseo-yo.*
See you tomorrow.	내일 뵙겠어요.	*Nae-il poep-kke-sseo-yo.*
I must go now.	지금 가야 돼요.	*Chi-geum ka-ya twae-yo.*
Thank you for the delicious food.	잘 먹었어요.	*Chal meo-geo-sseo-yo.*
Thank you for the nice time.	잘 지냈어요.	*Chal chi-nae-sseo-yo.*
Give my regards to your family.	가족한테 안부 전해 주세요.	*Ka-jok-han-t'e an-bu cheon-hae chu-se-yo.*

FAMILY

Family relationships are an important part of Korean life. You will often be asked about members of your family. Here are some useful words.

grandfather	할아버지	*ha-ra-beo-ji*
grandmother	할머니	*hal-meo-ni*
father	아버지	*a-beo-ji*
mother	어머니	*eo-meo-ni*
husband	남편	*nam-p'yeon*
wife	아내	*a-nae*

daughter	딸	*ttal*
son	아들	*a-deul*
older brother (of a female)	오빠	*o-ppa*
older sister (of a female)	언니	*eon-ni*
older brother (of a male)	형	*hyeong*
older sister (of a male)	누나	*nu-na*
younger brother (of both sexes)	남동생	*nam-dong-saeng*
younger sister (of both sexes)	여동생	*yeo-dong-saeng*

GIFT GIVING AND RECEIVING

It is customary in Korea to give gifts to friends, business associates, and acquaintances. You will no doubt receive your share of gifts in Korea—from small souvenirs to more expensive items. Although a return gift is not expected, some type of reciprocity, such as dinner at a restaurant, will show your appreciation. If you choose to give gifts to Koreans, a small souvenir from your native country is fine. The gift should be wrapped. The expense of the item is not important. It's the thought that counts.

When giving or receiving a gift in Korea, it is polite to use both hands. If you wish to open your gift, ask if you may do so. Generally, Koreans do not open gifts in front of the giver; however, if you would like to have your gifts opened, encourage the recipients to do so. They will be happy to oblige since they know this is a Western custom.

GIVING

Here's a gift for you.	선물이에요. *Seon-mu-ri-e-yo.*
It's from California.	캘리포니아에서 샀어요. *K'ael-li-p'o-ni-a-e-seo sa-sseo-yo.*
It's a small thing. (to express modesty)	약소합니다. *Yak-so-ham-ni-da.*
I hope you enjoy it.	마음에 드셨으면 좋겠어요. *Ma-eum-e teu-shyeo-sseu-myeon cho-k'e-sseo-yo.*
Please open it.	열어 보세요. *Yeo-reo po-se-yo.*

RECEIVING

Thank you very much.	정말 감사합니다. *Cheong-mal kam-sa-ham-ni-da.*
This wasn't necessary.	안그러셔도 되는데요. *An-keu-reo-shyeo-do toe-neun-de-yo.*
May I open it?	열어 봐도 될까요 ? *Yeo-reo pwa-do toel-kka-yo?*
I'll enjoy <u>using</u> it.	잘 <u>쓰겠어요</u>. *Chal <u>sseu-ge-sseo-yo</u>.*
▉ eating	먹겠어요 *meok-kke-sseo-yo*

WHEN YOU ARRIVE

PASSPORT AND CUSTOMS

    Once you arrive in Korea, you will be required to clear immigration and customs. You will need a valid passport. For U.S. citizens, visa requirements depend on your length of stay. You should check with the U.S. Department of State, the Embassy of the Republic of Korea in Washington, DC, or one of the Korean Consulates in major cities of the U.S. to prepare for your trip. You may also wish to consult with your physician in advance of your travel to obtain any information about immunizations.

    The following expressions will help as you go through the various areas of the airport:

airport	공항	*kong-hang*
airplane	비행기	*pi-haeng-gi*
flight number	항공번호	*hang-gong-beon-ho*
passenger	승객	*seung-gaek*
port	항구	*hang-gu*
ship	배	*pae*
ferry	페리	*p'e-ri*

IMMIGRATION

My name is _____.	제 이름은 _____ 이에요. *Che i-reum-eun _____-i-e-yo.*

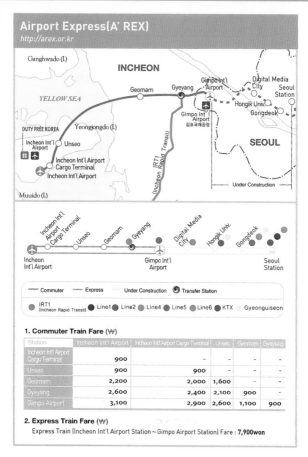

Airport Express(A' REX)
http://arex.or.kr

1. Commuter Train Fare (₩)

Station	Incheon Int'l Airport	Incheon Int'l Airport Cargo Terminal	Unseo	Geomam	Gyeyang
Incheon Int'l Airport Cargo Terminal	900	–	–	–	–
Unseo	900	900	–	–	–
Geomam	2,200	2,000	1,600	–	–
Gyeyang	2,600	2,400	2,100	900	–
Gimpo Airport	3,100	2,900	2,600	1,100	900

2. Express Train Fare (₩)

Express Train (Incheon Int'l Airport Station ~ Gimpo Airport Station) Fare : **7,900won**

I'm <u>American</u>.	저는 미국 사람이에요.	*Cheo-neun Mi-guk sa-ram-i-e-yo.*
■ Canadian	캐나다 사람	*K'ae-na-da sa-ram*

■ British	영국 사람	*Yeong-guk sa-ram*
■ Australian	호주 사람	*Ho-ju sa-ram*

I'm staying at a hotel. 호텔에 묵고 있어요. *Ho-t'e-re muk-kko i-sseo-yo.*

Here's my passport. 여권 여기 있어요. *Yeo-kkweon yeo-gi i-sseo-yo.*

Here are my documents. 서류 여기 있어요. *Seo-ryu yeo-gi i-sseo-yo.*

I'm on a business trip. 사업차 왔어요. *Sa-eop-ch'a wa-sseo-yo.*

I'm here as a tourist. 관광하러 왔어요. *Kwan-gwang-ha-reo wa-sseo-yo.*

I'll be staying here for <u>a few days</u>. 여기서 <u>며칠</u> 머물 거예요. *Yeo-gi-seo myeo-ch'il meo-mul kkeo-ye-yo.*

■ a week	일 주일	*il jju-il*
■ two weeks	두 주일	*tu chu-il*
■ a month	한 달	*han tal*
■ two months	두 달	*tu tal*

I'm traveling <u>alone</u>. <u>혼자</u> 여행하고 있어요. *<u>Hon-ja</u> yeo-haeng-ha-go i-sseo-yo.*

■ with my husband	남편과 함께	*nam-p'yeon-gwa ham-kke*
■ with my wife	아내와 함께	*a-nae-wa ham-kke*
■ with my family	가족이 함께	*ka-jok-i ham-kke*

BAGGAGE CLAIM

Where is the baggage claim? 수하물이 어디 있어요? *Su-ha-mu-ri eo-di i-sseo-yo?*

This is my bag. 여기 제 가방이 있어요. *Yeo-gi che ka-bang-i i-sseo-yo.*

I can't find my luggage.	제 짐을 못 찾겠어요. *Che chim-eul mot ch'at-kke-sseo-yo.*
My luggage is lost.	제 짐이 없어졌어요. *Che chim-i eop-sseo-jyeo-sseo-yo.*

CUSTOMS

Where's customs?	어디서 통관하지요 ? *Eo-di-seo t'ong-gwan-ha-ji-yo?*
Here's my customs declaration form.	세관 신고서 여기 있어요. *Se-gwan shin-go-seo yeo-gi i-sseo-yo.*
This is my luggage.	제 짐이 여기 있어요. *Che chim-i yeo-gi i-sseo-yo.*
This is all I have.	이게 전부예요. *I-ge cheon-bu-ye-yo.*
I have nothing to declare.	신고할 것이 없어요. *Shin-go-hal keo-shi eop-sseo-yo.*
I have <u>two cartons of cigarettes</u>.	<u>담배 두 상자가</u> 있어요. <u>*Tam-bae tu sang-ja-ga*</u> *i-sseo-yo.*
■ two bottles of whiskey	위스키 두 병이 *wi-seu-k'i tu pyeong-i*
These are my personal effects.	이것들은 제 사물이에요. *I-geot-deu-reun che sa-mul-i-e-yo.*
It's not new.	새 것이 아니에요. *Sae geo-shi a-ni-e-yo.*
These are gifts.	이것들은 선물이에요. *I-geot-deu-reun seon-mul-i-e-yo.*
May I close the bag now?	이제 가방을 닫아도 돼요 ? *I-je ka-bang-eul ta-da-do twae-yo?*
Do I have to pay duty?	관세를 내야 돼요 ? *Kwan-se-reul nae-ya twae-yo?*
How much do I pay?	얼마예요 ? *Eol-ma-ye-yo?*

Where do I pay?	어디에 내지요 ? *Eo-di-e nae-ji-yo?*
Can I pay with dollars?	달러로 내도 돼요 ? *Ttal-leo-ro nae-do twae-yo?*

MONEY EXCHANGE

Once you have cleared customs, you will be ready to leave the airport for your destination in Korea. You may need some Korean currency to hold you over until you can exchange more money at a bank or hotel, where exchange rates may be better. Korean currency is in the form of won. Here are some expressions you may need for exchanging currencies.

Where can I exchange money?	돈을 어디에서 바꿔요 ? *Ton-eul eo-di-e'seo pa-kkweo-yo?*
Will you change travelers checks?	여행자 수표를 바꿔 주시겠어요 ? *Yeo-haeng-ja su-p'yo-reul pa-kkweo chu-shi-ge-sseo-yo?*
Please change these dollars into won. (Korean currency).	이 달러를 원으로 좀 바꿔 주세요. *I ttal-leo-reul won-eu-ro chom pa-kkweo chu-se-yo.*
How much is the exchange rate?	달러의 환율이 어떻게 되지요 ? *Ttal-leo-eui hwan-yu-ri eo-tteo-k'e toe-ji-yo?*
Could I have some change?	잔돈 좀 바꿔 주세요. *Chan-don chom pa-kkweo chu-se-yo.*

PORTER

Where is the information counter?	안내소가 어디 있어요 ? *An-nae-so-ga eo-di i-sseo-yo?*
Where can I find a baggage cart?	카트가 어디 있어요 ? *K'a-t'eu-ga eo-di i-sseo-yo?*

Could you get me a porter?	짐꾼 좀 불러 주세요. *Chim-kkun chom pul-leo chu-se-yo.*
These are my bags.	제 짐이 여기 있어요. *Che chim-i yeo-gi i-sseo-yo.*
Put them <u>here</u>.	<u>여기에</u> 놓으세요. *Yeo-gi-e no-eu-se-yo.*
■ there	저기에 *cheo-gi-e*
Be careful with that one!	저것은 좀 조심해 주세요! *Cheo-geo-seun chom cho-shim-hae chu-se-yo!*
I'll carry this one myself.	이것은 제가 들겠어요. *I-geo-seun che-ga teul-ge-sseo-yo.*
How much do I owe you?	얼마 드리면 되겠어요? *Eol-ma teu-ri-myeon toe-ge-sseo-yo?*
Thank you.	수고하셨습니다./감사합니다. *Su-go-ha-shyeo-sseum-ni-da/Kam-sa-ham-ni-da.*

AIRPORT TRANSPORTATION

Taxis and buses can be used to get to your destination from the airport. Check with the information counter in the terminal to choose the right transportation. You may want to have the agent write in Korean the name of your hotel or the area to which you want to go.

Where can I get <u>a bus</u>?	<u>시내버스를</u> 어디서 타요? *Shi-nae-ppeo-seu-reul eo-di-seo t'a-yo?*
■ a hotel bus	호텔버스 *ho-t'el-ppeo-seu*
■ a taxi	택시 *t'aek-shi*

Please take me <u>downtown</u>.	시내 좀 가 주세요. *Shi-nae chom ka chu-se-yo.*
■ to this hotel	이 호텔에 *i ho-t'e-re*
■ to this location	이 곳에 *i ko-se*
How much is the fare?	요금이 얼마예요 ? *Yo-geum-i eol-ma-ye-yo?*

GREETINGS AND SEND-OFFS

Koreans feel a strong sense of obligation to meet friends when they arrive at the airport, as well as see them off when they leave. The following expressions will be helpful if you find yourself in these situations.

Thank you for meeting me at the airport.	마중을 나와 주셔서 감사합니다. *Ma-jung-eul na-wa chu-shyeo-seo kam-sa-ham-ni-da.*
Since you are so busy, please forget about seeing me off.	바쁘신데 전송 나오지 마세요. *Pa-ppeu-shin-de jeon-song na-o-ji ma-se-yo.*
Thank you for coming to see me off.	전송해 주셔서 감사합니다. *Cheon-song-hae chu-shyeo-seo kam-sa-ham-ni-da.*
Thank you for the farewell party last night.	어제밤 송별회 감사합니다. *Eo-je-ppam song-byeol-hoe kam-sa-ham-ni-da.*

BANKING AND MONEY MATTERS

The basic unit of currency in Korea is the won.
The symbol for won is W. Won comes in the following
denominations:

COINS	10 won	십원	*ship weon*
	50 won	오십원	*o-ship weon*
	100 won	백원	*paek weon*
	500 won	오백원	*o-baek weon*
NOTES	1,000 won	천원	*ch'eon weon*
	5,000 won	오천원	*o-ch'eon weon*
	10,000 won	만원	*man weon*

In Korea, banks, major tourist hotels, and airports all
exchange foreign currencies or travelers checks for won.
Banks usually offer the best rates.

Since exchange rates fluctuate, the following table might
be useful for you to keep track of your money.

Won	Your Own Currency
50	
100	
500	
1,000	
5,000	
10,000	

Koreans use bank checks (*su-p'yo*) to exchange large
sums of money. They are issued in fixed amounts according
to your needs. When cashing them, you may have to pay a
small fee and show your passport. They are available from
banks or ATMs. You may want to use the ATMs located in
banks in case you need assistance. Credit and debit cards are
accepted in most places except the smallest shops.

EXCHANGING MONEY

Where can I change money?	돈을 어디에서 바꿔요 ? *Ton-eul eo-di-e-seo pa-kkweo-yo?*
■ dollars	달러(를) *ttal-leo(reul)*
■ pounds	파운드(를) *p'a-un-deu(reul)*
■ travelers checks	여행자 수표(를) *yeo-haeng-ja su-p'yo(reul)*
■ a personal check	개인 수표(를) *kae-in su-p'yo(reul)*

Where is there a bank?	은행이 어디 있어요 ? *Eun-haeng-i eo-di i-sseo-yo?*
■ ATM	현금자동출납기(가) *hyeon-geum-ja-dong-ch'ul-nap-kki(ga)*

At what time does it open?	몇 시에 문 열어요 ? *Myeot shi-e mun yeo-reo-yo?*
■ close	닫아요 *ta-da-yo*

What is the current exchange rate?	달러의 환율이 어떻게 돼요 ? *Ttal-leo-eui hwan-yu-ri eo-tteo-k'e twae-yo?*

I'd like to cash this check.	이 수표를 원으로 바꿔 주세요. *I su-p'yo-reul weon-eu-ro pa-kkweo chu-se-yo.*

Where do I sign?	싸인을 어디에 하지요 ? *Ssa-in-eul eo-di-e ha-ji-yo?*

Here's my passport.	여권은 여기 있어요. *Yeo-kkweon-eun yeo-gi i-sseo-yo.*

I'd like the money in large bills.	큰 돈으로 주세요. *K'eun ton-eu-ro chu-se-yo.*
■ in small bills	작은 돈으로 *cha-geun ton-eu-ro*
■ in check form	수표로 *su-p'yo-ro*

Please give me a check for 100,000 won.	십만원짜리 수표 한 장 주세요. *Shim-man-weon-jja-ri su-p'yo han jang chu-se-yo.*
Please give me small change for this.	잔돈으로 주세요. *Chan-don-eu-ro chu-se-yo.*
Please give me <u>one 10,000 won bill.</u>	<u>만원 짜리 한 장 주세요.</u> *Man-weon jja-ri han chang chu-se-yo.*
■ two 5,000	오천원 짜리 두 장 *o-ch'eon weon jja-ri tu chang*
■ three 1,000	천원 짜리 세 장 *ch'eon-weon jja-ri se chang*

TIPPING

It is generally not necessary to tip in Korea. Tipping is required only in bars and other drinking establishments in which you are served by hostesses. At hotels and Western restaurants, tips are included in the service charge added to your bill. When someone has treated you exceptionally well, a smile, slight bow, and a courteous *kam-sa-ham-ni-da* will do.

AT THE HOTEL

Accommodations are varied in style as well as price. For those who prefer all the comforts of home, Korea has numerous super deluxe hotels with private baths and all the other conveniences. In addition to the super deluxe hotels, there are deluxe, first-, second-, and third-class Western-style hotels and motels, which offer many of the same features at less expensive rates. The rose of Sharon, Korea's national flower, is used as a symbol of quality. The number of flowers varies from two to five, reflecting the level of quality. Deluxe hotels display five flowers, first-class four, second-class three, and two flowers appear on economy-class hotels. In addition to Western-style rooms, many hotels and motels offer Korean-style rooms in which you can sleep on the *ondol* floor. For other unique experiences, you may want to consider staying in a Buddhist temple, private condominium, or private home. Contact the Korea Tourism Organization for more information. Youth hostels are also scattered throughout the country.

The following expressions will help you regardless of the accommodations you choose.

HOTEL

GETTING TO YOUR HOTEL

I'd like to go to the hotel.	호텔에 가고 싶어요. *Ho-t'e-re ka-go shi-p'eo-yo.*
Where can I get a taxi?	택시를 어디서 타지요 ? *T'aek-shi-reul eo-di-seo t'a-ji-yo?*
Where is the bus stop?	버스 정류장이 어디 있어요 ? *Ppeo-seu cheong-nyu-jang-i eo-di i-sseo-yo?*
How much is the fare?	요금이 얼마예요 ? *Yo-geum-i eol-ma-ye-yo.*

CHECKING IN

Hotels add a service charge to the final bill. Registration forms are in English as well as Korean.

I have a reservation.	예약이 되어 있는데요.	*Ye-yak-i toe-eo in-neun-de-yo.*
Here is my confirmation.	확인서가 여기 있어요.	*Hwa-gin-seo-ga yeo-gi i-sseo-yo.*
I don't have a reservation, but can I get a room?	예약을 안 했는데, 방이 있어요?	*Ye-yak-eul an haen-neun-de, pang-i i-sseo-yo?*
Could you call another hotel to see if they have something?	다른 호텔에 전화 좀 걸어 주시겠어요?	*Ta-reun ho-t'e-re cheon-hwa chom keo-reo chu-shi-ge-sseo-yo?*
I'd like a <u>single</u> room.	독방으로 주세요.	*<u>Tok</u>-ppang-eu-ro chu-se-yo.*
■ double	이인용	*i-in-yong*
■ Western-style	침대	*ch'im-dae*
■ Korean-style	온돌	*on-dol*
I'd like a room <u>with twin beds</u>.	침대가 두 개 있는 방을 주세요.	*<u>Ch'im-dae-ga tu kae in-neun</u> pang-eul chu-se-yo.*
■ with bath	욕실이 달린	*yok-shi-ri tal-lin*
■ with a shower	샤워실이 달린	*sha-weo-shi-ri tal-lin*
■ with a good view	전망이 좋은	*cheon-mang-i cho-eun*
■ facing the mountain	산이 보이는	*san-i po-i-neun*
■ facing the ocean	바다가 보이는	*pa-da-ga po-i-neun*
■ facing the garden	정원이 보이는	*cheong-weon-i po-i-neun*

What's the daily rate?	방 값이 하루에 얼마예요 ? *Pang kkap-shi ha-ru-e eol-ma-ye-yo?*
Does the rate include the service charge?	서비스료가 포함이 돼요 ? *Seo-bi-seu-ryo-ga p'o-ham-i twae-yo?*
Do you have anything cheaper?	더 싼 방이 있어요 ? *Teo ssan pang-i i-sseo-yo?*
Does it have <u>air conditioning</u>?	방에 에어콘 있어요 ? *Pang-e e-eo-k'on i-sseo-yo?*
■ a bathroom	화장실 *hwa-jang-shil*
▨ television	텔레비전 *t'el-le-bi-jeon*
I'll be staying <u>just tonight</u>.	<u>오늘만</u> 있을 거예요. *O-neul-man i-sseul kkeo-ye-yo.*
■ a few days	며칠 *myeo-ch'il*
■ a week	일 주일 *il jju-il*
▨ a month	한 달 *han tal*
What floor is it on?	방이 몇 층에 있어요 ? *Pang-i myeot ch'eung-e i-sseo-yo?*
May I see the room?	방을 구경해도 될까요 ? *Pang-eul ku-gyeong-hae-do toel-kka-yo?*
Can I get the room right now?	방을 지금 얻을 수 있어요 ? *Pang-eul chi-geum eo-deul su i-sseo-yo?*

CHANGING THE ROOM

Could I get a different room?	방을 바꿔 주시겠어요 ? *Pang-eul pa-kkweo chu-shi-ge-sseo-yo?*
It's too <u>big</u>.	방이 너무 <u>커요</u>. *Pang-i neo-mu k'eo-yo.*
■ small	작아요 *cha-ga-yo*

■ dark	어두워요	*eo-du-weo-yo*
■ noisy	시끄러워요	*shi-kkeu-reo-weo-yo*

Do you have a <u>better</u> room?　더 좋은 방 없어요 ? 　*Teo cho-eun pang eop-sseo-yo?*

■ larger	더 큰	*teo k'eun*
■ smaller	더 작은	*teo cha-geun*
■ quieter	더 조용한	*teo cho-yong-han*

I'd like a room <u>with more light</u>.　더 밝은 방으로 주세요. 　*Teo pal-geun pang-eu-ro chu-se-yo.*

■ on a higher floor	더 높은 층에 있는	*teo no-p'eun ch'eung-e in-neun*
■ on a lower floor	더 낮은 층에 있는	*teo na-jeun ch'eung-e in-neun*
■ with a better view	전망이 더 좋은	*cheon-mang-i teo cho-eun*
■ with an Internet connection	인터넷이 되는	*In-t'eo-ne-shi toe-neun*

HOTEL INFORMATION

Is room service available?	룸 서비스가 있어요 ? 　*Rum sseo-bi-seu-ga i-sseo-yo?*
Can you get me a baby-sitter?	아이 보는 사람을 구해 주시겠어요 ? 　*A-i po-neun sa-ram-eul ku-hae chu-shi-ge-sseo-yo?*
Is a massage therapist available?	맛사지사 부를 수 있어요 ? 　*Mas-sa-ji-sa pu-reul su i-sseo-yo?*
Is there a <u>restaurant</u> in the hotel?	호텔에 식당이 있어요 ? 　*Ho-t'e-re shik-ttang-i i-sseo-yo?*
■ bar	빠(가) 　*ppa(ga)*
■ coffee shop	커피 숍(이) 　*k'eo-p'i shyop(i)*
■ barber shop	이발소(가) 　*i-bal-so(ga)*

■ beauty salon	미장원(이)	*mi-jang-weon(i)*
■ pharmacy	약방(이)	*yak-ppang(i)*
■ shopping arcade	상점(이)	*sang-jeom(i)*

Where is it? 어디 있어요? *Eo-di i-sseo-yo?*

Is there an English-language interpreter available? 영어 통역할 사람이 있어요? *Yeong-eo t'ong-yeok-k'al sa-ram-i i-sseo-yo?*

What's the charge? 통역비가 얼마예요? *T'ong-yeok-bi-ga eol-ma-ye-yo?*

Do you have a business center? 비지니스 센터가 있습니까? *Pi-ji-ni-seu sen-t'eo-ga i-sseum-ni-kka?*

Where's the <u>elevator</u>? 엘리베이터가 어디 있어요? *El-li-be-i-t'eo-ga eo-di i-sseo-yo?*

■ telephone	전화(가)	*cheon-hwa(ga)*
■ dining room	식당(이)	*shik-ttang(i)*
■ ladies' room	여자 화장실(이)	*yeo-ja hwa-jang-shil(i)*
■ men's room	남자 화장실(이)	*nam-ja hwa-jang-shi(i)*

IN THE ROOM

The <u>air conditioner</u> doesn't work. 에어콘 고장났어요. *E-eo-k'on ko-jang-na-sseo-yo.*

■ heater 히터 *hi-t'eo*

Where can I plug in my <u>electric razor</u>? 면도기 어디에 끼워요? *Myeon-do-gi eo-di-e kki-weo-yo?*

■ hair dryer 드라이기 *teu-ra-i-gi*

Please call the <u>bellhop</u>. 벨보이 좀 불러 주세요. *Pel-bo-i chom pul-leo chu-se-yo.*

■ maid	청소부	*ch'eong-so-bu*
■ manager	지배인	*chi-bae-in*

Please send <u>breakfast</u> to my room.
아침 식사 방으로 갖다 주세요. *A-ch'im shik sa pang-eu-ro kat-tta chu-se-yo.*

■ some towels   타올   *t'a-ol*

■ some soap   비누   *pi-nu*

■ some hangers   옷걸이   *ot-kkeo-ri*

■ a pillow   베개   *pe-gae*

■ a blanket   이불   *i-bul*

■ some ice   얼음   *eo-reum*

■ some ice water   찬 물   *ch'an mul*

■ some toilet paper   휴지   *hyu-ji*

Who is it?   누구세요 ?   *Nu-gu-se-yo?*

Just a minute.   잠깐만요.   *Cham-kkan-man-yo.*

Come in.   들어오세요.   *Teu-reo-o-se-yo.*

Put it on the <u>table</u>, please.
테이블위에 놓으세요. *T'e-i-beul wi-e no-eu-se-yo.*

■ bed   침대   *ch'im-dae*

I'd like <u>room service</u>, please.
룸서비스 좀 보내 주세요. *Rum-sseo-bi-seu chom po-nae chu-se-yo.*

■ a massage therapist   맛사지사   *mas-sa-ji-sa*

■ a babysitter   아이 보는 사람   *a-i po-neun sa-ram*

I'd like a 6 o'clock wakeup call, please.
여섯시에 좀 깨워 주세요. *Yeo-seot-shi-e chom kkae-weo chu-se-yo.*

PROBLEMS

There's no electricity.   방에 전기가 안 들어와요.   *Pang-e cheon-gi-ga an teu-reo-wa-yo.*

The light doesn't work.   불이 고장났어요.   *Pu-ri ko-jang-na-sseo-yo.*

The <u>television</u> doesn't work.	텔레비전 안 나와요. *T'el-le-bi-jyeon an na-wa-yo.*
▓ radio	라디오 *ra-di-o*
The electric fan doesn't work.	선풍기 고장났어요. *Seon-p'ung-gi ko-jang-na-sseo-yo.*
There's no <u>running water</u>.	방에 수돗물이 안나와요. *Pang-e su-don-mul-i an-na-wa-yo.*
▓ hot water	더운 물 *teo-un mul*
The toilet won't flush.	변기가 고장났어요. *Pyeon-gi-ga ko-jang-na-sseo-yo.*
The <u>toilet</u> is stopped up.	변기가 고장났어요. *Pyeon-gi-ga ko-jang-na-sseo-yo.*
▓ sink	세면기 *se-myeon-gi*
The bathtub won't drain properly.	목욕통 물이 잘 안 내려가요. *Mo-gyok-t'ong mu-ri chal an nae-ryeo-ga-yo.*
Can you fix it?	고쳐 주시겠어요? *Ko-ch'yeo chu-shi-ge-sseo-yo?*
I need a new lightbulb.	새 전구 하나 주세요. *Sae cheon-gu ha-na chu-se-yo.*
The window won't <u>open</u>.	방에 창문이 안 <u>열려요</u>. *Pang-e ch'ang-mun-i an yeol-lyeo-yo.*
▓ close	닫혀요 *ta-ch'yeo-yo*
I've locked myself out.	방에 열쇠를 놓고 문을 잠갔어요. *Pang-e yeol-soe-reul no-k'o mun-eul cham-ga-sseo-yo.*
I've lost my key.	제 열쇠를 잃어버렸어요. *Che yeol-soe-reul i-reo-beo-ryeo-sseo-yo.*
These shoes aren't mine.	이 신발 제 것이 아니에요. *I shin-bal che keo-shi a-ni-e-yo.*

| Is my laundry ready? | 제 빨래가 다 되었어요 ? *Che ppal-lae-ga ta toe-eo-sseo-yo?* |
| This laundry isn't mine. | 이 빨래는 제 것이 아니에요. *I ppal-lae-neun che keo-shi a-ni-e-yo.* |

WITH THE DESK CLERK

I would like to keep this in your safe.	이것을 금고에 맡기고 싶은데요. *I-geo-seul keum-go-e ma-kki-go shi-p'eun-de-yo.*
May I have my things from the safe?	제가 맡긴 것 좀 주시겠어요 ? *Che-ga ma-kkin keot chom chu-shi-ge-sseo-yo?*
The key for room 500, please.	오백 호실 열쇠를 주세요. *O-baek ho-shil yeol-soe-reul chu-se-yo.*
Are there any messages for me?	저한테 연락온 거 없어요 ? *Cheo-han-t'e yeol-lak-on keo eop-sseo-yo?*
Do I have any letters?	편지 안 왔어요 ? *P'yeon-ji an wa-sseo-yo?*

ON THE TELEPHONE

Hello, I'd like to make a long distance call.	여보세요, 시외전화하고 싶은데요. *Yeo-bo-se-yo, shi-woe-jeon-hwa-ha-go shi-p'eun-de-yo.*
Hello, I was cut off.	여보세요 ! 전화가 그냥 끊어졌어요. *Yeo-bo-se-yo! Cheon-hwa-ga keu-nyang kkeun-eo-jyeo-sseo-yo.*
Could you try it again?	다시 걸어 보시겠어요 ? *Ta-shi keo-reo po-shi-ge-sseo-yo?*

CHECKING OUT

I'm checking out <u>this morning</u>.	오늘 아침에 계산하겠어요.	*O-neul a-ch'im-e kye-san-ha-ge-sseo-yo.*
■ soon	곧	*kot*
■ around noon	열두시 쯤	*yeol-ttu-shi jjeum*
■ early tomorrow	내일 아침 일찍	*nae-il a-ch'im il-jjik*
■ tomorrow morning	내일 아침에	*nae-il a-ch'im-e*

Would you send someone to carry my luggage down?
짐꾼 좀 불러 주시겠어요 ? *Chim-kkun chom pul-leo chu-shi-ge-sseo-yo?*

May I have my bill, please?
계산서 좀 주세요. *Kye-san-seo chom chu-se-yo.*

My room is 600.
제 방은 육백 호실이에요. *Che pang-eun yuk-ppaek ho-shil-i-e-yo.*

There seems to be an error in the bill.
계산이 잘못된 것 같아요. *Kye-san-i chal-mot-doen keot ka-t'a-yo.*

Could you check it again, please?
다시 한번 봐 주시겠어요 ? *Ta-shi han-beon pwa chu-shi-ge-sseo-yo?*

Could you get me a taxi?
택시 좀 불러 주시겠어요 ? *T'aek-shi chom pul-leo chu-shi-ge-sseo-yo?*

Can I check my baggage until <u>noon</u>?
제 짐을 열두시까지 보관해 주시겠어요 ? *Che chim-eul yeol-ttu-shi-kka-ji po-gwan-hae chu-shi-ge-sseo-yo?*

■ this evening
오늘 저녁 *o-neul cheo-nyeok*

YOUTH HOSTELS

Youth hostels are scattered throughout the country and rates are reasonable. If you are interested in staying at one, you should make arrangements in advance. Further information can be obtained from the Korea Youth Hostels Association in Seoul.

Is there a youth hostel nearby?	이 근처에 유스 호스텔이 있어요 ? *I keun-ch'eo-e yu-seu ho-seu-t'e-ri i-sseo-yo?*
I want to become a member.	회원이 되고 싶은데요. *Hoe-weon-i toe-go shi-p'eun-de-yo.*
When is meal time?	식사 시간이 어떻게 돼요 ? *Shik-sa shi-gan-i eo-tteo-k'e twae-yo?*
Where's the dining room?	식당이 어디 있어요 ? *Shik-ttang-i eo-di i-sseo-yo?*
Can I cook for myself?	직접 해 먹어도 돼요 ? *Chik-jjeop hae meo-geo-do twae-yo?*
Is there a bath time?	목욕 시간이 있어요 ? *Mo-gyok shi-gan-i i-sseo-yo?*
Can I use my sleeping bag?	제 침낭을 써도 돼요 ? *Che ch'im-nang-eul sseo-do twae-yo?*
Is there a curfew?	통행금지가 있어요 ? *T'ong-haeng-geum-ji-ga i-sseo-yo?*

GETTING AROUND TOWN

If you need assistance traveling around Seoul, you can call 1330 for the Information Help Line. The service is available 24/7 in English, Korean, and other languages. If you need help outside Seoul, just enter the area code of that region, then press 1330. You may also visit the Tourist Information Center, operated by the Korea Tourism Organization, located at the Incheon International Airport and in downtown Seoul.

TAXIS

Taxis are a convenient and inexpensive way of getting around Korean cities. The two most common types are regular and deluxe. Fares of deluxe taxis, which offer a higher standard of service, are almost twice that of regular ones. Taxi drivers do not expect tips. You can get a taxi on the street by sticking out your hand, palm down, and moving your hand toward you. Available taxis show a red light just inside the passenger's side or by the cap light on top. You can also go to a taxi stand, usually with a yellow canopy with "TAXI" written near the top, and wait in line for the next available taxi. When you need taxis for special purposes, you can phone "call taxis." Such taxis include jumbo taxis for several passengers and taxis that may be rented for extended periods of time. Because of the complexity of the arrangements, you may want to ask a Korean friend or colleague to help you.

Many taxi drivers do not speak English. You should always be prepared with the name and address of your destination written in Korean. Someone at your hotel can help with this. It is also a good idea to always carry a card or piece of paper with the name, address, and telephone number of the place in which you are staying. This will help the taxi driver, or anyone else, get you back home. A map to your destination will be helpful not only to the driver but also to you.

Please draw me a map.	약도 좀 그려 주세요.	*Yak-tto chom keu-ryeo chu-se-yo.*
Where can I get a taxi?	어디서 택시 타지요 ?	*Eo-di-seo t'aek-shi t'a-ji-yo?*
Are you available? (to the driver)	이 택시 타도 돼요 ?	*I t'aek-shi t'a-do twae-yo?*
Please take me to <u>Gyeongbokgung</u>.	<u>경복궁</u>으로 좀 가 주세요.	<u>*Kyeong-bok-kkung*</u>*-eu-ro chom ka chu-se-yo.*
■ Changdeokgung	창덕궁	*Ch'ang-deok-kkung*
■ Namsan Park	남산 공원	*Nam-san kong-weon*
■ City Hall	시청	*Shi-ch'eong*
■ South Gate Market	남대문 시장	*Nam-dae-mun shi-jang*
■ Itaewon	이태원	*I-t'ae-weon*
Take me to this address. (pointing to a map or location in Korean)	이 주소로 좀 가 주세요.	*I chu-so-ro chom ka chu-se-yo.*
How long does it take to get there?	얼마나 걸려요 ?	*Eol-ma-na keol-lyeo-yo?*
Go straight, please.	똑바로 가세요.	*Ttok-ppa-ro ka-se-yo.*
Turn to the <u>right</u> at the next corner.	다음 길에서 <u>오른쪽</u>으로 가세요.	*Ta-eum kil-e-seo* <u>*o-reun-jjok*</u>*-eu-ro ka-se-yo.*
■ left	왼쪽	*woen-jjok*

Would you drive more slowly?	좀 더 천천히 가 주시겠어요 ? *Chom teo ch'eon-ch'eon-hi ka chu-shi-ge-sseo-yo?*
Stop here, please.	여기서 세워 주세요. *Yeo-gi-seo se-weo chu-se-yo.*
Would you wait for me, please?	여기서 기다려 주시겠어요 ? *Yeo-gi-seo ki-da-ryeo chu-shi-ge-sseo-yo?*
How much do I owe you?	얼마예요 ? *Eol-ma-ye-yo?*

SUBWAYS

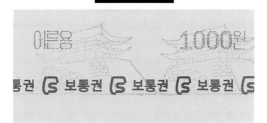

Several cities operate subway systems. The most extensive, the Seoul Metropolitan Subway, is clean, safe, efficient, and easy to use. It gets crowded during rush hour, so be prepared to stand and be jostled if you ride during this time. Most lines run from 6 A.M. to 11 P.M. and are easily identified by their numbers and colors. Station entrances, platforms, and destinations are color-coded and marked in Korean and English. Large subway maps, located in the stations and in each car, are also marked in English and Korean. Many stations have free subway maps that you can take and keep.

Purchase a ticket at a vending machine or ticket window in the subway station. Be sure you have Korean won to pay for the fare, as foreign currency is not accepted. To board the subway, insert the ticket and pick it up as you go through the turnstile. Be sure to keep it to use at the destination turnstile. Each subway car has seats reserved for seniors, people with disabilities, and pregnant women. Use these seats only if you qualify.

Do you have a subway map in English?	영어로 된 지하철 지도가 있어요 ? *Yeong-eo-ro toen chi-ha-ch'eol chi-do-ga i-sseo-yo?*
Where is there a subway station?	지하철역이 어디 있어요 ? *Chi-ha-ch'eol yeok-i eo-di i-sseo-yo?*
Which line goes to _____?	_____에 가려면 어느 차를 타지요 ? *_____-e ka-ryeo-myeon eo-neu ch'a-reul t'a-ji-yo?*
How much is the fare?	요금이 얼마예요 ? *Yo-geum-i eol-ma-ye-yo?*
Where is the ticket machine?	차표 자동 판매기가 어디 있어요 ? *Ch'a-p'yo cha-dong p'an-mae-gi-ga eo-di i-sseo-yo?*
Where should I get off to go to _____?	_____에 가려면 어디서 내려야 돼요 ? *_____e ka-ryeo-myeon eo-di-seo nae-ryeo-ya twae-yo?*
Do I have to change?	갈아 타야 돼요 ? *Ka-ra t'a-ya twae-yo?*
Please tell me where to get off.	어디서 내리는지 알려 주세요. *Eo-di-seo nae-ri-neun-ji al-lyeo chu-se-yo.*
I'm getting off. Excuse me.	내립니다. *Nae-rim-ni-da.*
Where is the lost and found office?	분실물 취급소는 어디 있어요 ? *Pun-shil-mul ch'wi-geup-so-neun eo-di i-sseo-yo?*

I left my <u>bag</u> on the train.	차 안에 <u>가방</u>을 놓고 내렸어요. *Ch'a an-e <u>ka-bang</u>-eul no-k'o nae-ryeo-sseo-yo.*
■ camera	카메라 *k'a-me-ra*

BUSES

While city buses are an interesting way to get around, they are not as easy to use as the subway due to the lack of language support. If you want to use the bus system in Seoul, call 1330 (02-1330 from a cell phone) for information on how to reach a specific destination. Buses use a numbering system and are color-coded to indicate departure and destination points in Seoul and the surrounding suburbs. Fares are based on the distance traveled and are integrated with the subway system. Fares are deposited in the fare terminal as you get on the bus.

Where can I get a bus to City Hall?	시청에 가는 버스를 어디서 타요 ? *Shi-ch'eong-e ka-neun ppeo-seu-reul eo-di-seo t'a-yo?*
Does this bus go to Gwanghwamun?	이 버스 광화문에 가요 ? *I ppeo-seu Kwang-hwa-mun-e ka-yo?*
Where do I get off to go to the American Embassy?	미국 대사관에 가려면 어디서 내려요 ? *Mi-guk tae-sa-gwan-e ka-ryeo-myeon eo-di-seo nae-ryeo-yo?*
Do I need to change buses to go to Itaewon?	이태원에 가려면 버스를 갈아타야 돼요 ? *I-t'ae-weon-e ka-ryeo-myeon ppeo-seu-reul ka-ra-t'a-ya twae-yo?*
How much is the fare?	요금이 얼마예요 ? *Yo-geum-i eol-ma-ye-yo?*
Please tell me where to get off.	어디서 내리는지 알려 주세요. *Eo-di-seo nae-ri-neun-ji al-lyeo chu-se-yo.*

   If you plan to rely on public transportation in Seoul, it is most economical to use a transportation card called T-money. The T-money card is a discounted fare card for use on the subway or bus. A T-money card can be purchased at subway stations, kiosks near the stations, and at many convenience stores. If necessary, you can get the card recharged by a clerk or a recharging machine, which has instructions in English. To use the card, simply place it on the sensor located to the right of each subway turnstile or on the fare terminal inside the bus. The display will tell you how much has been deducted and indicate the balance on your card. When getting off the bus or subway, place the card on the sensor again to determine any additional fare. Balances on cards may be refunded by any T-money card vendor.

Where can I buy a T-money card?	교통카드를 어디에서 살 수 있어요? *Kyo-t'ong-k'a-deu-reul eo-di-e-seo sal su i-sseo-yo?*
Would you please <u>recharge</u> my T-money card?	교통카드를 좀 <u>충전</u>해 주시겠어요? *Kyo-t'ong-k'a-deu-reul chom <u>ch'ung-jeon</u>-hae chu-shi-ge-sseo-yo?*
▓ refund the balance on	잔액을 환불 *chan-aek-eul hwan-bul*

SIGHTSEEING

Korea is a country to experience through the senses. Everywhere one goes, there is something to see, smell, hear, taste, or touch. As a visitor, you will constantly be aware of new and different sights and sounds, while learning about the country's 5,000 years of history and culture. Your problem will be to decide which of the myriad things you are most interested in experiencing during your stay.

Do not let the language hold you back. Koreans love to have you try to speak their language and will encourage you at the slightest utterance of a Korean sound. In fact, the openness and friendly manner in which Koreans respond to foreigners will be a real incentive for you to use whatever Korean you want to try. Remember also that most Koreans have studied English in school and may be able to communicate with you at some level in English. Given the convenience of domestic travel, Korea is an easy country in which to get around, and wherever you go there will be people happy to assist you in your adventure.

INQUIRIES

Where can I buy a guidebook for <u>Seoul</u>?	서울 관광 안내서를 어디서 살 수 있어요 ?	<u>Seo-ul</u> kwan-gwang an-nae-seo-reul eo-di-seo sal su i-sseo-yo?
■ Gyeongju	경주	*Kyeong-ju*
■ Busan	부산	*Pu-san*
■ Jeju Island	제주도	*Che-ju-do*
Could you tell me the points of interest in Seoul?	서울에서 볼 만한 데가 어디 있어요 ?	*Seo-u-re-seo pol man-han te-ga eo-di i-sseo-yo?*
I'm interested in <u>antiques</u>.	골동품에 관심이 있어요.	<u>Kol-ttong-p'um</u>-e kwan-shim-i i-sseo-yo.
■ art	미술	*mi-sul*

■ architecture	건축	*keon-ch'uk*
■ Buddhist temples	절	*cheol*
■ ceramics	도자기	*to-ja-gi*
■ festivals	축제	*ch'uk-jje*
■ folk art	민속예술	*min-sok ye-sul*
■ Korean history	한국역사	*Han-guk yeok-sa*
■ royal palaces	궁전/왕궁	*kung-jeon/wang-gung*
■ calligraphy	서예	*seo-ye*
■ sports	운동	*un-dong*
■ Korean martial arts	태권도	*t'ae-kkweon-do*

Where is the <u>tourist information center</u>? 관광 <u>안내소</u>가 어디 있어요 ? *<u>Kwan-gwang an-nae-so-ga</u> eo-di i-sseo-yo?*

■ Korea Tourism Organization (KTO)	한국 관광 공사	*Han-guk kwan-gwang kong-sa*
■ KTO Tourist Information Center (TIC)	종합 관광 안내 센터	*Chong-hap kwan-gwang an-nae sen-t'eo*
■ Tourist Complaint Center	관광 불편 신고 센터	*Kwan-gwang pul-p'yeon shin-go sen-t'eo*

I'd like to see the <u>market</u>. <u>시장</u>을 보고 싶어요. *<u>Shi-jang-eul</u> po-go shi-p'eo-yo.*

■ downtown area	시내(를)	*shi-nae(reul)*
■ museum	박물관(을)	*pang-mul-gwan(eul)*
■ park	공원(을)	*kong-weon(eul)*
■ temple	절(을)	*cheol(eul)*
■ university	대학교(를)	*tae-hak-kkyo(reul)*

SIGHTSEEING TOURS

Sightseeing tours are a convenient way to see Korea, especially if your time is limited. The Korea Tourism Organization or travel agencies, located in most first-class hotels, can help you arrange a trip to any part of the country. Staff in other hotels will be able to help with day trips and other local sites. Group tours are reasonably priced and have the added advantage of a bilingual guide.

Are there tours to Gyeongju?	경주에 가는 차편이 있어요 ?	*Kyeong-ju-e ka-neun ch'a-p'yeon-i i-sseo-yo?*
■ the Korean Folk Village	민속촌	*Min-sok-ch'on*
■ Independence Hall	독립 기념관	*Tong-nip ki-nyeom-gwan*
■ Gangwha Island	강화도	*Kang-wha-do*
■ Seoraksan National Park	설악산 국립공원	*Seo-rak-san kung-nip-gong-weon*
■ Jeju Island	제주도	*Che-ju-do*
What kind of transportation do you use?	어떻게 갈 거예요 ?	*Eo-tteo-k'e kal kkeo-ye-yo?*
Are the meals and lodging included in the tour fare?	관광요금에 숙박비와 식비가 포함이 돼요 ?	*Kwan-gwang yo-geum-e suk-ppak-ppi-wa shik-ppi-ga p'o-ham-i twae-yo?*
Are the meals Western or Korean?	음식은 양식이에요, 한식이에요 ?	*Eum-shik-eun yang-shik-i-e-yo, han-shik-i-e-yo?*
Is the hotel Western style?	호텔은 서양식이에요 ?	*Ho-t'e-reun seo-yang-shik-i-e-yo?*

<u>How many hours</u> does the tour take?	관광여행은 몇 시간 걸려요 ? *Kwan-gwang yeo-haeng-eun <u>myeot shi-gan</u> keol-lyeo-yo?*
■ how many days	며칠 *myeo-ch'il*
When does the tour <u>start</u>?	관광은 몇 시에 <u>출발해요</u> ? *Kwan-gwang-eun myeot shi-e <u>ch'ul-bal-hae-yo</u>?*
■ return	돌아와요 *to-ra-wa-yo*
Will the bus pick me up at my hotel?	호텔로 관광 버스가 와요 ? *Ho-t'el-lo kwan-gwang ppeo-seu-ga wa-yo?*
Where can I join the tour?	관광을 어디서부터 할 수 있어요 ? *Kwan-gwang-eul eo-di-seo-bu-t'eo hal su i-sseo-yo?*
Is there any free time for shopping?	쇼핑할 수 있는 시간이 있어요 ? *Shyo-p'ing-hal su in-neun shi-gan-i i-sseo-yo?*
How much is the fare for the tour?	관광요금은 얼마예요 ? *Kwan-gwang yo-geum-eun eol-ma-ye-yo?*
I'd like <u>one ticket</u> for the tour.	관광권을 <u>한 장</u> 주세요. *Kwan-gwang-kkweon-eul <u>han chang</u> chu-se-yo.*
■ two tickets	두 장 *tu chang*
■ three tickets	세 장 *se chang*

SIGHTSEEING ON YOUR OWN

For those travelers who prefer to see things on their own, the following phrases may be used.

What time does it <u>open</u>?	몇 시에 문을 <u>열어요</u> ? *Myeot shi-e mun-eul <u>yeo-reo-yo</u>?*
■ close	닫아요 *ta-da-yo*

Is it open on <u>Saturdays</u>?	토요일에 열어요 ? *T'o-yo-i-re yeo-reo-yo?*
■ on Sundays	일요일에 *i-ryo-i-re*
■ today	오늘 *o-neul*

Is there an admission fee?	입장료가 있어요 ? *Ip-jjang-nyo-ga i-sseo-yo?*

How much is the admission?	입장료가 얼마예요 ? *Ip-jjang-nyo-ga eol-ma-ye-yo?*

Is there a discount for <u>students</u>?	학생들에게 할인해 줘요 ? *Hak-ssaeng-deul-e-ge ha-rin-hae chweo-yo?*
■ senior citizens	노인들 *no-in-deul*
■ children	아이들 *a-i-deul*

Am I allowed to take pictures inside?	안에서 사진을 찍어도 돼요 ? *An-e-seo sa-jin-eul jjik-eo-do twae-yo?*

Where is the <u>entrance</u>?	입구가 어디에요 ? *Ip-kku-ga eo-di-e-yo?*
■ gift shop	선물 가게 *seon-mul ka-ge*
■ exit	출구 *ch'ul-gu*

Should I take off my shoes?	구두를 벗을까요 ? *Ku-du-reul peo-seul-kka-yo?*

Can I just look around?	구경해도 괜찮아요 ? *Ku-gyeong-hae-do kwaen-ch'an-a-yo?*

Is there an English-speaking guide available?	영어 할 줄 아는 안내원이 있어요 ? *Yeong-eo hal jjul a-neun an-nae-weon-i i-sseo-yo?*

POINTS OF INTEREST

Major sightseeing attractions include palaces, museums, temples, and national parks. Individual names of these attractions have been listed in their various categories for easy reference. This list is by no means exhaustive, and you may wish to consider other suggestions made by Korean friends or acquaintances. Categories are not exclusive. For example, many temples may be included as part of a national park.

NATIONAL MUSEUMS

Museums have large numbers of artifacts from archaeological excavations that have occurred over a number of years. The National Museum of Korea, located in the Yongsan area of Seoul, has an extensive collection of works of art. The National Palace Museum, located in the Gyeongbokgung area of Seoul, displays relics of the Joseon Dynasty (1392–1910).

Branches of the National Museum are located in Gyeongju (the ancient capital of the Silla period), Buyeo and Gongju (capitals during the old Baekje Kingdom), Chuncheon, Gimhae, Gwangju, Jinju, Jeonju, Cheongju, Daegu, and Jeju Island. These museums feature objects of regional importance, especially those items that were excavated from the tombs of Silla and Baekje kings.

In addition to national museums, other museums have been built to focus on specialized art forms. For example, the Jeju Haenyeo Museum honors the diving women of Jeju Island; the Andong Public Folk Village is where you can experience Confucian culture and traditional Korean games; and the Museum of Traditional Music in Seoul allows you to see and hear ancient musical instruments that were played in royal courts.

Jeju Haenyeo Museum Jeju Island	제주 해녀 박물관 *pang-mul-gwan*	*Che-ju hae-nyeo*

Jeju Folklore Museum Jeju Island	제주 민속 박물관	*Che-ju min-sok pang-mul-gwan*
Jinju National Museum Jinju	진주 국립 박물관	*Chin-ju kung-nip pang-mul-gwan*
Gongju National Museum Gongju	공주 국립 박물관	*Kong-ju kung-nip pang-mul-gwan*
Gwangju National Museum Gwangju	광주 국립 박물관	*Kwang-ju kung-nip pang-mul-gwan*
Gyeongju National Museum Gyeongju	경주 국립 박물관	*Kyeong-ju kung-nip pang-mul-gwan*
National Museum of Korea Seoul	한국 국립 박물관	*Han-guk kung-nip pang-mul-gwan*
National Palace Museum Seoul	국립 고궁 박물관	*Kung-nip ko-gung pang-mul-gwan*
National Folk Museum of Korea Seoul	국립 민속 박물관	*Kung-nip min-sok pang-mul-gwan*
Busan Museum Busan	부산 박물관	*Pu-san pang-mul-gwan*
Buyeo National Museum Buyeo	부여 국립 박물관	*Pu-yeo kung-nip pang-mul-gwan*
Sungkyunkwan University Museum Seoul	성균관 대학교 박물관	*Seong-gyun-gwan tae-hak-kkyo pang-mul-gwan*

Yonsei University Museum Seoul	연세 대학교 박물관 *Yeon-se tae-hak-kkyo pang-mul-gwan*
Andong Public Folk Village Andong	안동 민속촌 *An-dong min-sok-ch'on*
Museum of Traditional Music Seoul	전통음악 박물관 *Cheon-t'ong-eum-ak pang-mul-gwan*
Leeum Museum Seoul	리움 박물관 *Ri-um pang-mul-gwan*
Seoul National Science Museum Seoul	서울 국립 과학 박물관 *Seo-ul kung-nip kwa-hak pang-mul-gwan*
Museum of Art at Seoul National University Seoul	서울 대학교 미술관 *Seo-ul tae-hak-kyo mi-sul-gwan*
Seoul Museum of History Seoul	서울 역사 박물관 *Seo-ul yeok-sa pang-mul-gwan*

PALACES AND CITY GATES

Perhaps Korea's most magnificent architecture is seen in the city gates and royal palaces of Seoul. Seoul was once surrounded by a wall with four gates providing entrance into the city. The most famous gate, Namdaemun (South Gate), near Seoul Station has been designated as National Treasure Number 1 in Korea.

Royal palaces which were built during the Koryo (918–1392) and Yi (1392–1910) dynasties are open to visitors. The four palaces listed on the following page have been preserved. Although much of the structure of the four palaces was destroyed by war, they have been rebuilt to their original states. As you visit these palaces, you will notice that they face south or east, since people believed that positive powers came from these directions. The king was thought to receive guidance from heaven, which he transmitted to the people he ruled. Grounds of the palaces are splendid, and there are many other attractions within the walls.

Changdeokgung Palace Seoul	창덕궁	*Ch'ang-deok-kkung*
Changgyeonggung Palace Seoul	창경궁	*Ch'ang-gyeong-gung*
East Gate Seoul	동대문	*Tong-dae-mun*
Gyeongbokgung Palace Seoul	경복궁	*Kyeong-bok-kkung*
National Treasure No. 1	국보 일호	*Kuk-ppo il-ho*
South Gate Seoul	남대문	*Nam-dae-mun*
Deoksugung Palace Seoul	덕수궁	*Teok-su-gung*

CULTURAL AND HISTORICAL SITES

Jongmyo Royal Shrine Seoul	종묘	*Chong-myo*
Great King Sejong Memorial Hall Seoul	세종 문화 회관	*Se-jong mun-hwa hoe-gwan*

Chongwadae (home to the President) Seoul	청와대	Ch'eong-wa-dae
Hyeonchungsa Chungcheongnam-do	현충사	Hyeon-ch'ung-sa
Independence Hall Chungcheongnam-do	독립 기념관	Tong-nip ki-nyeom-gwan

NATIONAL PARKS

Koreans especially enjoy the outdoors and nature's beauty. The country has emphasized the development of the national parks located in the majestic mountain areas scattered around the nation. Buddhist temples, located in many of these parks, provide added attractions. A few of the more popular parks are listed below.

Jirisan National Park Jeollanam-do	지리산 국립 공원	Chi-ri-san kung-nip kong-weon
Juwangsan National Park Gyeongsangnam-do	주왕산 국립 공원	Chu-wang-san kung-nip kong-weon
Odaesan National Park Gangwon-do	오대산 국립 공원	O-dae-san kung-nip kong-weon
Songnisan National Park Chungcheongbuk-do	속리산 국립 공원	Song-ni-san kung-ni-san kong-weon
Seoraksan National Park, Gangwon-do	설악산 국립 공원	Seo-rak-san kung-nip kong-weon
Gyeryongsan National Park Chungcheongnam-do	계룡산 국립 공원	Kye-ryong-san kung-nip kong-weon

TEMPLES

Two thousand of the seven thousand Buddhist temples which once dotted the Korean countryside still exist. Temples are not only places of scenic beauty, but they are also an integral part of the culture. Buddhism flourished for centuries in Korea until it was replaced by Confucianism during the Yi Dynasty (1392–1910). Buddhism continues to be one of the major religions in Korea and can still be seen practiced in various temples.

The following list includes some of Korea's most popular temples. Try to see at least one temple during your visit in Korea. The colorful architectural style is unique to Korea and exemplifies a folk art not seen anywhere else in the world. Most temples are open seven days a week from early morning to evening. A number of temples participate in Temple Stay, a program designed to help people better understand Korean Buddhism.

Seoul and Vicinity
(The Korean word for temple is *sa*.)

Jogyesa	조계사	*Cho-gye-sa*
Bongwonsa	봉원사	*Pong-weon-sa*
Yongjusa	용주사	*Yong-ju-sa*

Busan and Gyeongju

Beomeosa	범어사	*Peom-eo-sa*
Bulguksa	불국사	*Pul-guk-sa*
Sokkuram Grotto	석굴암	*Seok-kku-ram*
Tongdosa	통도사	*T'ong-do-sa*

Central Region and Daegu Vicinity

Jikjisa	직지사	*Chik-jji-sa*
Haeinsa	해인사	*Hae-in-sa*
Beopjusa	법주사	*Peop-jju-sa*
Buseoksa	부석사	*Pu-seok-sa*

Southwest Region

Hwaeomsa	화엄사	*Hwa-eom-sa*
Geumsansa	금산사	*Keum-san-sa*
Songgwangsa	송광사	*Song-gwang-sa*

East Coast and Sorak Area

Naksansa	낙산사	*Nak-ssan-sa*
Sinheungsa	신흥사	*Shin-heung-sa*
Woljeongsa	월정사	*Weol-jjeong-sa*

RELIGIOUS SERVICES

Koreans practice a wide range of religions, including Buddhism, Christianity, and Confucianism, the three most popular. However, one can also find Jewish, Muslim, and other religious services in the country. Check the English-language newspapers for specific information. Should you be interested in attending a Korean service, the following expressions will help.

Shall we go to church together?	교회에 같이 갈까요 ?	*Kyo-hoe-e ka-ch'i kal-kka-yo?*
Is there a <u>Catholic church</u> near here?	이 근처에 <u>가톨릭 성당</u>이 있어요 ?	*I keun-ch'eo-e <u>Ka-t'ol-lik seong-dang</u>-i i-sseo-yo?*
■ Protestant church	교회(가)	*kyo-hoe(ga)*
■ synagogue	유태교 회당(이)	*yu-t'ae-gyo hoe-dang(i)*
■ mosque	회교 사원(이)	*hoe-gyo sa-weon(i)*
■ Buddhist temple	절(이)	*cheol(i)*
What time is the <u>service</u>?	예배가 몇 시에 있어요 ?	*Ye-bae-ga myeot shi-e i-sseo-yo?*
■ mass	미사	*mi-sa*

I'd like to speak to <u>a priest</u>.	신부님 뵙고 싶은데요. *Shin-bu-nim poep-kko shi-p'eun-de-yo.*
■ minister	목사님 *mok-ssa-nim*
■ monk	스님 *seu-nim*
■ rabbi	랍비님 *rap-ppi-nim*
I'd like to attend services here today.	오늘예배에 참석하고 싶어요. *O-neul ye-bae-e ch'am-seok-k'a-go shi-p'eo-yo.*
I enjoyed the services very much.	예배가 참 좋았어요. *Ye-bae-ga ch'am cho-a-sseo-yo.*
Are there any other activities here <u>today</u>?	오늘 다른 행사가 있어요 ? *O-neul ta-reun haeng-sa-ga i-sseo-yo?*
■ this week	이 번주에 *i peon-ju-e*
■ this month	이 달에 *i ta-re*
I'd like to come back again.	다시 오고 싶어요. *Ta-shi o-go shi-p'eo-yo.*
Thank you.	감사합니다. *Kam-sa-ham-ni-da.*

PLANNING TRIPS

Korea's extensive transportation system makes for convenient travel throughout the country. Depending on your destination, you can travel by bus, train, air, or ferry. Railway stations and bus terminals are centrally located in all major metropolitan areas. Air service links cities all over the country. Ferries may be used when traveling to Korea's islands. The efficiency of the system allows you to visit many places within a short period of time. If you need travel assistance and other information in Seoul, dial 1330 for the Information Help Line. The service is available 24/7 in English and other languages. For help outside Seoul, enter the area code of that region, and then press 1330. If you are interested in traveling to sites in North Korea while in South Korea, contact the Korea Tourism Organization.

TRAINS

The excellent railway network in Korea connects all major cities. Seoul Station, the major train station in Korea, offers service to such cities as Busan, Gyeongju, Jeonju, and Gwangju. Cheongnyangni Station has trains to destinations in the provinces of Gangwon-do and Gyeongsangbuk-do. These and other train stations are accessible by subway or taxi.

There are three types of train service. The KTX (Korea Train Express) is a high-speed train that links Seoul to Busan and other major cities. The Saemaeul train, offers a slower, yet comfortable and less expensive choice. The Mugunghwa train service is limited. In train stations, you can purchase tickets from an agent or from a vending machine.

INQUIRIES

Does the train leave from Seoul Station?

기차가 서울역에서 출발해요 ?
Ki-ch'a-ga Seo-ul-yeok-e-seo ch'ul-bal-hae-yo?

■ Cheongnyangni Station	청량리역	*Ch'eong-nyang-ni-yeok*

Where can I buy a ticket for the Saemaeul-ho?	새마을호 표를 어디서 사요 ?	*Sae-ma-eul-ho p'yo-reul eo-di-seo sa-yo?*

Where is the ticket window?	매표구가 어디에요 ?	*Mae-p'yo-gu-ga eo-di-e-yo?*

BUYING TICKETS

It is a good idea to buy tickets in advance, especially on weekends and holidays. Contact the Korea Tourism Organization for help with advance purchases.

Is the <u>KTX</u> train available to Daejeon?	<u>KTX</u>열차가 대전까지 갑니까 ?	*<u>KTX</u> yeol-ch'a-ga Tae-jeon-kka-ji kam-ni-kka?*
■ Saemaeul	새마을호	*Sae-ma-eul-ho*
■ Mugunghwa	무궁화호	*Mu-gung-hwa-ho*

Do I have to change trains?	기차를 갈아타야 돼요 ?	*Ki-ch'a-reul ka-ra-t'a-ya twae-yo?*

When is the <u>earliest train</u> of the day for Gwangju?	광주행 <u>첫차</u>가 몇 시예요 ?	*Kwang-ju-haeng <u>ch'eot-ch'a</u>-ga myeot shie-yo?*
■ last train	막차	*mak-ch'a*

I'd like a <u>round-trip ticket</u> to Daegu.	대구행 <u>왕복표</u>를 한 장 주세요.	*Tae-gu-haeng<u>wang-bok-p'yo</u>-reul han chang chu-se-yo.*
■ one-way ticket	편도표	*p'yeon-do-p'yo*
■ first-class ticket	일등 차표	*il-tteung ch'a-p'yo*
■ regular ticket	일반실 표	*il-ban-shil p'yo*
■ standing ticket	자유석 표	*cha-yu-seok p'yo*

Is there a <u>dining car</u> on the train?	열차에 식당차가 있습니까 ? *Yeol-ch'a-e shik-dang-ch'a-ga i-sseum-ni-kka?*
▦ sleeping car	침대차 *ch'im-dae-ch'a*
▦ movie car	영화객실 *yeong-hwa-gaek-shil*
How much is the fare?	요금이 얼마예요 ? *Yo-geum-i eol-ma-ye-yo?*

ON THE TRAIN

Is this the train to Jeonju?	전주행 열차예요 ? *Cheon-ju-haeng yeol-ch'a-ye-yo?*
Is this seat taken?	이 자리에 사람 있어요 ? *I cha-ri-e sa-ram i-sseo-yo?*
I think that's my seat.	그 자리는 제 자리인 것 같아요. *Keu cha-ri-neun che cha-ri-in keot ka-t'a-yo.*
Where's the dining car?	식당칸이 어디 있어요 ? *Shik-ttang-k'an-i eo-di i-sseo-yo?*
What time do we arrive at Jinju?	진주에 몇 시에 도착해요 ? *Chin-ju-e myeot shi-e to-ch'ak-k'ae-yo?*

REFRESHMENTS

Refreshments on the train are sold by vendors who pass through your car. Some serve beverages, others food. It is acceptable for you to bring your own food and drinks on the train.

May I have some <u>coffee</u>?	커피 주시겠어요 ? <u>*K'eo-p'i*</u> *chu-shi-ge-sseo-yo?*
▦ tea	차 *ch'a*
▦ milk	우유 *u-yu*
▦ cola	콜라 *k'ol-la*

■ juice	주스	*chu-seu*
■ beer	맥주	*maek-jju*
■ bottled water	생수	*saeng-su*
■ peanuts	땅콩	*ttang-k'ong*
■ cookies	과자	*kwa-ja*
■ ice cream	아이스크림	*a-i-seu-k'eu-rim*

Do you have a box
lunch?

도시락 있어요? *To-shi-rak i-sseo-yo?*

LOST AND FOUND

Where is the lost
and found office?

분실물 취급소가 어디 있어요?
Pun-shil-mul ch'wi-geup-so-ga eo-di i-sseo-yo?

I've lost my <u>camera</u>.

제 카메라를 잃어버렸어요. *Che k'a-me-ra-reul i-reo-beo-ryeo-sseo-yo.*

■ travelers' checks	여행자 수표	*yeo-haeng-ja su-p'yo*
■ passport	여권	*yeo-kkweon*
■ wallet	지갑	*chi-gap*
■ hand bag/briefcase	가방	*ka-bang*

LONG DISTANCE EXPRESS BUSES

Express bus service in Korea is comfortable and
convenient. Buses use expressways to connect to major
cities. Express bus terminals in Seoul are accessible by
subway and taxi.

I want to take an
express bus to
Gyeongju.

경주행 고속버스를 타고 싶은데요.
Kyeong-ju-haeng ko-sok-ppeo-seu-reul t'a-go ship-eun-de-yo.

What bus terminal do I use to go to Cheongju?	청주에 가려면 어느 터미널에 가야하지요 ? *Ch'eong-ju-e ka-ryeo-myeon eo-neu t'eo-mi-neol-e ka-ya-ha-ji-yo?*
Is this the bus to Chuncheon?	이 버스가 춘천행 버스입니까 ? *I peo-seu-ga Ch'un-ch'eon-haeng peo-seu-im-ni-kka?*

AIR TRAVEL

International routes are served by Incheon International Airport, and domestic routes by Gimpo Airport. Korea's domestic flight network links many major cities including Seoul, Busan, Daegu, Gwangju, Jeju Island, and the East Coast.

Is there a flight to <u>Busan</u>?	부산행 비행기가 있어요 ? <u>*Pu-san-haeng pi-haeng-gi-ga i-sseo-yo?*</u>
■ Ulsan	울산 *Ul-ssan*
■ Yeosu	여수 *Yeo-su*
Is there a daily flight to Jeju Island?	제주도행 비행기가 매일 있어요 ? *Che-ju-do-haeng pi-haeng-gi-ga mae-il i-sseo-yo?*
Which day of the week does the flight to Sokcho leave?	속초행 비행기가 무슨 요일에 있어요 ? *Sok-ch'o-haeng pi-haeng-gi-ga mu-seun yo-i-re i-sseo-yo?*
Should I buy my air ticket in advance?	표를 미리 사야 돼요 ? *P'yo-reul mi-ri sa-ya twae-yo?*
Can I get a ticket at the airport the day of the trip?	출발 하는날 공항에서 표를 살 수 있어요 ? *Ch'ul-bal ha-neun-nal kong-hang-e-seo p'yo-reul sal su i-sseo-yo?*

Can I get a ticket to Gwangju for <u>today</u>?	광주행 오늘 표를 살 수 있어요 ? *Kwang-ju-haeng o-neul p'yo-reul sal su i-sseo-yo?*
tomorrow	내일 *nae-il*
the day after tomorrow	모레 *mo-re*
April 4	사월 사일 *sa-weol sa-il*
I'd like a <u>one-way</u> ticket to Daegu.	대구행 비행기표 편도로 한 장 주세요. *Tae-gu-haeng pi-haeng-gi-p'yo p'yeon-do-ro han chang chu-se-yo.*
round-trip	왕복으로 *wang-bok-eu-ro*
<u>Two</u> tickets to Busan, please.	부산행 비행기표를 두 장 주세요. *Pu-san-haeng pi-haeng-gi-p'yo-reul tu chang chu-se-yo.*
three	세 *se*
four	네 *ne*
When is the next available flight to Gwangju?	다음 광주행 비행기가 언제 있어요 ? *Ta-eum Kwang-ju-haeng pi-haeng-gi-ga eon-je i-sseo-yo?*
Is there <u>an earlier</u> flight than that?	그 보다 더 이른 비행기가 있어요 ? *Keu po-da teo i-reun pi-haeng-gi-ga i-sseo-yo?*
a later	늦은 *neu-jeun*
What's the air fare to Seoul?	서울행 비행기 요금이 얼마예요 ? *Seo-ul-haeng pi-haeng-gi yo-geum-i eol-ma-ye-yo?*
What's the flying time to Sokcho?	속초까지 얼마나 걸려요 ? *Sok-ch'o-kka-ji eol-ma-na keol-lyeo-yo?*
Is there a limit on the number of bags?	수하물을 몇 개 부칠 수 있어요 ? *Su-ha-mu-reul myeot kkae pu-ch'il su i-sseo-yo?*

| When do I have to check in? | 탑승 수속은 몇 시까지 해야 돼요 ? |
| | *T'ap-seung su-sok-eun myeot shi-kka-ji hae-ya twae-yo?* |

| Do I need to re-confirm the reservation? | 예약을 재확인해야 돼요 ? *Ye-yak-eul chae-hwa-gin-hae-ya twae-yo?* |

GETTING TO THE AIRPORT

| Where is the airport? | 공항이 어디 있어요 ? *Kong-hang-i eo-di i-sseo-yo?* |

| Is it far? | 여기서 멀어요 ? *Yeo-gi-seo meo-reo-yo?* |

| How can I get to the airport? | 공항에 어떻게 가요 ? *Kong-hang-e eo-tteo-k'e ka-yo?* |

Is there a <u>bus</u> to the airport?	공항에 가는 버스가 있어요 ?
	Kong-hang-e ka-neun ppeo-seu-ga i-sseo-yo?
▨ shuttle bus	서틀버스 *shyeo-t'eul-beo-seu*
▨ taxi	택시 *taek-shi*

How much does the <u>taxi</u> to the airport cost?	공항까지 택시요금이 얼마예요 ?
	Kong-hang-kka-ji t'aek-shi yo-geum-i eol-ma-ye-yo?
▨ bus	버스 *ppeo-seu*

How long does the <u>taxi</u> take to the airport?	공항까지 택시로 얼마나 걸려요 ?
	Kong-hang-kka-ji t'aek-shi-ro eol-ma-na keol-lyeo-yo?
▨ bus	버스 *ppeo-seu*

AT THE AIRPORT

I'd like to check this suitcase.	이 가방을 좀 부쳐 주세요. *I ka-bang-eul chom pu-ch'yeo chu-se-yo.*
This is carry-on.	이 가방은 가지고 타겠어요. *I ka-bang-eun ka-ji-go t'a-ge-sseo-yo.*
Can I get a seat by the <u>window</u>?	창옆 좌석이 있어요 ? *Ch'ang-yeop chwa-seok-i i-sseo-yo?*
■ aisle	통로 *t'ong-no*
When is the departure?	몇 시에 출발해요 ? *Myeot shi-e ch'ul-bal-hae-yo?*
Where's the <u>departure</u> gate?	출발하는 데가 어디에요 ? *Ch'ul-bal-ha-neun te-ga eo-di-e-yo?*
■ arrival	도착하는 *to-ch'ak-k'a-neun*
What's the arrival time?	몇 시에 도착해요 ? *Myeot shi-e to-ch'ak-k'ae-yo?*

INTERNATIONAL AIR TRAVEL

I'd like a ticket to <u>Tokyo</u>.	동경행 비행기표 한 장 주세요. *Tong-gyeong-haeng pi-haeng-gi-p'yo han chang chu-se-yo.*
■ Hong Kong	홍콩 *Hong-k'ong*
When is the first available flight to <u>Bangkok</u>?	방콕행 첫 비행기가 몇 시예요 ? *Pang-k'ok-haeng ch'eot pi-haeng-gi-ga myeot shi ye-yo?*
■ Taipei	타이뻬이 *T'a-i-ppe-i*
Is there a direct flight to Manila from here?	여기서 마닐라행 직행이 있어요 ? *Yeo-gi-seo Ma-nil-la-haeng chik-haeng-i i-sseo-yo?*

What's the airfare to Los Angeles?	로스앤젤레스까지 비행기 요금이 얼마예요 ? *Ro-seu-aen-gel-le-seu-kka-ji pi-haeng-gi yo-geum-i eol-ma-ye-yo?*
How long does the flight take?	얼마나 걸리지요 ? *Eol-ma-na keol-li-ji-yo?*
Is there a charge if I change my flight?	비행기를 갈아탈때 요금을 냅니까 ? *Pi-haeng-gi-reul ka-ra-t'al-ttae yo-geum-eul naem-ni-kka?*
Are meals served on the flight?	기내식이 나옵니까 ? *Ki-nae-shik-i na-om-ni-kka?*
Is there a charge for meals?	식사에 요금을 내야 합니까 ? *Shik-sa-e yo-geum-eul nae-ya ham-ni-kka?*
When is the <u>departure</u> time?	출발 시간이 몇 시예요 ? *Ch'ul-bal shi-gan-i myeot shi-ye-yo?*
■ arrival	도착 *to-ch'ak*

FERRIES

Ferries give you interesting ways to see Jeju and many other islands of Korea.

Can I go to <u>Jeju</u> by ferry?	제주행 페리가 있어요 ? *Che-ju-haeng p'e-ri-ga i-sseo-yo?*
■ Chungmu	충무 *Ch'ung-mu*
When does the next ferry leave?	다음 페리가 몇 시에 있어요 ? *Ta-eum p'e-ri-ga myeot shi-e i-sseo-yo?*
Where is the <u>harbor</u>?	항구가 어디 있어요 ? *Hang-gu-ga eo-di i-sseo-yo?*
■ ticket office	매표실 *mae-p'yo-shil*
■ pier	부두 *pu-du*

How long does the trip take?	여행은 얼마나 걸려요 ? *Yeo-haeng-eun eol-ma-na keol-lyeo-yo?*
When do we board?	몇 시에 타요 ? *Myeot shi-e t'a-yo?*
Do we stop at any ports?	항구에 들러요 ? *Hang-gu-e teul-leo-yo?*
I'd like a <u>first-class ticket</u>.	<u>1등실표</u> 1장 주세요. *<u>Il-tteung-shil-p'yo</u> han-jang chu-se-yo.*
▨ second-class ticket	2등실표 *i-deung-shil-p'yo*
▨ third-class ticket	3등실표 *sam-deung-shil-p'yo*
Are meals served on board?	식사가 나와요 ? *Shik-sa-ga na-wa-yo?*
Can we buy something to eat on board?	배에서 먹는 것 팔아요 ? *Pae-e-seo meong-neun keot p'a-ra-yo?*
I don't feel well.	배멀미가 나요. *Pae-meol-mi-ga na-yo.*
Do you have something for seasickness?	멀미약 있어요 ? *Meol-mi yak i-sseo-yo?*
When do we arrive at Mokpo?	목포에 몇 시에 도착해요 ? *Mok-p'o-e myeot shi-e to-ch'ak-k'ae-yo?*

A FEW ITINERARIES

In this section, you will find suggested places to visit in Seoul as well as destinations to consider for trips of one day or more. A limited number of venues is presented to help you get started. Contact the Korea Tourism Organization for additional assistance.

SEOUL

Seoul has been the center of politics, economy, culture, and transportation of Korea since the Joseon Dynasty (1392–1910). Devastated during the Korean War (1950–1953), the city has become the symbol of Korea's rise as a major influence in the culture and economy of the world.

Apgujeong-dong

Fashionable shops, department stores, cafés, nightclubs, restaurants, galleries, and expensive residential areas draw people to this section of Gangnam, a major business and residential area south of the Han River. Apgujeong-dong and adjacent Cheongdam-dong are examples of the trend-setting culture of Korea. Nearby is the COEX Mall, an entertainment center of restaurants, exhibitions, a museum, an aquarium, and a theater. Bongeunsa, a Buddhist temple, is a short distance away.

Amusement Parks

Amusement parks are located in close proximity to Seoul. Lotte World, the closest to downtown, is an indoor theme park. Everland, the largest theme park, has a number of rides and a zoo. Seoul Land has a zoo and botanical garden.

Buddhist Temples

Many Buddhist temples in Korea invite foreign guests for tours as well as overnight programs. Jogyesa Temple in downtown Seoul offers tours as well as overnight stays. Contact the Korea Tourism Organization for details about temple stays.

Gyeongbokgung Palace

Gyeongbokgung, Korea's oldest palace, was the center of the Joseon Dynasty. Once inside the gates, you will be surrounded by the beauty of nature and fourteenth century Korean architecture. The National Folk Museum of Korea is located on the grounds of the palace. Adjacent to the palace is Cheongwadae, also known as the Blue House, the presidential mansion of Korea.

Hongik University Vicinity

Also known as *Hongdae*, the area is filled with uniquely decorated cafés, clubs, and art-related shops. It is especially popular among young people interested in music and art.

Huwon (Biwon)

Also called the Secret Garden, Huwon is one of Seoul's most beautiful examples of Korean landscaping. It is part of the Changdeokgung Palace, built in 1405.

Insadong

Insadong is the place to go to shop for items that reflect traditional Korean culture. Here you will find art galleries and antiques such as paintings, ceramics, paper crafts, and furniture. Also enjoyable are its restaurants and tea houses. From Insadong you can walk to Jongno, a major shopping and entertainment area by day and night. Further on is Cheonggyecheon Stream, a restored waterway that traverses the center of Seoul. Along the stream you can enjoy shops, restaurants, fountains, and historical sites.

Itaewon

Itaewon is a special tourism district with many shops as well as bars, nightclubs, ethnic restaurants, and hotels. Shops offer leather goods, bags, clothing, jewelry, and souvenirs.

Namdaemun Market

Namdaemun Market, in the center of Seoul, is a massive collection of shops specializing in clothing, children's wear, accessories, shoes, kitchen items, regional specialties, and more. Stores and stands prepare quick, inexpensive Korean snacks like noodles and pan-fried food. From the market, you can take an underground passage to Myeong-dong, a major shopping, restaurant, and financial center.

Namsan Park

In the heart of Seoul is Namsan Park, from which N Seoul Tower offers a panoramic view of the city. The park's walking paths, jogging courses, and lush flora make it an inviting place to visit.

National Museum of Korea

The museum, one of the largest in the world, contains an extensive collection of works of art that depict the history and culture of Korea and other selected countries. The museum building and grounds offer beautiful reinterpretations of Korea's traditional architecture.

Seoul Museum of History

The museum highlights Seoul's unique heritage and its place in Korea's history.

War Memorial of Korea

The War Memorial of Korea honors the country's heroes and documents the history of the Korean War as well as the other wars and military culture of Korea through its 5,000-year history.

Gyeongbokgung is really beautiful!	경복궁이 참 아름답군요. *Kyeong-bok-kkung-i ch'am a-reum-dap-kkun-yo.*
Was it built during the <u>Joseon</u> Dynasty?	조선시대에 지었어요 ? *Cho-seon-shi-dae-e chi-eo-sseo-yo?*
▨ Koryo	고려 *Ko-ryeo*
How large is the palace area?	왕궁이 얼마나 커요 ? *Wang-gung-i eol-ma-na k'eo-yo?*
How many rulers lived here?	여기서 왕들이 몇 분이나 살았어요 ? *Yeo-gi-seo wang-deu-ri myeot ppun-i-na sa-ra-sseo-yo?*
Is an English-speaking guide available?	영어 할 줄 아는 안내원이 있어요 ? *Yeong-eo hal jjul a-neun an-nae-won-i i-sseo-yo?*
What type of collections are they exhibiting at the National Museum?	국립 박물관에는 어떤 것을 전시해 놓았어요 ? *Kung-nip pang-mul-gwan-e-neun eo-tteon keo-seul cheon-shi-hae no-a-sseo-yo?*

How late is the museum open?	박물관을 몇 시까지 열어요 ? *Pang-mul-gwan-eul myeot shi-kka-ji yeo-reo-yo?*
Shall we take a picture?	사진을 찍을까요 ? *Sa-jin-eul jjik-eul-kka-yo?*
Would you take our picture?	사진 좀 찍어 주시겠어요 ? *Sa-jin chom jjik-eo chu-shi-ge-sseo-yo?*
Where's the Blue House? (President's residence)	청와대가 어디 있어요 ? *Ch'eong-wa-dae-ga eo-di i-sseo-yo?*
Is the Blue House open to visitors?	청와대를 구경할 수 있어요 ? *Ch'eong-wa-dae-reul ku-gyeong-hal su i-sseo-yo?*
When are the ceremonies at the Jogyesa Temple?	조계사에서는 몇 시에 의식이 있어요 ? *Cho-gye-sa-e-seo-neun myeot shi-e eui-shik-i i-sseo-yo?*
Are foreigners allowed to attend the ceremonies?	외국 사람들도 의식에 참석할 수 있어요 ? *Woe-guk sa-ram-deul-do eui-shik-e ch'am-seok-k'al su i-sseo-yo?*
How far is it to Secret Garden?	비원은 여기서 얼마나 멀어요 ? *Pi-weon-eun yeo-gi-seo eol-ma-na meo-reo-yo?*
How do I get to Insadong?	인사동을 어떻게 가면 좋아요 ? *In-sa-dong-eul eo-tteo-k'e ka-myeon cho-a-yo?*
Shall we go shopping in Apgujeong-dong?	압구정동에 쇼핑하러 갈까요 ? *Ap-kku-jeong-dong-e shyo-p'ing-ha-reo kal-kka-yo?*
Can I take a bus to Namsan Park?	남산 공원을 버스로 갈 수 있어요 ? *Nam-san kong-weon-eul ppeo-seu-ro kal su i-sseo-yo?*

How tall is Seoul Tower?	서울 타워는 얼마나 높아요 ? *Seo-ul t'a-weo-neun eol-ma-na no-p'a-yo?*

DAY TRIPS FROM SEOUL

Many interesting sites may be visited as a day trip from Seoul. You will find it refreshing to explore rural areas and experience the natural beauty of Korea's mountains, rivers, and seacoasts. Here are two suggested trips among many you may select.

Korean Folk Village

The Korean Folk Village is located in Gyeonggi-do Province, about 90 minutes from Seoul. The village allows you to experience life as it was during the Joseon Dynasty (1392–1910). Houses used by commoners and the upper-class have been recreated along with handicraft workshops, eateries, a pottery kiln, and a marketplace. A similar village is located in the city of Andong in Gyeongsangbuk-do Province. Andong is also considered the home of the development of Confucianism in Korea during the Joseon Dynasty.

Can I take a bus to the Korean Folk Village?	민속촌에 버스로 갈 수 있어요 ? *Min-sok-ch'on-e ppeo-seu-ro kal su i-sseo-yo?*
Does the subway go there?	지하철이 거기로 가나요 ? *Chi-ha-ch'eol-i keo-gi-ro ka-na-yo?*
What time does it <u>open</u>?	몇 시에 문을 <u>열어요</u> ? *Myeot shi-e mun-eul yeo-reo-yo?*
■ close	닫아요 *ta-da-yo*
How long should I plan to see the entire village?	다 보려면 얼마나 걸려요 ? *Ta po-ryeo-myeon eol-ma-na keol-lyeo-yo?*
When was the village built?	민속촌이 언제 생겼어요 ? *Min-sok-ch'on-i eon-je saeng-gyeo-sseo-yo?*

What province are these houses from?	이 집들은 어느 지방 것이에요 ? *I chip-deu-reun eo-neu chi-bang keo-shi-e-yo?*
Are there places to eat here?	여기 음식점이 있어요 ? *Yeo-gi eum-shik-jjeom-i i-sseo-yo?*

Panmunjeom

In 1953 the agreement ending the Korean War was signed in Panmunjeom, located in the Demilitarized Zone (DMZ). It is approximately 31 miles from Seoul on the 38th parallel. The area is patrolled by North and South Korean troops, surrounded by an ecosystem that has preserved rare plants and animal species. Contact the Korea Tourism Organization for tour information.

I'd like to go to Panmunjeom.	판문점에 가고 싶어요. *P'an-mun-jeom-e ka-go shi-p'eo-yo.*
How much are the tickets?	차표가 얼마예요 ? *Ch'a-p'yo-ga eol-ma-ye-yo?*
Is lunch included?	점심 식사비가 포함되어 있어요 ? *Cheom-shim shik-sa-bi-ga p'o-ham-doe-eo i-sseo-yo?*
How long is the tour?	관광이 얼마나 걸려요 ? *Kwan-gwang-i eol-ma-na keol-lyeo-yo?*

TWO-DAY TRIPS FROM SEOUL

Fast trains, express buses, taxis, and domestic airlines make it easy for you to see many places in Korea within a limited period of time. Here are two suggested venues. You may consider others, such as Busan, Gwangju, Incheon, and Jeju Island.

Gyeongju

Gyeongju and its surrounding area present numerous historical buildings, temples, burial mounds, and Buddhist artifacts. Located in Gyeongsangbuk-do Province in southeast Korea, it was the capital of the Silla Kingdom for 1,000 years (57 BC to AD 935). The Gyeongju National Museum is where you can view the cultural history of the area. The Emille Bell, one of Asia's largest bronze specimens, is part of the museum. Nearby, Bulguksa Temple and Seokguram Grotto are two of the most majestic structures from the Silla period. Daereung-won Tumuli Park, site of many royal tombs, is located in the middle of the city. Additional sites in Gyeongju include palaces, pavilions, Buddhist images, and Cheomseongdae, Asia's oldest standing observatory, built in the seventh century. A popular place to stay when visiting Gyeongju is Bomun Lake Resort, which offers attractive accommodations, shopping, dining, and recreation. Moderately priced accommodations are available in downtown Gyeongju.

Please take me to Cheomseongdae.	첨성대로 가 주세요. *Ch'eom-seong-dae-ro ka chu-se-yo.*
Can I walk to Seokguram Grotto from Bulguksa Temple?	불국사에서 석굴암까지 걸어갈 수 있어요? *Pul-guk-sa-e-seo Seo-kku-ram-kka-ji keo-reo-gal su i-sseo-yo?*
Is there a bus to downtown from Bulguksa Temple?	불국사에서 시내 가는 버스가 있어요? *Pul-guk-sa-e-seo shi-nae ka-neun ppeo-seu-ga i-sseo-yo?*
There are hotels downtown and at Bomun Lake Resort.	시내와 보문단지에 호텔이 있어요. *Shi-nae-wa Po-mun-dan-ji-e ho-t'e-ri i-sseo-yo.*
What time does the Gyeongju National Museum open?	경주 국립 박물관은 몇 시에 열어요? *Kyeong-ju kung-nip pang-mul-gwan-eun myeot shi-e yeo-reo-yo?*

Gangwon-do Province

Mt. Seoraksan and the East Sea are highlights in this province, located in the mid-eastern part of the Korean peninsula. Here you will find towering mountains, beaches, and coastal villages. Outdoor activities include skiing, hiking, camping, rafting, and swimming. Gyeongpodae Beach is one of the most popular summer escapes in Korea. Yongpyeong Dragon Valley, a two-hour drive from Seoul, is Korea's largest ski resort. About thirty minutes away, Mt. Odaesan National Park has rich forests and beautiful creeks. Nearby is Daegwallyeong Sheep Farm, a vast grassland in Korea, well-known as a location for filming internationally famous Korean dramas. Chuncheon, the capital of the province, is ninety minutes from Seoul by bus or train. It is a popular riverside destination where you can enjoy lakes and mountains and a respite from fast-paced urban life.

Can I swim at Gyeongpodae?	경포대에서 수영해도 돼요 ? *Kyeong-p'o-dae-e-seo su-yeong-hae-do twae-yo?*
How far is Mt. Seoraksan from Sokcho?	속초에서 설악산까지 얼마나 멀어요 ? *Sok-ch'o-e-seo seo-rak-san-kka-ji eol-ma-na meo-reo-yo?*
Are camping facilities available?	캠프 시설이 있어요 ? *K'aem-p'eu shi-seo-ri i-sseo-yo?*
Skiing is my favorite sport.	제일 좋아하는 운동이 스키예요. *Che-il cho-a-ha-neun un-dong-i seu-k'i-ye-yo.*
The fall colors are beautiful on the East Coast.	동해안에는 단풍이 참 아름다워요. *Tong-hae-an-e-neun tan-p'ung-i ch'am a-reum-da-weo-yo.*
Where is a good seafood restaurant?	생선요리 잘하는 음식점이 어디 있어요 ? *Saeng-seon yo-ri chal-ha-neun eum-shik-jjeom-i eo-di i-sseo-yo?*

ENTERTAINMENT AND DIVERSIONS

Entertainment comes in many forms in Korea from traditional, colorful Korean dances to an evening of Beethoven. Whatever your interest, you can find something to entertain you in Korea.

CULTURAL EVENTS

Updated schedules of events are printed in various English-language publications distributed to most hotels. Staff at theaters can also provide current information, including how to buy tickets. The English-language newspapers also publish schedules of cultural events.

SCHEDULES AND TICKETS

Where can I buy an English-language newspaper?	영자 신문을 어디서 살 수 있어요 ? *Yeong-jja shin-mun-eul eo-di-seo sal su i-sseo-yo?*
Where can I get an entertainment guide?	공연 안내서를 어디서 구할 수 있어요 ? *Kong-yeon an-nae-seo-reul eo-di-seo ku-hal su i-sseo-yo?*
Where can I buy tickets?	표를 어디서 살 수 있어요 ? *P'yo-reul eo-di-seo sal su i-sseo-yo?*

FILMS AND THEATER

A variety of films and plays can be seen in Korea. Plays may be traditional or contemporary Korean works, or they could be productions of European or American playwrights. Large-scale performance halls are located in various parts of Seoul within easy access to public transportation. Some examples of theaters with large stages are the Sejong Center

for the Performing Arts, National Theater of Korea, Seoul
Arts Center, LG Art Center, and Olympic Park. Shows that are
famous throughout the world as well as those produced by
Koreans are always available.

Daehangno, or University Street, is an entertainment
area popular with young people in Seoul. Movie theaters,
performance centers, quaint cafes, and pubs are scattered
throughout the area. It is possible to enjoy live entertainment
throughout Seoul, including free performances. Check
posters along the street for information.

The Korean wave, or *Hallyu*, is a term used to describe
South Korea's popular culture in other countries, especially in
Asia. Movies, part of the Korean wave, have a large following
in Korea. International film festivals are held in Busan,
Jeonju, and Bucheon. English-language movies usually have
the original soundtrack with Korean subtitles. The Jongno
area in Seoul is where most movie theaters are located.

Shall we go see a <u>movie</u>?	영화 보러 갈까요 ? *Yeong-hwa po-reo kal-kka-yo?*
■ play	연극 *yeon-geuk*
Could you recommend a good <u>film</u>?	좋은영화를 좀 소개해 주시겠어요 ? *Cho-eun yeong-hwa-reul chom so-gae-hae chu-shi-ge-sseo-yo?*
■ play	연극 (을) *yeon-geuk(eul)*
Where's the Munye Theater?	문예회관이 어디예요 ? *Mun-ye-hoe-gwan-i eo-di-ye-yo?*
What's the title of the <u>film</u>?	그 영화 제목이 뭐예요 ? *Keu yeong-hwa che-mok-i mwoe-ye-yo?*
■ play	연극 *yeon-keuk*
Is it a <u>comedy</u>?	코메디예요 ? *K'o-me-di-ye-yo?*
■ historical drama	사극 *sa-geuk*
■ musical	뮤지칼 *myu-ji-k'al*
■ mystery	미스테리 *mi-seu-t'e-ri*

■ romance   애정물   *ae-jeong-mul*

■ science fiction film   공상 과학영화   *kong-sang kwa-hak yeong-hwa*

■ thriller/horror movie   공포영화   *kong-p'o yeong-hwa*

■ tragedy   비극   *pi-geuk*

■ Western movie   서부영화   *seo-bu yeong-hwa*

■ war film   전쟁영화   *cheon-jaeng yeong-hwa*

Is it <u>a Korean</u> film?   한국영화예요 ?   <u>*Han-guk*</u> *yeong-hwa-ye-yo?*

■ an American   미국   *Mi-guk*

■ a British   영국   *Yeong-guk*

■ Hong Kong   홍콩   *Hong-k'ong*

Does it have English subtitles?   영어 자막이 나와요 ?   *Yeong-eo cha-mak-i na-wa-yo?*

Are the actors Korean or American?   배우가 한국 사람이에요, 미국 사람이에요 ?   *Pae-u-ga Han-guk sa-ram-i-e-yo, Mi-guk sa-ram-i-e-yo?*

Do they perform in English or Korean?   상영은 영어로 해요, 한국말로 해요 ?   *Sang-yeong-eun yeong-eo-ro hae-yo, Han-gung-mal-lo hae-yo?*

What time does the <u>first</u> show begin?   첫 공연은 몇 시에 시작해요 ?   *Ch'eot kong-yeon-eun myeot shi-e shi-jak-k'ae-yo?*

■ last   마지막   *ma-ji-mak*

What time does the show end?   상영은 몇 시에 끝나요 ?   *Sang-yeong-eun myeot shi-e kkeun-na-yo?*

How long will it run?   언제까지 상영할 거예요 ?   *Eon-je-kka-ji sang-yeong-hal kkeo-ye-yo?*

Is there a matinee?   낮 상영이 있어요 ?   *Nat sang-yeong-i i-sseo-yo?*

Where can I buy a ticket?	표를 어디서 살 수 있어요 ?	*P'yo-reul eo-di-seo sal su i-sseo-yo?*
Where's the box office?	매표소가 어디 있어요 ?	*Mae-p'yo-so-ga eo-di i-sseo-yo?*
Do you have any tickets left for <u>tonight</u>?	<u>오늘 밤</u> 표가 남았어요 ?	<u>*O-neul ppam*</u> *p'yo-ga nam-a-sseo-yo?*
▓ the next show	다음 공연	*ta-eum kong-yeon*
I'd like to buy <u>a ticket</u> for tonight.	오늘 밤 <u>표 한 장</u> 주세요.	*O-neul ppam* <u>*p'yo han chang*</u> *chu-se-yo.*
▓ two tickets	표 두 장	*p'yo tu chang*
▓ three tickets	표 세 장/표 석 장	*p'yo se chang/ p'yo seok chang*
▓ four tickets	표 네 장/표 넉 장	*p'yo ne chang/ p'yo neok chang*
I'd like to buy a ticket for <u>tomorrow</u> night.	<u>내일</u> 밤 표 한 장 주세요.	<u>*Nae-il*</u> *ppam p'yo han chang chu-se-yo.*
▓ Friday	금요일	*keum-yo-il*
▓ Saturday	토요일	*t'o-yo-il*
▓ Sunday	일요일	*i-ryo-il*
▓ Monday	월요일	*weo-ryo-il*
▓ Tuesday	화요일	*hwa-yo-il*
▓ Wednesday	수요일	*su-yo-il*
▓ Thursday	목요일	*mo-gyo-il*
Do you have seats in the <u>orchestra</u>?	<u>특별석</u>이 있어요 ?	<u>*T'euk-ppyeol-seok-i*</u> *i-sseo-yo?*
▓ balcony	이층석	*i-ch'eung-seok*
Do you have better seats than that?	그보다 좋은 자리 좀 없어요 ?	*Keu-bo-da cho-eun cha-ri chom eop-sseo-yo?*

Do you have seats a little more <u>forward</u>?	더 앞 자리 좀 없어요 ?	*Teo ap jja-ri chom eop-sseo-yo?*
■ to the rear	뒷	*twit*
■ toward the center	가운데	*ka-un-de*

Is there a program in English?	영어로 된 프로그램 있어요 ? *Yeong-eo-ro toen p'eu-ro-geu-raem i-sseo-yo?*

Please show me to my seat.	내 자리 좀 찾아 주세요. *Nae cha-ri chom ch'a-ja chu-se-yo.*

OPERA, BALLET, AND CONCERTS

Opera and ballet performances are held at such places as the Sejong Center for the Performing Arts, the National Theater of Korea, and the Seoul Arts Center.

Seoul's symphony orchestra features many fine musicians who perform to packed audiences. In addition, world famous troupes often include Seoul as a stopover. As a result, a variety of musical performances is available.

I'd like to attend <u>a ballet</u>.	발레를 보고 싶어요. *Pal-le-reul po-go shi-p'eo-yo.*
■ an opera	오페라 *o-p'e-ra*
■ a concert	연주회 *yeon-ju-hoe*

How should I dress?	어떤 옷을 입을까요 ? *Eo-tteon o-seul i-beul-kka-yo?*

I prefer <u>chamber music</u>.	실내악을 좋아해요. *Shil-lae-ak-eul cho-a-hae-yo.*
■ classical music	고전음악 (을) *ko-jeon-eum-ak(eul)*
■ concertos	피아노 협주곡 (을) *p'i-a-no hyeop-jju-gok(eul)*
■ country music	칸츄리 뮤직 (을) *k'an-ch-yu-ri myu-jik(eul)*
■ folk songs	대중가요 (를) *tae-jung-ga-yo(reul)*

■ jazz   째즈(를)   *jjae-jeu(reul)*

■ modern music   현대 음악(을)   *hyeon-dae eum-ak(eul)*

■ popular songs   팝송(을)   *p'ap-ssong(eul)*

■ rock'n'roll   로큰롤(을)   *ro-k'eun-rol(eul)*

■ symphonies   교향곡(을)   *kyo-hyang-gok(eul)*

■ classical ballet   고전 발레(를)   *ko-jeon bal-le(reul)*

■ modern ballet   현대 발레(를)   *hyeon-dae bal-le(reul)*

■ modern dance   현대 무용(을)   *hyeon-dae mu-yong(eul)*

Where's the <u>Sejong Center for the Performing Arts</u>?   세종문화회관이 어디에 있습니까 ?   *<u>Se-jong-mun-hwa-hoe-gwan</u>-i eo-di-e i-sseum-ni-kka?*

■ National Theater   국립극장(이)   *Kung-nip-geuk-jjang(i)*

■ Seoul Arts Center   예술의 전당(이)   *Ye-sul-eui cheon-dang(i)*

■ LG Art Center   LG 아트센터(가)   *LG a-t'eu-sen-t'eo(ka)*

What's the orchestra playing?   오케스트라가 무슨 곡을 연주해요 ?   *O-k'e-seu-t'eu-ra-ga mu-seum kok-eul yeon-ju-hae-yo?*

Who's <u>conducting</u>?   누가 지휘해요 ?   *Nu-ga <u>chi-hwi</u>-hae-yo?*

■ dancing   무용   *mu-yong*

■ playing   연주   *yeon-ju*

■ singing   노래   *no-rae*

What time does tonight's performance start?   오늘 밤 공연은 몇 시에 시작해요 ?   *O-neul ppam kong-yeon-eun myeot shi-e shi-jak-k'ae-yo?*

Are tonight's tickets <u>sold out</u>?	오늘 밤 표가 다 팔렸어요 ? *O-neul ppam p'yo-ga <u>ta p'al-lyeo-sseo-yo</u>?*
▦ still available	남아 있어요 *nam-a i-sseo-yo*
Should I get tickets in advance?	표를 미리 사야 돼요 ? *P'yo-reul mi-ri sa-ya twae-yo?*
How much are the least expensive seats?	제일 싼 자리가 얼마예요 ? *Che-il ssan cha-ri-ga eol-ma-ye-yo?*
I'd like to get good seats.	좋은 자리를 구했으면 좋겠어요. *Cho-eun cha-ri-reul ku-hae-sseu-myeon cho-k'e-sseo-yo.*
How much are the front row seats?	앞줄에 있는 자리가 얼마예요 ? *Ap-jju-re in-neun cha-ri-ga eol-ma-ye-yo?*

KOREAN MUSIC AND DANCE

An evening of Korean music and dance is a delightful form of entertainment. Dances range from the lively folk dances like the farmer's band, to the more courtly dances that were performed for royalty during dynastic rule. Korean mask dance is an interesting combination of traditional dance and drama. Folk music includes percussion ensembles and solo performances on such instruments as the *gayageum* and *geomungo*. Outdoor performances of authentic Korean traditional music and dance can be seen at the National Theater in Seoul, in the Seoul Nori Madang near Jamsil, and throughout Korea during festivals and holidays.

Korea House, near the Daehan Theater on Toegyero in Seoul, offers an excellent opportunity to see performances of Korean dance and music, as well as to sample some of Seoul's best Korean food. In addition, you can enjoy traditional architecture while shopping for folk art objects. You may also have a chance to see one of the traditional Korean wedding ceremonies held here. A visit to Korea House is a good way to get an introduction to Korean culture.

I'm interested in <u>farmers' music and dance</u>.

농악에 관심이 있어요. *Nong-ak-e kwan-shim-i i-sseo-yo.*

■ dramatic song 판소리 *p'an-so-ri*

■ mask dance 탈춤 *t'al-ch'um*

■ monk's dance 승무 *seung-mu*

■ drum dance 장고춤 *chang-go-ch'um*

■ crane dance 학춤 *hak-ch'um*

■ twelve-string zither 가야금 *ka-ya-geum*

■ six-string zither 거문고 *keo-mun-go*

What's playing at the <u>Sejong Center for the Performing Arts</u>?

세종문화회관에서 무슨 공연을 하고 있나요 ? *Se-jong-mun-hwa-hoe-gwan-e-seo mu-seun kong-yeon-eul ha-go in-na-yo?*

■ Seoul Nori Madang 서울놀이마당 *Seo-ul-no-ri-ma-dang*

■ Munye Theater 문예회관 *Mun-ye-hoe-gwan*

Outdoor performances are given at <u>Korean Folk Village</u>.

민속촌에서 야외공연이 있어요. *Min-sok-ch'on-e-seo ya-woe-gong-yeon-i i-sseo-yo.*

■ Seoul Nori Madang 서울 놀이 마당 *Seo-ul no-ri ma-dang*

■ Gyeongju 경주 *Kyeong-ju*

<u>Shall we eat at Korea House</u>?

한국의 집에서 <u>식사할까요</u> ? *Han-guk-eui chip-e-seo <u>shik-sa-hal-kka-yo</u>?*

■ take pictures 사진 찍을까요 *sa-jin jjik-eul-kka-yo*

■ see a performance 공연을 볼까요 *kong-yeon-eul pol-kka-yo*

How much is the admission for the performance?

입장료가 얼마예요 ? *Ip-jjang-nyo-ga eol-ma-ye-yo?*

RADIO AND TELEVISION

Radio programming is mostly in Korean, but it is possible to get English stations on both AM and FM. American Forces Network (AFN) stations broadcast news, music, and sports 24 hours a day. The government-operated radio station, KBS, airs broadcasts in multiple languages, including Korean and English.

Cable TV has a wide range of English-language programs. In addition, Arirang, a Korean cultural channel, offers original programs in English as well as some Korean programs with English subtitles. Movies in English are broadcast on a number of channels as are some English-language programs from the United States, Great Britain, and Australia. A large number of TV networks operate in Korean, including KBS, MBC, and SBS.

Watching Korean telecasts can be entertaining. Even without much knowledge of the language, you will find that many shows are easy to understand. You can see sports events, game shows, variety shows, and soap operas. Reruns of American series are also fun to watch in Korean. AFN television, seen in most parts of the country, provides contemporary programming and daily news from the U.S.

NIGHT LIFE

You should have many opportunities to enjoy the night life of Korea. Koreans look forward to relaxing in the evening after a hard day of work and will enjoy showing you their favorite spots. Establishments can be expensive, particularly salons and nightclubs. To avoid having an evening of fun end on a sour note, check with the hotel staff or an acquaintance to get an estimate of the cost. They can help you choose a place that is suited to your taste.

When settling the bill, paying individually is not a common practice. Only one person usually pays when two or more people go out for food or drink. Others may put up a convincing fight, but if you are hosting, you must be sure to get to the cashier first to pay the bill. If you have been someone's guest, you should make every effort to reciprocate on another occasion. If your time in Korea is limited, you might invite your host to another place that day for coffee and dessert or another drink.

The following expressions will be helpful for different kinds of night life. Refer to the Food and Drink section for information on how to order specific items.

TRADITIONAL DRINKING ESTABLISHMENTS

Koreans choose their drinking establishments according to the alcoholic beverages they wish to consume, the desired ambiance, and the amount of money they want to spend. The *sojujip* is where they enjoy one of their most favored spirits, *soju*, made from rice and a combination of wheat, barley, or sweet potatoes. A less expensive traditional establishment is the *minsokjujeom*, which serves *makkeolli*, a milky wine made of rice and barley, *dongdongju*, a clearer, more expensive form of *makkeolli*, other traditional spirits, and beer. Since drinking and eating go hand-in-hand in Korea, *anju* (appetizers) such as vegetables, meat, fish, and various spicy dishes are available for a charge. An interesting place to enjoy food and drink is with a nighttime street vendor, called *pojangmacha*. It offers a kind of standing buffet of inexpensive and delicious snack foods.

The *gisaeng* house, where female staff entertain guests with songs and food, is declining in popularity, replaced by the less formal *dallanjujeom*, a kind of karaoke where hostesses serve alcoholic beverages. Eating and drinking at traditional establishments is an interesting way to experience Korean culture, but you should get a recommendation for places that match your taste and budget.

Here are tips about Korean drinking etiquette. (1) Never pour a drink from a bottle into your own glass, and never allow other persons in the group to pour their own; (2) if you notice that another person's glass is empty or nearly so, offer to fill the glass; and (3) when pouring for someone older than you or of higher status, pour holding the bottle with two hands. When someone pours for you, hold your glass with two hands. Your two hands may be on the bottle or glass, or you may hold the bottle or glass with your right hand and place your left hand at your right wrist. The hand placements apply to other exchanges, such as soft drinks, giving and receiving gifts, or passing objects such as a book or pen. If you prefer not to drink alcohol, you may excuse yourself by gracefully declining or suggesting health reasons.

Shall we have a glass of makkeolli?	막걸리 한 잔 할까요?	*Mak-kkeol-li han chan hal-kka-yo?*
▨ tongdongju	동동주	*tong-dong-ju*
▨ soju	소주	*so-ju*
▨ beer	맥주	*maek-jju*

I'd like to have some makkeolli. 막걸리 마시고 싶어요. *Mak-kkeol-li ma-shi-go shi-p'eo-yo.*

Do you have a favorite place? 단골집이 있어요? *Tan-gol-jjip-i i-sseo-yo?*

It's famous for its appetizers. 그 집 안주가 유명해요. *Keu chip an-ju-ga yu-myeong-hae-yo.*

▨ small fried octopus 낙지볶음(이) *nak-ji-po-kkeum*

▨ mung bean pancakes 빈대떡(이) *pin-dae-tteok(i)*

We'll have to have "hangover soup" later. 나중에 해장국을 먹어야겠어요. *Na-jung-e hae-jang-kkuk-eul meok-eo-ya-ge-sseo-yo.*

BARS AND BEER HALLS

Bars range from those serving beer or liquor to upscale places that serve mixed drinks, cocktails, wine, bottled beer, and whole bottles of spirits. Beer halls, many decorated along a European theme, are also popular places to drink and meet friends. Hofs (from German *hofbrau*) serve draft beer, and many brew their own beer on site. Rock cafés are Western-style bars with a dance floor that serve mixed drinks, cocktails, and bottled beer. As with any drinking establishment, appetizers are available and commonly eaten.

Is there an inexpensive <u>beer hall</u> nearby?	이 근처에 싼 <u>비어홀</u>이 있어요 ? *I keun-ch'eo-e ssan <u>pi-eo-hol</u>-i i-sseo-yo?*
▨ bar	바 *pa*
▨ hof	호프집 *ho-p'eu-jip*
▨ rock café	락카페 *rak-k'a-p'e*
Do you know one <u>with a nice atmosphere</u>?	<u>분위기가 좋은</u> 데를 아세요 ? <u>*Pun-wi-gi-ga cho-eun*</u> *de-reul a-se-yo?*
▨ with good music	음악이 좋은 *eum-ak-i cho-eun*
▨ that's quiet	조용한 *cho-yong-han*
Will they charge more than <u>20,000</u> won per person?	1인당 <u>2만</u>원 이상 내야 하나요 ? *I-rin-dang <u>i-man</u>-weon i-sang nae-ya ha-na-yo?*
▨ 30,000	삼만 *sam-man*
▨ 40,000	사만 *sa-man*
▨ 50,000	오만 *o-man*
▨ 100,000	십만 *shim-man*
Do they serve meals?	식사가 나와요 ? *Shik-sa-ga na-wa-yo?*
What kind of food do they have?	무슨 음식이 있어요 ? *Mu-seun eum-shik-i i-sseo-yo?*
What kind of entertainment do they have?	무슨 쇼를 하지요 ? *Mu-seun shyo-reul ha-ji-yo?*

NIGHTCLUBS AND ROOM SALONS

These forms of entertainment feature private rooms, liquor, and elaborate *anju* appetizer selections. Nightclubs, which are usually located in hotels, are generally the most elaborate and therefore the most expensive. Music is provided and you may also dance. Large tips are required for hostesses who pour drinks, provide conversation, and dance with customers. You should explore these establishments based on a recommendation or with a Korean acquaintance.

Let's go to a <u>nightclub</u>.	나이트 클럽으로 갑시다. <u>Na-i-t'eu k'eul-leop-eu-ro kap-shi-da.</u>
■ room salon	룸살롱 *rum-sal-long*
How much will it cost per person?	일인당 얼마예요 ? *I-rin-dang eol-ma-ye-yo?*
Do they have a cover charge?	입장료가 있어요 ? *Ip-jjang-nyo-ga i-sseo-yo?*
How much is the hostess fee?	도우미팁이 얼마입니까 ? *To-u-mi-t'ip-i eol-ma-im-ni-kka?*
Are private rooms available?	별실이 있어요 ? *Pyeol-shi-ri i-sseo-yo?*
Can we sing in the room?	방에서 노래할 수 있나요 ? *Pang-e-seo no-rae-hal su in-na-yo?*
I'd like to see a floor show.	쇼를 보고 싶어요. *Shyo-reul po-go shi-p'eo-yo.*
What time does the floor show start?	쇼가 몇 시에 시작하지요 ? *Shyo-ga myeot shi-e shi-jak-k'a-ji-yo?*

NORAEBANG

Koreans love to sing. As a result, a popular source of entertainment is a *noraebang* (singing room). Recorded background music (*karaokke*) is provided as the customer supplies the words to a favorite song. Many songs are in English; however, you will be a big hit with your Korean counterparts if you join in with a Korean song. One of the most popular traditional songs, "Arirang," is included near the end of this book, in the section titled Notes about Korean Language and Culture. The *dallanjujeom* is an establishment that combines a *noraebang* with a hostess bar setting. Tips are required for the hostesses who pour drinks and provide conversation.

Where can I find a singing room?	노래방이 어디에 있을까요 ? *No-rae-bang-i eo-di-e i-sseul-kka-yo?*
Could you recommend a good hostess bar singing room?	도우미가 나오는 노래방을 추천해 주시겠어요 ? *To-u-mi-ga na-o-neun no-rae-bang-eul ch'u-ch'eon-hae chu-shi-ge-sseo-yo?*
Is there a service charge?	봉사료가 따로 있습니까 ? *Pong-sa-ryo-ga tta-ro i-seum-ni-kka?*
How much should I tip the hostess?	도우미에게 얼마 줘야 하지요 ? *To-u-mi-e-ge eol-ma chweo-ya ha-ji-yo?*

DVD ROOM

A DVD room (*DVD bang*) is a small room furnished with a large television screen and comfortable furniture. You can choose from a large selection of DVD movies in the reception area and view the movie privately in the room.

Where can I find a DVD room?	디비디방이 어디에 있을까요 ? *Ti-bi-di-bang-i eo-di-e i-sseul-kka-yo?*
How much does it cost?	얼마지요 ? *Eol-ma-ji-yo?*
Do you have movies in English?	영어가 나오는 영화가 있습니까 ? *Yeong-eo-ga na-o-neun yeong-hwa-ga i-sseum-ni-kka?*
Do you have Korean movies with English subtitles?	영어자막이 나오는 한국영화가 있습니까 ? *Yeong-eo-ja-mak-i na-o-neun Han-guk-yeong-hwa-ga i-sseum-ni-kka?*

RESTAURANTS

Restaurants are also a common form of entertainment with many of the same features as drinking places. Different types of restaurants and how to order are covered under Food and Drink.

GAMES

Games represent an important part of Korean culture. The following are traditional and modern games that Koreans currently enjoy. In addition to these, you should try to see some of the traditional outdoor group games involving masses of people. For example, tug-of-war (*chul-da-ri-gi*) can be seen performed during festivals and holidays in such places as Gyeongju and the Korean Folk Village.

BADUK AND JANGGI

These two traditional board games are still popular in Korea. *Baduk*, the Korean version of the Japanese *go*, is a game that has been played since ancient times. White and black stones are used by opposing players in a game of strategy. The object is for one player to surround the other's pieces, paralyzing any movement. *Janggi*, a form of chess, also remains popular among Koreans.

Do you play <u>baduk</u>?	바둑 둘 줄 아세요 ?	*Pa-duk tul jjul a-se-yo?*
■ Korean chess	장기	*chang-gi*
Could you teach me how to play baduk?	바둑 좀 가르쳐 주시겠어요 ?	*Pa-duk chom ka-reu-ch'yeo chu-shi-ge-sseo-yo?*
Is it difficult to learn Korean chess?	장기 배우기 어려워요 ?	*Chang-gi pae-u-gi eo-ryeo-weo-yo?*

How do you decide the winner?	어떻게 승부를 결정하지요 ? *Eo-tteo-k'e seung-bu-reul kyeol-jjeong-ha-ji-yo?*
How do you capture your opponent's stones?	상대방 말을 어떻게 잡아요 ? *Sang-dae-bang ma-reul eo-tteo-k'e chab-a-yo?*
Is there a place to play baduk here?	여기 기원이 있어요 ? *Yeo-gi ki-weon-i i-sseo-yo?*

HWATU

Hwatu is a popular card game played with a deck of 48 small cards. A little gambling livens up the game.

I don't know how to play hwatu.	화투할 줄 몰라요. *Hwa-t'u-hal jjul mol-la-yo.*
Is it easy to learn?	배우기 쉬워요 ? *Pae-u-gi shwi-weo-yo?*
Gambling makes it interesting.	내기를 해야 재미있어요. *Nae-gi-reul hae-ya chae-mi-i-sseo-yo.*
Where can I buy a set of hwatu cards?	화투를 어디서 사지요 ? *Hwa-t'u-reul eo-di-seo sa-ji-yo?*

YUT

Yut is similar to backgammon. It is played with four sticks which are tossed in the air to determine the number of moves that each player should make. The first player to move all four sticks to the goal is the winner.

Those people are playing yut.	저 사람들은 윷놀이 하고 있어요. *Cheo sa-ram-deu-reun yun-no-ri ha-go i-sseo-yo.*
It looks very interesting.	재미있어 보여요. *Chae-mi-i-sseo po-yeo-yo.*

SPECTATOR SPORTS

Koreans are great sport enthusiasts and enjoy participating as well as watching. Following are expressions to use when discussing popular spectator sports.

TAEKWONDO

This well-known Korean martial art can be found world-wide. The emphasis on kicking distinguishes it from *kungfu* and *karate*.

How is taekwondo different from karate?	태권도와 가라데가 어떻게 달라요 ? *T'ae-kkweon-do-wa ka-ra-de-ga eo-tteo-k'e tal-la-yo?*
Is there a place where I can learn taekwondo?	태권도장이 있어요 ? *T'ae-kkweon-do-jang-i i-sseo-yo?*
Where can I see a taekwondo demonstration?	태권도 시범을 어디서 볼 수 있어요 ? *T'ae-kkweon-do shi-beom-eul eo-di-seo pol su i-sseo-yo?*
What degree black belt does the player have?	저 선수는 검은 띠 몇 단이에요 ? *Cheo seon-su-neun keom-eun tti myeot tan-i-e-yo?*

SSIRUM

This traditional form of wrestling, in which participants wear only shorts and cloth belts around their waists, attracts many spectators. Wrestlers compete in different weight classes in a sand-filled arena.

I'm interested in ssirum.	씨름에 관심이 있어요. *Sshi-reum-e kwan-shim-i i-sseo-yo.*
Where can I see a ssirum match?	씨름 경기를 어디서 볼 수 있어요 ? *Sshi-reum kyeong-gi-reul eo-di-seo pol su i-sseo-yo?*

Can I get something to eat there?	거기서 뭘 사먹을 수 있어요 ? *Keo-gi-seo mweol sa-meok-eul su i-sseo-yo?*
Is he the champion?	저 사람이 우승자예요 ? *Cheo sa-ram-i u-seung-ja-ye-yo?*
What's that wrestler's name?	저 씨름 선수 이름이 뭐예요 ? *Cheo sshi-reum seon-su i-reum-i mweo-ye-yo?*
How much does he weigh?	저 사람 몸무게가 얼마예요 ? *Cheo sa-ram mom-mu-ge-ga eol-ma-ye-yo?*
How tall is he?	저 사람 키가 얼마예요 ? *Cheo sa-ram k'i-ga eol-ma-ye-yo?*

SOCCER

Korea has some of the most competitive professional soccer teams in Asia. The skill of the players has attracted a large following of fans.

Is this the soccer season?	요즘이 축구 씨즌이에요 ? *Yo-jeum-i ch'uk-kku sshi-jeun-i-e-yo?*
Is there a soccer match <u>today</u>?	<u>오늘</u> 축구 시합이 있어요 ? *<u>O-neul</u> ch'uk-kku shi-hap-i i-sseo-yo?*
■ tomorrow	내일 *nae-il*
■ this weekend	이번 주말에 *i-beon chu-ma-re*
Is the soccer game televised?	축구 경기를 텔레비전에서 중계해요 ? *Ch'uk-kku kyeong-gi-reul t'el-le-bi-jeon-e-seo chung-gye-hae-yo?*
Where is the soccer stadium?	축구장이 어디 있어요 ? *Ch'uk-kku-jang-i eo-di i-sseo-yo?*
Which teams are playing?	어느 팀이 나와요 ? *Eo-neu t'im-i na-wa-yo?*

| Can I buy tickets at the stadium on the day of the game? | 시합 당일에 축구장에서 표를 살 수 있어요 ? *Shi-hap tang-i-re ch'uk-kku-jang-e-seo p'yo-reul sal su i-sseo-yo?* |

BASEBALL AND BASKETBALL

The country has a large number of professional baseball and basketball teams, most owned by major business corporations. Several foreign players participate in both sports.

I like to watch baseball.	야구 구경을 좋아해요. *Ya-gu ku-gyeong-eul cho-a-hae-yo.*
Do you have a professional team in this city?	이 도시에 프로 팀이 있어요 ? *I to-shi-e p'eu-ro t'im-i i-sseo-yo?*
Where is the ball park?	야구장이 어디에요 ? *Ya-gu-jang-i eo-di-e-yo?*
Can I buy tickets at the ball park?	야구장에서 표를 살 수 있어요 ? *Ya-gu-jang-e-seo p'yo-reul sal su i-sseo-yo?*
I'd like seats <u>behind home plate</u>.	특석으로 주세요. *T'euk-seok-eu-ro chu-se-yo.*
■ on the first base side	일루석 *il-lu-seok*
■ on the third base side	삼루석 *sam-nu-seok*
Where can I buy tickets for the basketball game?	야구표를 어디에서 살 수 있을까요 ? *Ya-gu-p'yo-reul eo-di-e-seo sal su i-sseul-kka-yo?*
Where is the stadium?	경기장은 어디에 있습니까 ? *Kyeong-gi-jang-eun eo-di-e i-sseum-ni-kka?*

Can I get seats close to the court?	앞자리표를 살 수 있을까요 ? *Ap-jja-ri-p'yo-reul sal su i-sseul-kka-yo?*

VOLLEYBALL

Volleyball is another popular sport with a large following. Women's volleyball teams have been especially successful in international competitions.

Where can I see a volleyball game?	배구 시합을 어디서 볼 수 있어요 ? *Pae-gu shi-hap-eul eo-di-seo pol su i-sseo-yo?*
I'd like to see the best team.	제일 강한 팀을 보고 싶어요. *Che-il kang-han t'im-eul po-go shi-p'eo-yo.*
She's a good player!	그 여자가 참 잘 해요 ! *Keu yeo-ja-ga ch'am chal hae-yo!*

PARTICIPATORY SPORTS

GOLF

Golf courses are available throughout Korea. Green fees can be very expensive, so you may want to compare prices. Courses are especially busy on weekends.

Do you play golf?	골프 치세요 ? *Kol-p'eu ch'i-se-yo?*
Where do you play?	어디서 치세요 ? *Eo-di-seo ch'i-se-yo?*
Can I play there?	저도 거기서 칠 수 있어요 ? *Cheo-do keo-gi-seo ch'il su i-sseo-yo?*
How much are the green fees?	요금이 얼마예요 ? *Yo-geum-i eol-ma-ye-yo?*

Do I have to hire a caddie?	캐디를 써야 돼요 ? *K'ae-di-reul sseo-ya twae-yo?*
Can I rent <u>golf clubs</u>?	골프채를 빌릴 수 있어요 ? <u>*Kol-p'eu-ch'ae-reul pil-lil su i-sseo-yo?*</u>
▪ a golf cart	카트 *k'a-t'eu*
Is it a <u>difficult</u> course?	코스가 어려워요 ? *K'o-seu-ga <u>eo-ryeo-weo-yo</u>?*
▪ an easy	쉬워요 *shwi-weo-yo*
What's par?	파가 얼마예요 ? *P'a-ga eol-ma-ye-yo?*
Can I use the clubhouse facilities?	골프장 시설물을 써도 돼요 ? *Kol-p'eu-jang shi-seol-mu-reul sseo-do twae-yo?*

TENNIS

Since many Koreans play tennis, you may be invited to play with a friend or acquaintance. There are both private and public courts made of clay and asphalt. You may want to consider playing during a weekday, if possible, since courts tend to be crowded on weekends.

I love to play tennis.	테니스를 참 좋아해요. *T'e-ni-seu-reul ch'am cho-a-hae-yo.*
Do you play tennis?	테니스 치세요 ? *T'e-ni-seu ch'i-se-yo?*
Where do you play tennis?	어디서 치세요 ? *Eo-di-seo ch'i-se-yo?*
Is the court public or private?	공설 테니스장이에요, 사설 테니스장이에요 ? *Kong-seol t'e-ni-seu-jang-i-e-yo, sa-seol t'e-ni-seu-jang-i-e-yo?*

Where can I buy a racket?	라켓을 어디서 살 수 있어요 ? *Ra-k'e-seul eo-di-seo sal su i-sseo-yo?*
Can you play this weekend?	이번 주말에 칠 수 있으세요 ? *I-beon chu-ma-re ch'il su i-sseu-se-yo?*

TABLE TENNIS

A popular sport among young and old alike is table tennis. Public indoor facilities can be found in any city and the fees are inexpensive.

Is there a place to play table tennis near here?	이 근처에 탁구장이 있어요 ? *I keun-ch'eo-e t'ak-kku-jang-i i-sseo-yo?*
How much does it cost for an hour?	한 시간에 얼마예요 ? *Han shi-gan-e eol-ma-ye-yo?*
Shall we play?	같이 칠까요 ? *Ka-ch'i ch'il-kka-yo?*
You're an extraordinary player!	실력이 보통이 아닌데요 ! *Shil-lyeok-i po-t'ong-i a-nin-de-yo!*

SKIING

Ski resorts in Korea offer good skiing as well as comfortable accommodations. Several resorts can be reached easily from Seoul.

Do you like skiing?	스키를 좋아하세요 ? *Seu-k'i-reul cho-a-ha-se-yo?*
Where do you go for skiing?	스키를 어디서 타세요 ? *Seu-k'i-reul eo-di-seo t'a-se-yo?*
Are the conditions there good now?	지금 거기 상태가 좋아요 ? *Chi-geum keo-gi sang-t'a'e-ga cho-a-yo?*
How can I get there?	거기를 어떻게 가지요 ? *Keo-gi-reul eo-tteo-k'e ka-ji-yo?*

How long does it take?	얼마나 걸려요 ? *Eol-ma-na keol-lyeo-yo?*
Is it crowded?	사람이 많아요 ? *Sa-ram-i man-a-yo?*
Should I make a reservation for a hotel?	호텔방을 예약해야 돼요 ? *Ho-t'el-bang-eul ye-yak-k'ae-ya twae-yo?*
Can I rent ski equipment?	스키 용품을 빌릴 수 있어요 ? *Seu-k'i yong-p'um-eul pil-lil su i-sseo-yo?*
Can I take lessons there?	거기서 스키 강습을 받을 수 있어요 ? *Keo-gi-seo seu-k'i kang-seup-eul pa-deul su i-sseo-yo?*

SWIMMING

Indoor and outdoor swimming pools are available, but your best opportunity may be at your hotel. Beaches also offer swimming and sightseeing.

Is there a swimming pool near here?	이 근처에 수영장이 있어요 ? *I keun-ch'eo-e su-yeong-jang-i i-sseo-yo?*
Is it heated?	물을 데워 줘요 ? *Mu-reul te-weo chweo-yo?*
Is there a nice beach around here?	이 근처에 좋은 해수욕장이 있어요 ? *I keun-ch'eo-e cho-eun hae-su-yok-jjang-i i-sseo-yo?*
How far is it?	여기서 얼마나 멀어요 ? *Yeo-gi-seo eol-ma-na meo-reo-yo?*
Are there lifeguards on duty?	인명구조원이 있어요 ? *In-myeong-gu-jo-weon-i i-sseo-yo?*

Is it safe for children?	아이들이 놀기에 안전해요 ? *A-i-deu-ri nol-gi-e an-jeon-hae-yo?*
What time is <u>high tide</u>?	몇 시에 <u>만조</u> 되요 ? *Myeot shi-e man-jo toe-yo?*
▦ low tide	간조 *kan-jo*
I want to rent <u>a folding chair</u>.	<u>접는 의자</u> 좀 빌려 주세요. *Cheom-neun eui-ja chom pil-lyeo chu-se-yo.*
▦ an air mattress	고무침대 *ko-mu-ch'im-dae*
▦ skin-diving equipment	스킨다이빙용 장비 *seu-k'in-da-i-bing-yong chang-bi*

CAMPING, HIKING, AND MOUNTAIN CLIMBING

Since 80 percent of Korea is mountainous, camping, hiking, and mountain climbing are favorite pastimes of many Koreans. These expressions will be useful in case you go with a Korean or decide to do some camping on your own.

I like camping at <u>a lake</u>.	<u>호수에서</u> 캠핑하기를 좋아해요. *Ho-su-e-seo k'aem-p'ing-ha-gi-reul cho-a-hae-yo.*
▦ a mountain	산 *san*
▦ the seashore	해변 *hae-byeon*
Can we camp here?	여기서 캠핑해도 돼요 ? *Yeo-gi-seo k'aem-p'ing-hae-do twae-yo?*
Is there <u>a shower</u>?	<u>샤워장</u>이 있어요 ? *Sha-weo-jang-i i-sseo-yo?*
▦ a toilet	화장실 (이) *hwa-jang-shil(i)*
▦ running water	수돗물 (이) *su-don-mul(i)*
▦ grocery	가게 (가) *ka-ge(ga)*
Is there a hiking trail nearby?	이 부근에 등산 코스가 있어요 ? *I pu-geun-e teung-san k'o-seu-ga i-sseo-yo?*

The view is breathtaking!	경치가 기가 막혀요 !	*Kyeong-ch'i-ga ki-ga ma-k'yeo-yo!*
Look at the <u>bridge</u>!	저 다리 좀 보세요 !	*Cheo <u>ta-ri</u> chom po-se-yo!*

- farm   농가   *nong-ga*
- fields   들판   *teul-p'an*
- flowers   꽃   *kkot*
- forest   숲   *sup*
- hill   언덕   *eon-deok*
- lake   호수   *ho-su*
- mountains   산   *san*
- ocean   바다   *pa-da*
- plants   화초   *hwa-ch'o*
- pond   연못   *yeon-mot*
- rice paddy   논   *non*
- river   강   *kang*
- stream   시냇물   *shi-naen-mul*
- temple   절   *cheol*
- thatched roof   초가집   *ch'o-ga-jip*
- trees   나무   *na-mu*
- valley   골짜기   *kol-jja-gi*
- village   마을   *ma-eul*
- waterfall   폭포   *p'ok-p'o*

Where does this road lead to?	이 길은 어디로 통해요 ?	*I ki-reun eo-di-ro t'ong-hae-yo?*
How far is it to _____?	_____까지 얼마나 멀어요 ?	*_____-kka-ji eol-ma-na meo-reo-yo?*
Can you tell me the way to _____?	_____에 가는 길을 좀 가르쳐 주세요.	*_____-e ka-neun ki-reul chom ka-reu-ch'yeo chu-se-yo.*

I'm lost.	길을 잃어버렸어요. *Ki-reul i-reo-beo-ryeo-sseo-yo.*

BICYCLING, JOGGING, AND WALKING

Most Koreans are health-conscious and participate in activities such as bicycling, jogging, or walking. Walking and jogging can be done outdoors, in a stadium, or in fitness clubs. Bike trails are also available in Seoul, especially along the riverside parks bordering the Han River and in other cities. Mountain biking is also popular.

Where <u>can</u> I <u>jog</u>?	어디에서 <u>조깅할 수</u> 있나요 ? *Eo-di-e-seo cho-ging-hal su in-na-yo?*
▨ walk	걸을 수 *keo-reul su*
▨ bike	자전거탈 수 *cha-jeon-geo-t'al su*
Can I rent a bicycle?	자전거를 빌릴 수 있습니까 ? *Cha-jeon-geo-reul pil-lil su i-sseum-ni-kka?*
Is there a <u>bicycle path</u> around here?	이 근처에 <u>자전거전용도로</u>가 있습니까 ? *I keun-ch'eo-e cha-jeon-geo-jeon-yong-do-ro-ga i-sseum-ni-kka?*
▨ fitness club	헬스클럽(이) *hel-seu-k'eul-leop(i)*
Where is a good place for mountain biking?	산악자전거를 탈 수 있는 곳이 어디 있나요 ? *San-ak-ja-jeon-geo-reul t'al su in-neun ko-shi eo-di in-na-yo?*

FOOD AND DRINK

Dining is a major source of Korean entertainment. From an exquisite meal in one of the finer restaurants to a quick stop at one of the street stands, you will find much to delight your palate.

Among the many different things in Korean-style eating that you will notice are the use of chopsticks, the distinctive foods, and the table manners. In some restaurants you will be given hot or cold towels after you have been seated. These are to be used to wipe your hands and face, if desired.

In those restaurants where required, a service charge will be added to your bill; otherwise, no tip is expected.

KOREAN RESTAURANTS

The diversity of Korean food is reflected in its varied tastes and textures. Garlic and red pepper are used liberally in many dishes, but many also contain less spicy ingredients and add a nice, subtle contrast to the stronger flavors.

A Korean meal is commonly composed of main dishes (*yo-ri*), soup (*kuk*), side dishes (*pan-ch'an*), rice, and one or more kinds of kimchi. You will be served your rice and soup in individual bowls, and all other dishes are placed in the middle of the table to be shared by everyone in your party.

Eating Korean food is incomplete without at least one of the several varieties of kimchi, a pickled cabbage/radish dish spiced with garlic and red pepper. Along with rice, kimchi is a staple of the Korean diet.

The following list provides some of the most popular Korean dishes.

MAIN DISHES

fried fish   생선전 *saeng-seon-jeon*

Bite-sized pieces of fish lightly seasoned, dipped in flour and beaten eggs, then fried until golden brown.

grilled fish 생선구이 *saeng-seon-gu-i*

A whole fish basted with a combination of soy sauce, sugar, sesame seeds, sesame oil, chopped green onion, minced garlic, and black pepper, then grilled.

skewered beef and 산적 *san-jeok*
vegetables

Thin strips of beef which have been seasoned with soy sauce, sugar, sesame seeds, sesame oil, garlic, ginger juice, and black pepper, then arranged with strips of spring onions, carrots and mushrooms on bamboo skewers and fried in a little oil until browned.

noodles with meat 잡채 *chap-ch'ae*
and vegetables

A combination of cooked vermicelli noodles, beef, pork, spinach, carrots, green onions, and mushrooms seasoned with soy sauce, sugar, sesame salt, black pepper, and sesame oil.

grilled beef 불고기 *pul-go-gi*

Bite-sized pieces of beef, marinated in soy sauce, sugar, sesame oil, sesame salt, black pepper, green onions, garlic, ginger, and rice wine, then grilled.

beef ribs 불갈비 *pul-gal-bi*

Beef ribs that have been marinated in the same mixture as pulgogi and grilled.

pork ribs 돼지갈비 *twae-ji-gal-bi*

Pork ribs that are prepared in the same manner as beef ribs.

rib stew 갈비찜 *kal-bi-jjim*

A stew made with beef ribs which have been marinated in a soy sauce mixture and boiled with carrots, mushrooms, water, and rice wine. Just before serving, the stew is sprinkled with gingko or pine nuts and decorated with strips of cooked egg.

| fancy meat and vegetable stew | 신선로 | *shin-seol-lo* |

This is food that was once reserved for Korean royalty. Today it is served on special occasions in a pot designed hundreds of years ago. The special pot has a hollow middle where some form of burning fuel keeps the food hot until all is eaten. The dish is made up of mixed vegetables, meat, fried fish and cooked strips of egg layered in the pot and covered with a seasoned beef broth.

| ginseng chicken | 삼계탕 | *sam-gye-t'ang* |

A small chicken stuffed with ginseng, glutinous rice, garlic, chestnuts, and jujubes. The chicken is then boiled in water flavored with garlic and salt to create a delicious broth that surrounds the chicken.

| mustard sauce salad | 겨자채 | *kyeo-ja-ch'ae* |

A cold dish usually made with strips of boiled squid, ham, cucumber, pear, egg, carrot, and Chinese cabbage served with a sauce made of hot mustard powder, vinegar, sugar, salt, soy sauce, and crushed sesame seeds.

ONE-DISH SPECIALTIES
(Served with Rice and Side Dishes)

| mixed rice and vegetables | 비빔밥 | *pi-bim-ppap* |

A mixture of cooked rice, fried egg, broiled meat, and assorted vegetables served with red pepper paste and sesame oil.

| cold noodles with beef and vegetables | 냉면 | *naeng-myeon* |

A food especially popular in summer. The noodles are usually made of buckwheat, placed in a cold beef broth and mixed with strips of beef, pear, cucumber and boiled egg. Vinegar, mustard, and red pepper powder are added for seasoning.

steamed rice with 　백반 *paek-ppan*
side dishes

A bowl of rice served with various side dishes such as kimchi, fish, soup, and some vegetables. This is the basic Korean meal.

rib soup 　갈비탕 *kal-bi-t'ang*

Ribs served in a mild broth made of soy sauce, water, leeks, garlic, sesame salt, and black pepper.

hot pepper fish soup 　매운탕 *mae-un-t'ang*

A very spicy soup made with fish, soybean curd, egg, vegetables, and seasoned with red pepper.

soy-bean paste stew 　된장찌개 *toen-jang-jji-gae*

A stew made with soy-bean paste, water, soy bean curd, Chinese cabbage, and leeks.

SOUP
(To Accompany Main Dishes)

spinach soup 　시금치국 *shi-geum-ch'i-kkuk*

A basic soup made with spinach, green onions, garlic, sesame oil, ground beef, soy sauce, black pepper, and water.

soy-bean paste soup 　된장국 *toen-jang-kkuk*

A light broth made with the same ingredients as the soy-bean paste stew.

kimchi soup 　김치국 *kim-ch'i-kkuk*

Soup made with kimchi, water, bean curd, green onions, beef and soy sauce.

seaweed soup 　미역국 *mi-yeok-kkuk*

Soup made with brown seaweed, thinly-sliced beef, garlic, sesame salt, soy sauce, sesame oil, and black pepper.

bean sprout soup   콩나물국   *k'ong-na-mul-kkuk*

Soup made with soy sauce, sesame oil, sesame salt, onions, black pepper, and bean sprouts.

meat dumpling soup   만두국   *man-du-kkuk*

Soup made of dumplings stuffed with a mixture of ground beef, bean sprouts, squash, bean curd, green pepper, garlic, sesame salt, sesame oil, soy sauce, leeks, carrots, mushrooms, salt and pepper. The dumplings are simmered in a mildly-seasoned broth.

SIDE DISHES

fried dried anchovies   멸치볶음   *myeol-ch'i-bokk-eum*

Anchovies stir-fried with soy sauce, sugar, and sesame salt.

bellflower root   도라지   *to-ra-ji*

A popular root mixed with salt, red pepper powder, chives, garlic, vinegar, sugar, soy sauce, sesame seeds, and salt.

toasted seaweed   김   *kim*

Sheets of seaweed that have been lightly brushed with sesame oil, salted and grilled on a griddle or skillet over low heat.

fried bean curd   두부부침   *tu-bu-bu-ch'im*

Bean curd fried in oil, then served with a mixture of soy sauce, green onions, and vinegar.

steamed bean curd   두부조림   *tu-bu-jo-rim*

Bean curd fried in oil, then seasoned with soy sauce, crushed sesame seed, sugar, minced green onion, crushed garlic, and water, then simmered.

fried stuffed peppers   풋고추전   *put-kko-ch'u-jeon*

Ground meat, mashed bean curd, soy sauce, salt, crushed sesame seed, sesame oil, green onion, and black pepper are mixed together and used as a stuffing for bell peppers or hot green peppers. After the sliced peppers have been stuffed, they are dipped in flour and beaten egg and fried in oil.

beef and bean curd patties   완자전   *wan-ja-jeon*

Ground beef, mashed bean curd, soy sauce, salt, green onion, garlic, sesame powder, sesame oil, and black pepper are mixed together and shaped into patties. The patties are rolled in flour, dipped in beaten egg, and fried in hot oil.

stuffed zucchini   호박전   *ho-bak-jeon*

Minced meat, soy sauce, salt, sesame powder, sesame oil, pepper, onion and garlic are mixed together. The mixture is stuffed into small pieces of zucchini. The zucchini is then slightly boiled in some water or broth, soy sauce, salt, pepper, chopped onion, red pepper threads, and strips of egg.

seasoned spinach   시금치나물   *shi-geum-ch'i-na-mul*

Blanched spinach is cut into pieces which are then seasoned with a mixture of soy sauce, sugar, sesame seed, sesame oil, and finely chopped green onion.

seasoned bean sprouts   콩나물   *k'ong-na-mul*

Blanched bean sprouts seasoned with soy sauce, sesame oil, sugar, sesame salt, chopped green onion, garlic, and red pepper.

TYPES OF KIMCHI

cabbage kimchi   김치   *kim-ch'i*

Chinese cabbage, turnip radishes, minari (like watercress), green onions and leeks seasoned with a sauce of red pepper, salt, sugar, garlic, and fresh ginger. Seafood such as tiny shrimp may also be added.

white cabbage kimchi (a less-spicy variety)   백김치   *paek-kkim-ch'i*

A combination of Chinese cabbage, leeks, salt, water, carrot, green onion, garlic, ginger, salt, and sugar.

radish and cabbage   나박 김치   *na-bak kim-ch'i*
kimchi

Radish or turnip, Chinese cabbage, minari, green onions, leeks, garlic, ginger, red pepper powder, hot red peppers, salt, sugar, and water are mixed together for this type of kimchi.

hot radish kimchi   깍두기   *kkak-ttu-gi*

This popular kimchi is made of large radishes or turnips, salt, ground red pepper, sugar, garlic, ginger, green onions, and red pepper threads.

cucumber kimchi   오이소박이   *o-i-so-bak-i*

Cucumbers are slit and stuffed with a combination of green onions, garlic, ginger, red pepper threads or powder, salt, and sugar.

small radish kimchi   총각 김치   *ch'ong-gak kim-ch'i*

Made with the same red pepper mixture as other kimchi dishes. This mixture is added to small white radishes.

CONDIMENTS

The following condiments are often requested to add to some of the above foods.

red pepper powder   고춧가루   *ko-ch'u-kka-ru*

red pepper paste   고추장   *ko-ch'u-jang*

soy sauce   간장   *kan-jang*

vinegar   식초   *shik-ch'o*

black pepper   후춧가루   *hu-ch'u-kka-ru*

ARRIVING

At most Korean restaurants, you have a choice of sitting in a chair at a table or sitting on the floor, Korean-style. If you choose Korean-style, you must remove your shoes before sitting on a cushion at a low table. Some restaurants also offer small rooms for dining.

Please come in. (greeting by restaurant host or hostess)	어서 오세요.	*Eo-seo o-se-yo.*
How many are in your party?	몇 분이세요 ?	*Myeot ppun-i-se-yo?*
There are <u>two</u> of us.	<u>두</u> 사람이에요.	<u>*Tu*</u> *sa-ram-i-e-yo.*
■ three	세	*se*
■ four	네	*ne*
Is there a room available?	방이 있어요 ?	*Pang-i i-sseo-yo?*
I'd like a table, please.	테이블 주세요.	*T'e-i-beul chu-se-yo.*

AT THE TABLE

You may want to order something to drink such as rice wine or beer before ordering your food. Western-style liquor and mixed drinks are generally not served in Korean restaurants. Whatever you decide to drink, here are some things to remember: (1) Never pour a drink into your own glass, and never allow other persons in the group to pour their own; (2) if you notice that another person's glass is empty or nearly so, offer to fill the glass; and (3) when pouring for someone older than you or of higher status, pour holding the bottle with two hands. When someone pours for you, hold your glass with two hands. Your two hands may be on the bottle or glass, or you may hold the bottle or glass with your right hand and place your left hand at your right wrist. The hand placements apply to other exchanges, such as passing items like plates of food or chopsticks. It is considered impolite to give or receive items with your left hand.

Is there a menu in English?	영어로된 메뉴가 있어요 ?	*Yeong-eo-ro-doen me-nyu-ga i-sseo-yo?*
May I have some <u>water</u>?	<u>물</u> 좀 주세요.	*<u>Mul</u> chom chu-se-yo.*
▦ beer	맥주	*maek-jju*
▦ rice wine	정종	*cheong-jong*
▦ cola	콜라	*k'ol-la*
▦ lemon-lime soda	사이다	*sa-i-da*
<u>Two</u> bottles of beer, please.	맥주 <u>두</u> 병 주세요.	*Maek-jju <u>tu</u> pyeong chu-se-yo.*
▦ three	세	*se*
▦ five	다섯	*ta-seot*
Please bring one more glass.	잔 하나 더 주세요.	*Chan ha-na teo chu-se-yo.*
We'd like some appetizers.	안주 좀 주세요.	*An-ju chom chu-se-yo.*
Do you have <u>sliced raw fish</u>?	생선회 있어요 ?	*<u>Saeng-seon-hoe</u> i-sseo-yo?*
▦ mung bean pancakes	빈대떡	*pin-dae-tteok*
▦ oysters	굴	*kul*
Is it <u>raw</u>?	생거예요 ?	*<u>Saeng-geo</u>-ye-yo?*
▦ cooked	익힌	*ik-k'in*

■ hot (spicy)   매운   *mae-un*

■ salty   짠   *jjan*

Is it <u>grilled</u>?   <u>구운</u>거예요 ?   <u>*Ku-un*</u>-*geo-ye-yo?*

■ fried   튀긴   *t'wi-gin*

■ boiled   삶은   *sal-meun*

What do you suggest?   뭐가 좋아요 ?   *Mweo-ga cho-a-yo?*

I'll have this.   이거 주세요.   *I-geo chu-se-yo.*

EATING THE KOREAN WAY: A FEW POINTERS

    Menus may not be available in English. You may want to point to a food item listed under the Main Dishes or One Dish Specialties sections of this book to see if it is served in the restaurant. You may also ask someone at your hotel to suggest a restaurant that serves a dish you would like to try.

    Desserts usually consist of seasonal fruit. At fancier restaurants, other items may be available, such as persimmon punch (*su-jeong-gwa*), fruit punch (*hwa-ch'ae*) or rice punch (*shik-k'ye*).

    Soy sauce is not poured over steamed rice. Rice is served in individual bowls and is eaten in combination with other pieces of food. Soy sauce is used for dipping bits of food (especially meat and fish) just before eating.

    Soup is usually served as part of every meal. It is served in individual bowls and is eaten with the spoon provided. Chopsticks may be needed to pick the meat, vegetables, or other pieces of food from the soup.

    Chopsticks are mastered with a little practice. Hold one stick at the base of the thumb and index finger and the end of the ring finger. It remains stationary. Hold the second stick with the ends of the thumb and the first two fingers. It is moved to grasp the pieces of food.

    If you need a toothpick at the end of a meal, it is considered polite to cover your mouth with one hand while using it.

If you eat with a Korean colleague or friend, paying individually is not a common practice. Only one person will pay when two or more people go out for food or drink. Others may put up a convincing fight, but if you are hosting, you must be sure to get to the cashier first to pay the bill. If you have been someone's guest, you should make every effort to reciprocate on another occasion. If your time in Korea is limited, you might invite your host to another place that day for coffee and dessert or another drink.

KINDS OF KOREAN RESTAURANTS

Korean food can be found in a variety of eating establishments. These include specialty restaurants, such as barbecue meat restaurants (*pul-go-gi-jjip*), hotel restaurants, outdoor garden restaurants, cafes, and various drinking houses. The following phrases will be useful in helping you order and enjoy your food.

FINDING A RESTAURANT

I'm hungry.	배가 고픈데요.	*Pae-ga ko-p'eun-de-yo.*
I want to go to a <u>barbecue meat restaurant</u>.	불고기집에 가고 싶어요.	*Pul-go-gi-jjip-e ka-go shi-p'eo-yo.*
■ vegetarian restaurant	채식 식당	*ch'ae-shik shik-dang*
■ dumpling restaurant	만두집	*man-du-jjip*
■ snack shop	분식집	*pun-shik-jjip*
■ steamed rice restaurant	백반집	*paek-ban-jjip*
■ raw fish restaurant	횟집	*hoe-jjip*
■ ginseng chicken restaurant	삼계탕집	*sam-gye-t'ang-jjip*

Do you have a favorite restaurant?	단골집이 있어요 ?	*Tan-gol-jjip-i i-sseo-yo?*
Let's go to a barbecue meat restaurant.	불고기집에 갑시다.	*Pul-go-gi-jjip-e kap-shi-da.*

AT THE RESTAURANT

Please come in.	어서 오세요.	*Eo-seo o-se-yo.*
Do you want a menu?	메뉴 드릴까요 ?	*Me-nyu teu-ril-kka-yo?*

Do you have <u>pulgogi</u>?	<u>불고기</u> 돼요 ?	<u>*Pul-go-gi*</u> *twae-yo?*
▧ dumpling soup	만두국	*man-du-kkuk*
▧ kimchi stew	김치찌개	*kim-ch'i-jji-gae*
▧ grilled fish	생선구이	*saeng-seon-gu-i*
▧ noodles with meat and vegetables	잡채	*chap-ch'ae*
▧ mixed rice and vegetables	비빔밥	*pi-bim-ppap*

I prefer vegetarian dishes.	저는 야채요리를 더 좋아해요. *Cheo-neun ya-ch'ae-yo-ri-reul teo cho-a-hae-yo.*

I'd like <u>beef ribs</u> for two.	<u>불갈비</u> 이 인분 주세요.	<u>*Pul-gal-bi*</u> *i in-bun chu-se-yo.*
▧ pork ribs	돼지갈비	*twae-ji-gal-bi*
▧ grilled beef	불고기	*pul-go-gi*

Please give me some <u>red pepper paste</u>.	<u>고추장</u> 좀 주세요.	<u>*Ko-ch'u-jang*</u> *chom chu-se-yo.*
▧ vinegar	식초	*shik-ch'o*
▧ black pepper	후춧가루	*hu-ch'u-kka-ru*
▧ red pepper powder	고춧가루	*ko-ch'u-kka-ru*

Please give me more kimchi.	김치 좀 더 주세요.	*Kimch'i chom teo chu-se-yo.*
▓ toasted seaweed	김	*kim*
▓ rice	밥	*pap*
▓ water	물	*mul*
▓ seasoned spinach	시금치나물	*shi-geum-ch'i-na-mul*

I hope you enjoy your meal. (Said by the host at the beginning and during the meal; literally, "Eat a lot.") 많이 잡수세요. *Ma-ni chap-su-se-yo.*

This looks delicious. (Said by the guest at the beginning of the meal; literally, "I will eat well.") 잘 먹겠습니다. *Chal meok-kke-sseum-ni-da.*

I've had plenty. 많이 먹었어요. *Ma-ni meo-geo-sseo-yo.*

It was really delicious. 맛있게 먹었어요. *Ma-shi-kke meo-geo-sseo-yo.*

I've had all I can eat. 다 먹었어요. *Ta meo-geo-sseo-yo.*

Thank you for a wonderful meal. 잘 먹었어요. *Chal meo-geo-sseo-yo.*

May I have the check, please? 계산서를 주시겠어요? *Kye-san-seo-reul chu-shi-ge-sseo-yo?*

CAFÉS

Cafés provide a wide assortment of non-alcoholic and alcoholic beverages. Snacks such as sandwiches, pastries, and ice cream are also available. Café owners try to establish an atmosphere that will appeal to a specific clientele. Those located near universities cater to young people, while those in residential areas are designed more for business people and families. Whether you want a place to snack, drink, or simply rest, you will find the café a fascinating experience.

I'd like some Western food.	양식을 먹고 싶은데요. *Yang-shik-eul meok-kko shi-p'eun-de-yo.*
Are there any cafés around here?	이 근처에 까페가 있어요 ? *I keun-ch'eo-e kka-p'e-ga i-sseo-yo?*
There is a café with a nice atmosphere in this alley.	이 골목에 분위기가 좋은 까페가 있어요. *I kol-mok-e pun-wi-gi-ga cho-eun kka-p'e-ga i-sseo-yo.*
What would you like?	무엇을 드릴까요 ? *Mu-eo-seul teu-ril-kka-yo?*
What is your specialty?	이 집 전문이 뭐예요 ? *I chip cheon-mun-i mweo-ye-yo?*
Our <u>pizza</u> is quite good.	피자를 아주 잘 해요. *P'i-ja-reul a-ju chal hae-yo.*
▨ omerice (fried rice, onions, and meat, wrapped in a thinly-fried omelet)	오므라이스(를) *o-meu-ra-i-seu(reul)*
▨ curry rice	카레라이스(를) *k'a-re-ra-i-seu(reul)*
I'll just have <u>coffee</u>.	저는 커피만 주세요. *Cheo-neun k'eo-p'i-man chu-se-yo.*
▨ tomato juice	토마토 쥬스 *t'o-ma-t'o chyu-seu*

▓ ice cream	아이스 크림	*a-i-seu k'eu-rim*
▓ red wine	적포도주	*cheok-p'o-do-ju*
▓ white wine	백포도주	*paek-p'o-do-ju*
▓ champagne	샴페인	*shyam-p'e-in*
▓ a sandwich	샌드위치	*saen-deu-wi-ch'i*
▓ a pastry	빵	*ppang*

COFFEE AND TEA HOUSES

From espressos to iced lattes, coffee is a very popular drink in Korea, and there are numerous local and international coffee house chains available in the larger cities. Many coffee houses are as popular for blended fruit drinks and ice cream as they are for coffee and tea. You can also find pastries, sandwiches, fruit, and other snacks.

If you are a tea drinker, look for a traditional tea house (*ch'a-jjip*) that specializes in a variety of Korean-style teas. The tea house is an excellent place to sample some unusual teas and be exposed to an authentic, traditional Korean atmosphere.

What would you like? (said by the hostess)	무엇을 드릴까요 ?	*Mu-eo-seul teu-ril-kka-yo?*

I'd like <u>coffee</u>, please.	<u>커피</u> 주세요.	<u>*K'eo-p'i*</u> *chu-se-yo.*
▓ tea	홍차	*hong-ch'a*
▓ green tea	녹차	*nok-ch'a*
▓ jujube tea	대추차	*tae-ch'u-ch'a*
▓ ginseng tea	인삼차	*in-sam-ch'a*
▓ ginger tea	생강차	*saeng-gang-ch'a*
▓ walnut tea	호두차	*ho-du-ch'a*
▓ sesame tea	들깨차	*teul-kkae-ch'a*
▓ Job's tears tea	율무차	*yul-mu-ch'a*

▧ arrowroot tea	칡차	*ch'ik-ch'a*
▧ herb tea	쌍화차	*ssang-hwa-ch'a*

Do you have strawberry juice? — 딸기 쥬스 있어요 ? *Ttal-gi chyu-seu i-sseo-yo?*

▧ peach juice	복숭아 쥬스	*pok-sung-a chyu-seu*
▧ orange juice	오렌지 쥬스	*o-ren-ji chyu-seu*
▧ milk and fruit blend	쉐이크	*shwe-i-k'eu*
▧ cola	콜라	*k'ol-la*
▧ lemon-lime soda	사이다	*sa-i-da*

How much is the check? — 얼마예요 ? *Eol-ma-ye-yo?*

INTERNATIONAL RESTAURANTS

Korea offers an extensive variety of international restaurants. While Chinese and Japanese restaurants are popular, it is easy to find a wide and varied selection of food from all over the world. There are many international chains as well as locally owned establishments that serve different types of ethnic food.

CHINESE RESTAURANTS

Is there a good Chinese restaurant near here? — 이 근처에 잘하는 중국집이 있어요 ? *I keun-ch'eo-e chal-ha-neun chung-guk-jjip-i i-sseo-yo?*

Please suggest an inexpensive one. — 값이 싼 데를 소개해 주세요. *Kap-shi ssan te-reul so-gae-hae chu-se-yo.*

I would like <u>sweet and sour pork</u>. — 탕수육 하나 주세요. *T'ang-su-yuk ha-na chu-se-yo.*

▧ seafood with vegetables	팔보채	*p'al-bo-ch'ae*

- fried chicken in oyster sauce 간풍기 *kkan-p'ung-gi*
- braised bean curd in spicy meat sauce 마파두부 *ma-p'a-du-bu*
- mustard sauce salad 양장피 *yang-jang-p'i*
- beef patties 난자완스 *nan-ja-wan-seu*
- spicy seafood noodle soup 짬뽕 *jjam-ppong*
- noodles with a black bean sauce 짜장면 *jja-jang-myeon*
- fried rice 볶음밥 *po-kkeum-bap*

Please give us two bottles of <u>Chinese liquor</u>. <u>고량주</u> 두 병 주세요. <u>*Ko-ryang-ju*</u> *tu pyeong chu-se-yo.*

- beer 맥주 *maek-jju*
- cola 콜라 *k'ol-la*

JAPANESE RESTAURANTS

I want to eat Japanese food. 일식을 먹고 싶은데요. *Il-shik-eul meok-kko shi-p'eun-de-yo.*

Where can I find a good Japanese restaurant? 잘하는 일식집이 어디 있어요 ? *Chal-ha-neun il-shik-jjip-i eo-di i-sseo-yo?*

I would like <u>raw fish</u>. <u>생선회</u> 주세요. <u>*Saeng-seon-hoe*</u> *chu-se-yo.*

- sushi 생선초밥 *saeng-seon-ch'o-bap*
- tempura 뎀뿌라 *tem-ppu-ra*
- noodle and vegetable soup 우동 *u-dong*
- sukiyaki 스끼야끼 *seu-kki-ya-kki*

■ pork cutlet	돈까스	*ton-kka-seu*
■ rice topped with meat and vegetables	덮밥	*teop-ppap*

Do you have <u>rice wine</u>?	정종 있어요 ?	*Cheong-jong i-sseo-yo?*
■ beer	맥주	*maek-jju*
■ lemon-lime soda	사이다	*sa-i-da*

May we have our check?	계산서를 주시겠어요 ?	*Kye-san-seo-reul chu-shi-ge-sseo-yo?*

OTHER INTERNATIONAL RESTAURANTS

Here are some expressions to use when enjoying the many international restaurants available in the larger cities of Korea. Many of these restaurants are found in major hotels while others are operated independently.

I'd like to have <u>American</u> food.	미국 음식을 먹고 싶어요.	<u>*Mi-guk*</u> *eum-shik-eul meok-kko shi-p'eo-yo.*
■ French	프랑스	*P'eu-rang-seu*
■ Italian	이태리	*I-t'ae-ri*
■ Indian	인도	*In-do*

Can you recommend <u>a nice</u> restaurant?	좋은 음식점을 좀 소개해 주세요.	<u>*Cho-eun*</u> *eum-shik-jjeom-eul chom so-gae-hae chu-se-yo.*
■ a first-class	고급	*ko-geup*
■ an inexpensive	비싸지 않은	*pi-ssa-ji an-eun*

Do they take credit cards?	크레딧 카드를 받을까요 ?	*K'eu-re-dit k'a-deu-reul pa-deul-kka-yo?*

What are their hours?	영업 시간이 어떻게 되지요 ?	*Yeong-eop shi-gan-i eo-tteo-k'e toe-ji-yo?*

Do you have the telephone number?	전화 번호를 아세요 ? *Cheon-hwa peon-ho-reul a-se-yo?*
Do I need to make a reservation?	예약해야 돼요 ? *Ye-yak-k'ae-ya twae-yo?*
Would you make the reservation for me?	저대신 예약 좀 해 주시겠어요 ? *Cheo-dae-shin ye-yak chom hae chu-shi-ge-sseo-yo?*
I'd like a reservation for four people at 7:00.	저녁 일곱시에 네 사람을 부탁해요. *Cheo-nyeok il-gop-shi-e ne sa-ram-eul pu-t'ak-k'ae-yo.*

AT THE RESTAURANT

Do you have our reservation?	예약을 받으셨어요 ? *Ye-yak-eul pa-deu-shyeo-sseo-yo?*
Can we get our table now?	지금 테이블로 가도 돼요 ? *Chi-geum t' e-i-beul-lo ka-do twae-yo?*
Shall we order drinks first?	먼저 마실 걸 주문할까요 ? *Meon-jeo ma-shil kkeol chu-mun-hal-kka-yo?*
Please bring us a bottle of wine and four glasses.	와인 한 병과 잔 네 개만 주세요. *Wa-in han pyeong-gwa chan ne kae-man chu-se-yo.*
Will you take our order?	주문 받으시겠어요 ? *Chu-mun pa-deu-shi-ge-sseo-yo?*
I'd like a salad.	샐러드를 주세요. *Sael-leo-deu-reul chu-se-yo.*
Can you bring us some bread?	빵을 주시겠어요 ? *Ppang-eul chu-shi-ge-sseo-yo?*
What <u>chicken</u> dishes do you have?	무슨 <u>닭고기</u> 요리가 있어요 ? *Mu-seun <u>tak-ko-gi</u> yo-ri-ga i-sseo-yo?*

■ fish	생선	*saeng-seon*
■ beef	쇠고기	*soe-go-gi*

Will you prepare it without <u>salt</u>?

소금 넣지말고 요리해 주시겠어요 ?
So-geum neo-ch'i-mal-go yo-ri-hae chu-shi-ge-sseo-yo?

■ butter or oil	버터나 기름	*peo-t'eo-na ki-reum*
■ MSG	화학 조미료	*hwa-hak cho-mi-ryo*

I'd like <u>potatoes</u>.　감자 주세요. *Kam-ja chu-se-yo.*

■ asparagus	아스파라거스	*a-seu-p'a-ra-geo-seu*
■ peas	완두콩	*wan-du-k'ong*
■ cauliflower	꽃양배추	*kkot-yang-bae-ch'u*
■ corn on the cob	옥수수	*ok-su-su*
■ carrots	당근	*tang-geun*
■ mixed vegetables	모듬야채	*mo-deum-ya-ch'ae*

What kind of desserts do you have?

디저트는 뭐가 있어요 ? *Ti-jeo-t'eu-neun mweo-ga i-sseo-yo?*

We have <u>ice cream</u>.

아이스 크림이 있어요. *A-i-seu k'eu-rim-i i-sseo-yo.*

■ cake	케이크(가)	*k'e-i-k'eu(ga)*
■ apple pie	사과 파이(가)	*sa-gwa p'a-i(ga)*
■ peach melba	피치 멜바(가)	*p'i-ch'i mel-ba(ga)*
■ fruit cocktail	프루트 칵테일(이)	*p'eu-ru-t'eu k'ak-t'e-il(i)*

I'll have some <u>coffee</u>.　커피 주세요. *K'eo-p'i chu-se-yo.*

■ brandy	브랜디	*peu-raen-di*
■ cognac	꼬냑	*kko-nyak*
■ port	포트와인	*p'o-t'eu wa-in*

ADDITIONAL REQUESTS

Excuse me.   여기요.   *Yeo-gi-yo.*
(To get the server's attention, use the expression, *Yeo-gi-yo,*
literally "here.")

Could you bring me a knife, please?	나이프 좀 주세요.	*Na-i-p'eu* chom *chu-se-yo.*
▥ a fork	포크	*p'o-k'eu*
▥ a spoon	숟가락	*su-kka-rak*
▥ chopsticks	젓가락	*cheo-kka-rak*
▥ a cup	컵	*k'eop*
▥ a glass	유리컵	*yu-ri-k'eop*
▥ a plate	접시	*cheop-shi*
▥ a bowl	밥그릇	*pap-kkeu-reut*
▥ a napkin	냅킨	*naep-k'in*
▥ some toothpicks	이쑤시개	*i-ssu-shi-gae*

Could you bring me some more water, please?	물 좀 더 주세요.	*Mul* chom teo *chu-se-yo.*
▥ bread	빵	*ppang*
▥ butter	버터	*peo-t'eo*
▥ wine	와인	*wa-in*

Show me the menu again, please.   매뉴 좀 다시 보여 주세요.   *Me-nyu chom ta-shi po-yeo chu-se-yo.*

COMPLAINTS

It's not what I ordered.   이것은 제가 주문한 게 아니에요.   *I-geo-seun che-ga chu-mun-han ke a-ni-e-yo.*

This is overcooked.   너무 익었어요.   *Neo-mu i-geo-sseo-yo.*

▥ under   덜   *Teol*

This isn't <u>hot</u>.	이것은 식었어요.	*I-geo-seun shi-geo-sseo-yo.*
■ cold	차지 않아요	*ch'a-ji an-a-yo*
■ fresh	싱싱하지 않아요	*shing-shing-ha-ji an-a-yo*
May I speak with the manager?	매니저 좀 불러 주세요.	*Mae-ni-jeo chom pul-leo chu-se-yo.*
May we have another table?	다른 테이블을 주시겠어요 ?	*Ta-reun t'e-i-beu-reul chu-shi-ge-sseo-yo?*

THE CHECK

Separate checks, please.	각자 계산해 주세요.	*Kak-jja kye-san-hae chu-se-yo.*
Do you take <u>credit cards</u>?	<u>크레딧 카드</u> 받아요 ?	<u>*K'eu-re-dit k'a-deu*</u> *pa-da-yo?*
■ traveler's checks	여행자수표	*yeo-haeng-ja-su-p'yo*
Which credit cards do you take?	어떤 크레딧 카드를 받아요 ?	*Eo-tteon k'eu-re-dit k'a-deu-reul pa-da-yo?*
Are the tax and service charge included?	세금하고 서비스료도 포함되어 있어요 ?	*Se-geum-ha-go seo-bi-seu-ryo-do p'o-ham-doe-eo i-sseo-yo?*
Is this correct?	계산이 맞아요 ?	*Kye-san-i ma-ja-yo?*
I don't think the bill is right.	계산이 틀린 것 같아요.	*Kye-san-i t'eul-lin keot ka-t'a-yo.*
What are these charges for?	이 요금은 뭐지요 ?	*I yo-geum-eun mweo-ji-yo?*
I didn't order this.	이것은 주문 안 했는데요.	*I-geo-seun chu-mun an haen-neun-de-yo.*

May I have a receipt, please?	영수증을 주시겠어요 ? *Yeong-su-jeung-eul chu-shi-ge-sseo-yo?*

OTHER BEVERAGES

Alcoholic

The following words will help you order Western-style drinks, called "cocktail" in Korean, when visiting a bar in your hotel or in the city.

gin	진 *chin*
gin and tonic	진토닉 *chin-t'o-nik*
rum	럼 *reom*
screwdriver	스크루드라이버 *seu-k'eu-ru-deu-ra-i-beo*
vodka	보드카 *po-deu-k'a*
tequila	테킬라 *t'e-kkil-la*
margarita	마가리타 *ma-ga-ri-t'a*
martini	마티니 *ma-t'i-ni*
Manhattan	맨하탄 *maen-ha-t'an*
whiskey on the rocks	위스키 온더락 *wi-seu-k'i on-deo-rak*
whiskey straight	위스키 스트레이트 *wi-seu-k'i seu-t'eu-re-i-t'eu*

Nonalcoholic

iced coffee	아이스 커피 *a-i-seu k'eo-p'i*
cola	콜라 *k'ol-la*
lemon lime soda	사이다 *sa-i-da*
orange juice	오렌지 쥬스 *o-ren-ji chyu-seu*
pineapple juice	파인애플 쥬스 *p'a-in-ae-p'eul chyu-seu*

| tomato juice | 토마토 쥬스 | *t'o-ma-t'o chyu-seu* |
| milk | 우유 | *u-yu* |

EATING ON THE GO

When you don't have time to stop in a restaurant, the following can help you choose foods which are fast and inexpensive. These items are available in supermarkets and small neighborhood stores anywhere in Korea.

Do you have _____?	_____있어요 ?	_____ *i-sseo-yo?*
▥ bread	빵	*ppang*
▥ shrimp chips	새우깡	*sae-u-kkang*
▥ candy	캔디	*k'aen-di*
▥ cookies	과자	*kwa-ja*
▥ ice cream	아이스크림	*a-i-seu-k'eu-rim*
▥ apples	사과	*sa-gwa*
▥ strawberries	딸기	*ttal-gi*
▥ peaches	복숭아	*pok-sung-a*
▥ persimmons	감	*kam*
▥ apple pears	배	*pae*
▥ tangerines	귤	*kyul*
▥ bananas	바나나	*ppa-na-na*

| How much is it? | 얼마예요 ? | *Eol-ma-ye-yo?* |

MEETING PEOPLE

Your travels throughout Korea will bring you in contact with Koreans from many different walks of life. Since Koreans are naturally friendly and interested in people from other countries, it will be easy for you to meet them and to get to know them as individuals. The expressions in this section will help you get the ball rolling and continue if you feel it is appropriate. See the section on The Land and the People for more information on Korean customs.

CONVERSATION STARTERS: WITH LOCAL PEOPLE

Do you live <u>here</u>?	여기 사세요 ?	<u>*Yeo-gi*</u> *sa-se-yo?*
■ in Seoul	서울에	*Seo-u-re*
■ in Chuncheon	춘천에	*Ch'un-ch'eon-e*
■ in Gyeongju	경주에	*Kyeong-ju-e*

How long have you lived here?　여기서 얼마동안 사셨어요 ? *Yeo-gi-seo eol-ma-dong-an sa-shyeo-sseo-yo?*

I've always wanted to visit Korea.　그 전부터 한국에 오고 싶었어요. *Keu cheon-bu-t'eo Han-guk-e o-go shi-p'eo-sseo-yo.*

It's a beautiful place.　참 아름다워요. *Ch'am a-reum-da-weo-yo.*

I really like it here.　아주 마음에 들어요. *A-ju ma-eu-me teu-reo-yo.*

I've been to Daegu, Busan, and Jeju-do.　대구, 부산, 제주도에 가 봤어요. *Tae-gu, Pu-san, Che-ju-do-e ka pwa-sseo-yo.*

I plan to go to Mt. Seoraksan, the East Sea, and Panmunjeom.	설악산, 동해, 판문점에 갈 예정이에요. *Seo-rak-san, Tong-hae, P'an-mun-jeom-e kal ye-jeong-i-e-yo.*
What do you think about my plans?	제 계획이 어때요 ? *Che kye-hoek-i eo-ttae-yo?*
Could you recommend any other sites I should see?	다른 가 볼 만한 데를 소개해 주세요. *Ta-reun ka pol man-han te-reul so-gae-hae chu-se-yo.*
Could you explain about ____?	____에 대해서 설명해 주세요. *____-e tae-hae-seo seol-myeong-hae chu-se-yo.*
Can you recommend a good <u>restaurant</u>?	잘하는 <u>음식점</u>을 소개해 주세요. *Chal-ha-neun <u>eum-shik-jjeom</u>-eul so-gae-hae chu-se-yo.*
■ hotel	호텔(을) *ho-t'el(eul)*
■ souvenir shop	선물 가게(를) *seon-mul ka-ge(reul)*

CONVERSATION STARTERS: WITH OUT-OF-TOWN PEOPLE

How long have you been here?	여기오신 지 얼마나 되셨어요 ? *Yeo-gi-o-shin chi eol-ma-na toe-shyeo-sseo-yo?*
I've been here <u>two days</u>.	이틀 되었어요. *<u>I-t'eul</u> toe-eo-sseo-yo.*
■ three days	사흘 *sa-eul*
■ a week	일 주일 *il jju-il*

Are you here for sightseeing?	관광하러 오셨어요 ?	*Kwan-gwang-ha-reo o-shyeo-sseo-yo?*
I'm here on business.	사업차 왔어요.	*Sa-eop-ch'a wa-sseo-yo.*
Is this your first time here?	이번이 처음이세요 ?	*I-beon-i ch'eo-eum-i-se-yo?*
I was here <u>last year</u>.	<u>작년</u>에 왔었어요.	*<u>Chang-nyeon-e</u> wa-sseo-sseo-yo.*
■ two years ago	이년 전	*i-nyeon cheon*
■ four years ago	사년 전	*sa-nyeon cheon*

FOLLOW-UP

Are you enjoying your visit?	여행이 즐거우세요 ?	*Yeo-haeng-i cheul-geo-u-se-yo?*
I like it very much here.	아주 좋아요.	*A-ju cho-a-yo.*
What have you seen here?	어디 가보셨어요 ?	*Eo-di ka-bo-shyeo-sseo-yo?*
I recommend you go to _____.	_____에 가면 좋아하실 거예요.	*_____-e ka-myeon cho-a-ha-shil kkeo-ye-yo.*
Are you alone?	혼자 오셨어요 ?	*Hon-ja o-shyeo-sseo-yo?*
I'm <u>with my wife</u>.	<u>아내와 함께</u> 왔어요.	*<u>A-nae-wa ham-kke</u> wa-sseo-yo.*
■ with my husband	남편과 함께	*nam-p'yeon-gwa ham-kke*
■ with my family	가족과 함께	*ka-jok-kkwa ham-kke*
■ with my friend	친구와 함께	*ch'in-gu-wa ham-kke*
Where are you from?	어느 나라에서 오셨어요 ?	*Eo-neu na-ra-e-seo o-shyeo-sseo-yo?*

I'm from the United States.	미국에서 왔어요. *Mi-guk-e-seo wa-sseo-yo.*
▓ Hong Kong	홍콩 *Hong-k'ong*
▓ Australia	호주 *Ho-ju*

| Where are you staying? | 어디에 묵고 계세요? *Eo-di-e muk-kko kye-se-yo?* |

| Let me introduce myself. | 제 소개를 하지요. *Che so-gae-reul ha-ji-yo.* |

| My name is _____ | 제 이름은 _____에요. *Che i-reum-eun _____ye-yo.* |

I'm a student.	저는 학생이에요. *Cheo-neun hak-ssaeng-i-e-yo.*
▓ businessperson	사업가 *sa-eop-kka*
▓ teacher	선생 *seon-saeng*

| What are you studying? | 무엇을 공부하세요? *Mu-eo-seul kong-bu-ha-se-yo?* |

| Do you have any pictures of your family? | 가족 사진이 있으세요? *Ka-jok sa-jin-i i-sseu-se-yo?* |

TAKING PICTURES

| May I take your picture? | 사진을 찍어도 될까요? *Sa-jin-eul jjik-eo-do toel-kka-yo?* |

| Would you like me to take a picture for you? | 사진을 찍어 드릴까요? *Sa-jin-eul jjik-eo teu-ril-kka-yo?* |

| Please stand here. | 여기 서세요. *Yeo-gi seo-se-yo.* |

| Don't move. | 움직이지 마세요. *Um-jik-i-ji ma-se-yo.* |

Kimchi! 김치！ *Kim-ch'i!*
(Koreans often say, "Kimchi" as the alternative expression for Americans' use of "Cheese")

That's all. 됐어요. *Twae-sseo-yo.*

Would you take a picture of me, please? 사진 좀 찍어 주시겠어요？ *Sa-jin chom jjik-eo chu-shi-ge-sseo-yo?*

Thank you. 감사합니다. *Kam-sa-ham-ni-da.*

GETTING TOGETHER

Shall we get together again? 또 만날까요？ *Tto man-nal-kka-yo?*

Here's my name, hotel, and telephone number. 제 이름과 호텔 그리고 전화 번호를 드리지요. *Che i-reum-gwa ho-t'el keu-ri-go cheon-hwa peon-ho-reul teu-ri-ji-yo.*

Will you call me if you have time? 시간이 있으면 전화하세요. *Shi-gan-i i-sseu-myeon cheon-hwa-ha-se-yo.*

May I have your <u>telephone number</u>? <u>전화 번호를 주시겠어요？</u> <u>*Cheon-hwa peon-ho-reul chu-shi-ge-sseo-yo?*</u>
■ address 주소(를) *chu-so(reul)*
■ business card 명함(을) *myeong-ham(eul)*

Are you doing anything <u>this afternoon</u>? <u>오늘 오후에</u> 시간이 있으세요？ <u>*O-neul o-hu-e*</u> *shi-gan-i i-sseu-se-yo?*
■ this evening 오늘 저녁에 *o-neul cheo-nyeok-e*
■ tomorrow 내일 *nae-il*

I'd like to invite you for dinner.	저녁 식사에 초대하겠어요. *Cheo-nyeok shik-sa-e ch'o-dae-ha-ge-sseo-yo.*
Oh, you don't have to do that.	아, 안 그러셔도 되는데요. *A, an keu-reo-shyeo-do toe-neun-de-yo.*
Where shall we meet?	어디서 만날까요 ? *Eo-di-seo man-nal-kka-yo?*
What time shall we meet?	몇 시에 만날까요 ? *Myeot shi-e man-nal-kka-yo?*
Shall we meet at <u>six</u> ?	<u>여섯</u> 시에 만날까요 ? <u>*Yeo-seot*</u> *shi-e man-nal-kka-yo?*
■ seven	일곱 *il-gop*
■ eight	여덟 *yeo-deol*
See you then.	그 때 뵙지요. *Keu ttae poep-jji-yo.*
Do you have time to meet tomorrow?	내일 만날 시간이 있으세요 ? *Nae-il man-nal shi-gan-i i-sseu-se-yo?*
No, I have another appointment.	아니요, 다른 약속이 있어요. *A-ni-yo, ta-reun yak-sok-i i-sseo-yo.*
How about the day after tomorrow?	모레는 어떨까요 ? *Mo-re-neun eo-tteol-kka-yo?*
Yes, that would be fine.	네, 좋아요. *Ne, cho-a-yo.*
Thanks to you, I had a nice time.	덕분에 즐거웠어요. *Teok-ppun-e cheul-geo-weo-sseo-yo.*

SAYING GOOD-BYE

I hope I'll see you again.	또 뵙기를 바랍니다. *Tto poep-kki-reul pa-ram-ni-da.*
See you later.	나중에 뵙겠어요. *Na-jung-e poep-kke-sseo-yo.*
See you tomorrow.	내일 뵙겠어요. *Nae-il poep-kke-sseo-yo.*
I'm sure we'll meet each other again.	또 만나뵙게 되겠지요. *Tto man-na-boep-kke toe-get-jji-yo.*

SHOPPING

Korea offers shoppers a wide variety of opportunities to purchase everything from famous brand names to inexpensive, locally made items. You can shop in specialty stores, malls, department stores, and traditional markets. You can also find shopping malls that integrate shopping, dining, and entertainment. In addition, there are 24-hour convenience stores located throughout the cities. A visit to a supermarket will give you fascinating insights into the food culture of Korea.

I'd like to go shopping today.	쇼핑하러 가고 싶어요.	*Shyo-p'ing-ha-reo ka-go shi-p'eo-yo.*
Where can I find a/an _____?	_____(이/가)어디 있어요 ?	*_____(i/ga) eo-di i-sseo-yo?*

- antique shop 　골동품점(이) 　*kol-ttong-p'um-jeom(i)*
- art gallery 　화랑(이) 　*hwa-rang(i)*
- bakery 　빵집(이) 　*ppang-jjip(i)*
- bookstore 　서점(이) 　*seo-jeom(i)*
- camera shop 　카메라점(이) 　*k'a-me-ra-jeom(i)*
- ceramics store 　도자기점(이) 　*to-ja-gi-jeom(i)*
- convenience store 　편의점(이) 　*p'yeon-eui-jeom(i)*
- department store 　백화점(이) 　*paek-k'wa-jeom(i)*
- dressmaker (traditional Korean *hanbok*) 　한복집(이) 　*han-bok-jjip(i)*
- drugstore 　약국(이) 　*yak-kkuk(i)*
- electrical appliance store 　전자제품점(이) 　*cheon-ja-je-p'um-jeom(i)*
- filling station 　주유소(가) 　*chu-yu-so(ga)*
- fish market 　수산물 시장(이) 　*su-san-mul shi-jang(i)*

▓ florist	꽃집 (이)	*kkot-jjip(i)*
▓ frame shop (for creating frames, screens, and scrolls for art work)	표구사 (가)	*p'yo-gu-sa(ga)*
▓ ginseng shop	인삼가게 (가)	*in-sam-ga-ge(ga)*
▓ grocery store	식료품점 (이)	*shing-nyo-p'um-jeom(i)*
▓ hardware store	철물점 (이)	*ch'eol-mul-jjeom(i)*
▓ herbal medicine shop	건재약국 (이)	*keon-jae-yak-kkuk(i)*
▓ jewelry store	보석상 (이)	*po-seok-sang(i)*
▓ leather goods store	가죽제품점 (이)	*ka-juk-che-p'um-jeom(i)*
▓ market (traditional)	시장 (이)	*shi-jang(i)*
▓ newsstand	신문 판매대 (가)	*shin-mun p'an-mae-dae(ga)*
▓ optician	안경점 (이)	*an-gyeong-jeom(i)*
▓ photography studio	사진관 (이)	*sa-jin-gwan(i)*
▓ post office	우체국 (이)	*u-ch'e-guk(i)*
▓ shoe repair shop	구두방 (이)	*ku-du-ppang(i)*
▓ shopping mall	쇼핑몰 (이)	*shyo-p'ing-mol(i)*
▓ souvenir shop	선물가게 (가)	*seon-mul-ga-ge(ga)*
▓ sporting goods store	스포츠용품점 (이)	*seu-p'o-ch'eu-yong-p'um-jeom(i)*
▓ stationery store	문방구점 (이)	*mun-bang-gu-jeom(i)*
▓ supermarket	수퍼마켓 (이)	*su-p'eo-ma-k'et(i)*
▓ tailor	양복점 (이)	*yang-bok-jjeom(i)*
▓ tobacco shop	담배가게 (가)	*tam-bae-ga-ge(ga)*
▓ toy store	완구점 (이)	*wan-gu-jeom(i)*
▓ travel agency	여행사 (가)	*yeo-haeng-sa(ga)*

■ vending machine	자동판매기(가)	*cha-dong-p'an-mae-gi(ga)*
■ watch and clock store	시계방(이)	*shi-gye-ppang(i)*

INQUIRIES ABOUT SHOPPING

Where's the nearest _____?	제일 가까운 _____(이/가) 어디 있어요?	*Che-il ka-kka-un _____-(i/ga) eo-di i-sseo-yo?*
Would you recommend a _____?	_____(을/를) 좀 소개해 주시겠어요?	*_____-(eul/reul) chom so-gae-hae chu-shi-ge-sseo-yo?*
I'd like to go to <u>a market</u>.	시장에 가고 싶어요.	*Shi-jang-e ka-go shi-p'eo-yo.*
■ an arcade	상가/아케이드	*sang-ga/ a-k'e-i-deu*
■ a department store	백화점	*paek-k'wa-jeom*
Is it far?	여기서 멀어요?	*Yeo-gi-seo meo-reo-yo?*
Please tell me how to get there.	가는 길을 좀 가르쳐 주세요.	*Ka-neun ki-reul chom ka-reu-ch'yeo chu-se-yo.*

THE CLERK

These expressions may be used by the clerk while you are shopping. Should you be unsure about exactly what is being said, you can have the clerk point to the expression in the book.

Welcome.	어서 오세요.	*Eo-seo o-se-yo.*

What are you looking for?	뭘 찾으세요 ?	*Mweol ch'a-jeu-se-yo?*
What <u>color</u> do you want?	무슨 색깔을 원하세요 ?	*Mu-seun saek-kkal-eul weon-ha-se-yo?*
▓ size	사이즈(를)	*sa-i-jeu(reul)*
I'm sorry. We don't have it/any.	미안합니다. 없는데요.	*Mi-an-ham-ni-da. Eom-neun-de-yo.*
Would you like us to order it for you?	주문해 드릴까요 ?	*Chu-mun-hae teu-ril-kka-yo?*
Please write your name and phone number.	성함과 전화 번호를 좀 써 주세요.	*Seong-ham-gwa cheon-hwa peon-ho-reul chom sseo chu-se-yo.*
How long will it take?	얼마나 걸릴까요 ?	*Eol-ma-na keol-lil-kka-yo?*
It should be here <u>in a few days</u>.	며칠안에 올 거예요.	*Myeo-ch'il-a-ne ol kkeo-ye-yo.*
▓ next week	다음주에	*ta-eum-jju-e*
We'll call you when it's here.	오면 전화해 드릴께요.	*O-myeon cheon-hwa-hae teu-ril-kke-yo.*
That will be _____ won, please.	_____원이에요.	*_____ weon-i-e-yo.*
I'm sorry. We don't accept credit cards.	미안합니다. 크레딧 카드를 안 받아요.	*Mi-an-ham-ni-da. K'eu-re-dit k'a-deu-reul an pa-da-yo.*
We accept <u>Diners Club</u>.	다이너스 클럽을 받아요.	*Da-i-neo-seu k'eul-leop-eul pa-da-yo.*
▓ American Express	아메리칸 엑스프레스(를)	*A-me-ri-k'an ek-seu-p'eu-re-seu(reul)*
▓ Visa	비자(를)	*Pi-ja(reul)*

▓ Master Card	마스터 카드(를)	*Ma-seu-t'eo k'a-deu(reul)*
Here's your receipt.	영수증 여기 있어요.	*Yeong-su-jeung yeo-gi i-sseo-yo.*
Thank you.	감사합니다.	*Kam-sa-ham-ni-da.*
Come again.	또 오세요.	*Tto o-se-yo.*

IN THE STORE

Here are some expressions for you to use while shopping.

Excuse me.   여기요.   *Yeo-gi-yo.*
(To get the clerk's attention, use the expression *Yeo-gi-yo*, literally, "here.")

Can you help me?	좀 도와 주시겠어요?	*Chom to-wa chu-shi-ge-sseo-yo?*
I'd like to see some _____.	_____ 좀 보여 주세요.	_____ *chom po-yeo chu-se-yo.*
Do you have any _____?	_____ 있어요?	_____ *i-sseo-yo?*
I'm just looking.	그냥 구경하고 있어요.	*Keu-nyang ku-gyeong-ha-go i-sseo-yo.*
I'd like something for <u>a child</u>.	어린이용품이 있어요?	<u>*Eo-rin-i yong-p'um-i*</u> *i-sseo-yo?*
▓ a 5-year-old boy	다섯 살 난 남자 아이	*ta-seot ssal lan nam-ja a-i*
▓ a 10-year-old girl	열 살 난 여자 아이	*yeol ssal lan yeo-ja a-i*

I'd like to see <u>that one</u>.	저것 좀 보여 주세요. *Cheo-geot chom po-yeo chu-se-yo.*
▣ this one	이것 *i-geot*
▣ the one in the window	쇼윈도에 있는 것 *shyo-win-do-e in-neun keot*
May I <u>exchange</u> this?	이것 좀 바꿔 주시겠어요 ? *I-geot chom pa-kkweo chu-shi-ge-sseo-yo?*
▣ return	물러 *mul-leo*
May I have a refund?	돈을 좀 돌려 주시겠어요 ? *Ton-eul chom tol-lyeo chu-shi-ge-sseo-yo?*
Here's my receipt.	영수증 여기 있어요. *Yeong-su-jeung yeo-gi i-sseo-yo.*
I'm interested in something <u>inexpensive</u>.	<u>비싸지 않은 것</u>을 사고 싶어요. *Pi-ssa-ji an-eun keo-seul sa-go shi-p'eo-yo.*
▣ handmade	수제품(을) *su-je-p'um(eul)*
▣ Korean	국산품(을) *kuk-ssan-p'um(eul)*
Do you have any others?	다른 것 없어요 ? *Ta-reun keot eop-sseo-yo?*
Please give me the <u>large</u> one.	큰 것으로 주세요. *K'eun keo-seu-ro chu-se-yo.*
▣ small	작은 *cha-geun*
▣ cheap	싼 *ssan*
▣ good	좋은 *cho-eun*
▣ better	더 좋은 *teo cho-eun*
▣ less expensive	덜 비싼 *teol pi-ssan*
▣ more expensive	더 비싼 *teo pi-ssan*
How much is <u>this one</u>?	이것은 얼마예요 ? *I-geo-seun eol-ma-ye-yo?*
▣ that one	저것은 *cheo-geo-seun*

Could you write it down?	좀 써 주시겠어요 ? *Chom sseo chu-shi-ge-sseo-yo?*
I want to spend about _____ won.	_____원 정도면 괜찮아요. _____ *weon cheong-do-myeon kwaen-ch'an-a-yo.*
May I try it on?	입어 봐도 될까요 ? *I-beo pwa-do toel-kka-yo?*
I'll take this.	이것으로 주세요. *I-geo-seu-ro chu-se-yo.*
May I use a <u>credit card</u>?	크레딧 카드를 써도 돼요 ? *K'eu-re-dit k'a-deu-reul sseo-do twae-yo?*
■ travelers check	여행자 수표 *yeo-haeng-ja su-p'yo*
Which cards do you accept?	어느 크레딧 카드를 받으세요 ? *Eo-neu k'eu-re-dit k'a-deu-reul pa-deu-se-yo?*
Please give me a receipt.	영수증을 주세요. *Yeong-su-jeung-eul chu-se-yo.*
Will you wrap it?	포장해 주시겠어요 ? *P'o-jang-hae chu-shi-ge-sseo-yo?*
Could you send it to my hotel?	제 호텔로 배달해 주시겠어요 ? *Che ho-t'el-lo pae-dal-hae chu-shi-ge-sseo-yo?*
Please send it to this address.	이 주소로 부쳐 주세요. *I chu-so-ro pu-ch'yeo chu-se-yo.*
Please send it by sea.	배로 부쳐 주세요. *Pae-ro pu-ch'yeo chu-se-yo.*
Please send it by air.	항공으로 부쳐 주세요. *Hang-gong-eu-ro pu-ch'yeo chu-se-yo.*

How much would it cost?	얼마예요 ?	*Eol-ma-ye-yo?*
That's all.	다 됐어요.	*Ta twae-sseo-yo.*
Thank you.	고맙습니다.	*Ko-map-sseum-ni-da.*

DEPARTMENT STORES

Department stores throughout Korea feature a mix of Korean and international items, with luxury brands well represented. Prices are fixed, with no bargaining. The stores usually have a collection of diverse restaurants and cafes, and their food courts and supermarkets give you inexpensive options for eating.

Where's the <u>men's clothing</u> department?	<u>신사복</u> 코너가 어디 있어요 ? <u>*Shin-sa-bok*</u> *k'o-neo-ga eo-di i-sseo-yo?*
▧ women's clothing	숙녀복 *sung-nyeo-bok*
▧ children's clothing	아동복 *a-dong-bok*
▧ shoe	신발 *shin-bal*
▧ housewares	가정용품 *ka-jeong-yong-p'um*
▧ china	도자기 *to-ja-gi*
▧ jewelry	보석 *po-seok*
▧ notions	장신구 *chang-shin-gu*
▧ furniture	가구 *ka-gu*
▧ luggage	가방 *ka-bang*
▧ handicrafts	수공예품 *su-gong-ye-p'um*
▧ food	식료품 *shing-nyo-p'um*
Where's the <u>ladies' room</u>?	여자 <u>화장실</u>이 어디 있어요 ? <u>*Yeo-ja hwa-jang-shil*</u>*-i eo-di i-sseo-yo?*
▧ men's room	남자 화장실(이) *nam-ja hwa-jang-shil(i)*

■ elevator	엘리베이터 (가)	*el-li-be-i-t'eo(ga)*
■ escalator	에스컬레이터 (가)	*e-seu-k'eol-le-i-t'eo(ga)*
■ food court	지하음식상가 (가)	*chi-ha-eum-shik-sang-ga(ga)*
■ coffee shop	커피숖 (이)	*k'eo-p'i-shyop(i)*
■ restaurant	음식점 (이)	*eum-shik-jjeom(i)*
■ supermarket	수퍼마켓 (이)	*su-p'eo-ma-k'et(i)*
■ telephone	전화 (가)	*cheon-hwa(ga)*
■ information desk	안내소 (가)	*an-nae-so(ga)*
■ Will you help me find someone who speaks English?	영어 통역하시는 분 좀 불러주세요.	*Yeong-eo t'ong-yeok-ha-shi-neun pun chom pul-leo-ju-se-yo.*

MARKETS AND SHOPS

Korea's traditional markets allow you to experience the country's unique shopping culture and observe many aspects of Korean life. Namdaemun, located in central Seoul, offers a wide range of goods, including clothing, ceramics, household items, jewelry, and street food. Bargaining in markets like Namdaemun is usually acceptable, but you should ask before you begin haggling. Do not expect to cut the price more than 5 to 20%. Before you begin bargaining, be relatively sure that you want the item. It is discourteous to haggle the price lower, only to change your mind and walk away. The more you buy from a vendor, the easier it is to cut the price.

Dongdaemun Market is known for its many retail and wholesale clothing markets and modern malls. Its shops carry fabrics, leather goods, bedding, housewares, and sporting goods. As in Namdaemun, shopkeepers stay open until daybreak.

Insadong is an historical shopping area of art galleries and antique shops that carry paintings, ceramics, paper crafts, traditional clothing, and furniture. For a shopping venue that caters to foreigners, visit Itaewon, where you will find clothing, leather goods, bags, jewelry, and antiques.

Where is Dongdaemun Market?	동대문 시장이 어디 있어요 ? *Tong-dae-mun shi-jang-i eo-di i-sseo-yo?*
▓ Namdaemun Market	남대문 시장 *Nam-dae-mun shi-jang*
▓ Insadong	인사동 *In-sa-dong*
▓ Itaewon	이태원 *I-t'ae-won*

Where is the market in this city?	이 도시에 시장이 어디 있어요 ? *I to-shi-e shi-jang-i eo-di i-sseo-yo?*

Where can I buy silk?	실크를 어디서 팔아요 ? *Shil-k'eu-reul eo-di-seo p'a-ra-yo?*
▓ cotton goods	면제품 (을) *myeon-je-p'um(eul)*
▓ handicrafts	수공예품 (을) *su-gong-ye-p'um(eul)*
▓ inlaid lacquerware	나전칠기 (를) *na-jeon-ch'il-gi(reul)*
▓ mountain climbing gear	등산용품 (을) *teung-san-yong-p'um(eul)*
▓ fish	생선 (을) *saeng-seon(eul)*
▓ bags	가방 (을) *ka-bang(eul)*
▓ cushions	방석 (을) *pang-seok(eul)*
▓ umbrellas	우산 (을) *u-san(eul)*
▓ belts	혁대 (를) *hyeok-ttae(reul)*
▓ dolls	인형 (을) *in-hyeong(eul)*
▓ fans	부채 (를) *pu-ch'ae(reul)*
▓ traditional Korean dresses (*hanbok*)	한복 (을) *han-bok(eul)*
▓ porcelain	도자기 (를) *to-ja-gi(reul)*

Do you have _____?   _____ (이/ 가) 있어요 ?   _____
-(i/ ga) i-sseo-yo?

How much is it?   얼마예요 ?   *Eol-ma-ye-yo?*

That's a little expensive.   조금 비싸요.   *Cho-geum pi-ssa-yo.*

Can you sell it cheaper?   좀 깎아 주세요.   *Chom kka-kka chu-se-yo.*

Will you sell it for _____ won?   _____원에 해 줄 수 있어요 ?   _____ *weon-e hae chul su i-sseo-yo?*

How much would it be if I buy several?   여러 개 사면 얼마까지 해 줄 수 있어요 ?   *Yeo-reo kae sa-myeon eol-ma-kka-ji hae jul su i-sseo-yo?*

Let's settle it at 15,000 won.   15,000원에 합시다.   *Man-o-ch'eon-weon-e hap-shi-da.*

Good-bye. *(literally, "Work hard.")*   수고하세요.   *Su-go-ha-se-yo.*

Where can I buy <u>roasted peanuts</u>?   땅콩을 어디서 살 수 있어요 ?   *Ttang-k'ong-eul eo-di-seo sal su i-sseo-yo?*

- mung bean pancakes   빈대떡 (을)   *pin-dae-tteok(eul)*

- pork sausage   순대 (를)   *sun-dae(reul)*

- roasted chestnuts   군밤 (을)   *kun-bam(eul)*

The peanuts are on that pushcart.   땅콩은 저 손수레에 있어요.   *Ttang-k'ong-eun cheo son-su-re-e i-sseo-yo.*

BOOKS, NEWSSTANDS, AND STATIONERY STORES

Koreans are avid readers and intensely interested in education, so it is easy to find stores that sell books, magazines, and stationery supplies. Large bookstore chains carry many titles in English and other languages. Stationery stores provide stamps and fax service in addition to other supplies. You can buy newsmagazines and newspapers in English at your hotel or from street vendors. Two popular English-language newspapers, the *Korea Times* and the *Korea Herald*, are online and widely available in print form.

BOOKS

Where is a nearby <u>bookstore</u>?	이 근처에 <u>서점</u>이 어디 있어요 ?	*I keun-ch'eo-e <u>seo-jeom</u>-i eo-di i-sseo-yo?*
▓ stationery store	문방구 (가)	*mun-bang-gu(ga)*
▓ newsstand	신문 판매대 (가)	*shin-mun p'an-mae-dae(ga)*
Do you have books in <u>English</u>?	<u>영어</u> 책이 있어요 ?	*<u>Yeong-eo</u> ch'aek-i i-sseo-yo?*
▓ French	불어	*Pu-reo*
▓ Italian	이태리어	*I-t'ae-ri-eo*
▓ Japanese	일본어	*Il-bon-eo*
I want to buy <u>a Korean-English</u> dictionary.	<u>한영</u> 사전을 사고 싶어요.	*<u>Han-yeong</u> sa-jeon-eul sa-go shi-p'eo-yo.*
▓ an English-Korean	영한	*Yeong-han*
▓ a pocket	포켓	*p'o-k'et*
Do you have a <u>guidebook</u>?	<u>안내서</u>가 있어요 ?	*<u>An-nae-seo</u>-ga i-sseo-yo?*
▓ a map of this city	시내 지도 (가)	*shi-nae chi-do(ga)*

■ a road map　　　　도로 지도(가)　*to-ro chi-do(ga)*

■ a map of Korea　　한국 지도(가)　*Han-guk chi-do(ga)*

■ a book for learning　한국어 책(이)　*Han-guk-eo Korean　　　　　　ch'aek(i)*

Do you have English　유명한 한국 작가 작품 중에서 영어로
translations of any　번역된 것이 있어요 ?　*Yu-myeong-*
famous Korean　　*han Han-guk chak-ga chak-p'um*
authors?　　　　　*chung-e-seo Yeong-eo-ro peon-yeok-doen keo-shi i-sseo-yo?*

The title of the book　이 책의 제목이 ＿＿＿＿ 이에요.
is ＿＿＿＿.　　　*I ch'aek-eui che-mok-i ＿＿＿＿ i-e-yo.*

The author of the　이 책의 저자가 ＿＿＿＿ 이에요.
book is ＿＿＿＿.　　*I ch'aek-eui cheo-ja-ga ＿＿＿＿ i-e-yo.*

I'll take these books.　이 책을 사겠어요.　*I ch'aek-eul sa-ge-sseo-yo.*

NEWSSTANDS

Whare can I buy the　코리아 타임스를 어디서 팔아요 ?
<u>Korea Times</u>?　*K'o-ri-a t'a-im-seu-reul eo-di-seo p'a-ra-yo?*

■ Korea Herald　　코리아 헤럴드　*K'o-ri-a he-reol-deu*

Do you sell news　영자 뉴스 잡지를 팔아요 ?　*Yeong-*
magazines in　　*jja nyu-seu chap-jji-reul p'a-ra-yo?*
English?

How much are they?　얼마예요 ?　*Eol-ma-ye-yo?*

STATIONERY STORES

I want to buy <u>an address book</u>.	주소적는 책을 사고싶어요. *Chu-so-cheong-neun ch'aek-eul sa-go-shi-p'eo-yo.*

- a ball point pen — 볼펜(을) *pol-p'en(eul)*
- some cellophane tape — 스카치 테이프(를) *seu-k'a-ch'i t'e-i-p'eu(reul)*
- some envelopes — 봉투(를) *pong-t'u(reul)*
- some paper — 편지지(를) *p'yeon-ji-jji(reul)*
- a pocket notebook — 수첩(을) *su-ch'eop(eul)*
- some postcards — 엽서(를) *yeop-sseo(reul)*
- some string — 끈(을) *kkeun(eul)*
- some wrapping paper — 포장지(를) *p'o-jang-ji(reul)*
- some labels — 라벨(을) *ra-bel(eul)*

Would you please fax this for me?	이것을 팩스로 보내주시겠어요? *I-geo-seul p'aek-seu-ro po-nae-ju-shi-ge-sseo-yo?*

CLOTHING

Clothing of high quality and diverse styles is available in Korea, but sizes suitable for foreigners may be limited. Tailor-made suits and dresses are less common, as Koreans usually purchase their clothes ready-made. Department stores offer the greatest selection. In Seoul, you may want to visit areas that cater to foreigners, such as Itaewon and the markets at Dongdaemun and Namdaemun. If you decide to try tailor-made clothing, you should get recommendations from a Korean associate so that you can better guarantee quality and price.

I'd like to buy a (an / some) belt.	혁대를 사고 싶은데요.	_Hyeok-ttae-reul sa-go shi-p'eun-de-yo._
▤ blouse	블라우스(를)	_peul-la-u-seu(reul)_
▤ bra	브래지어(를)	_peu-rae-ji-eo(reul)_
▤ dress	드레스(를)	_teu-re-seu(reul)_
▤ evening dress	이브닝 드레스(를)	_i-beu-ning teu-re-seu(reul)_
▤ gloves	장갑(을)	_chang-gap(eul)_
▤ handkerchiefs	손수건(을)	_son-su-geon(eul)_
▤ hat	모자(를)	_mo-ja(reul)_
▤ jacket	자켓(을)	_cha-k'et(eul)_
▤ jeans	청바지(를)	_ch'eong-ba-ji(reul)_
▤ long underwear	내복(을)	_nae-bok(eul)_
▤ overcoat	외투(를)	_weo-t'u(reul)_
▤ pajamas	잠옷(을)	_cham-ot(eul)_
▤ pantyhose	팬티스타킹(을)	_p'aen-t'i-seu-t'a-k'ing(eul)_
▤ raincoat	우비(를)	_u-bi(reul)_
▤ robe	까운(을)	_kka-un(eul)_
▤ scarf	스카프(를)	_seu-k'a-p'eu(reul)_
▤ shirt	와이샤쓰(를)	_wa-i-shya-sseu(reul)_
▤ skirt	스커트(를)	_seu-k'eo-t'eu(reul)_
▤ slacks	바지(를)	_pa-ji(reul)_
▤ slip	속치마(를)	_sok-ch'i-ma(reul)_
▤ slippers	슬리퍼(를)	_seul-li-p'eo(reul)_
▤ socks	양말(을)	_yang-mal(eul)_
▤ suit (men's)	남자양복(을)	_nam-ja-yang-bok(eul)_
▤ sweater	스웨터(를)	_seu-we-t'eo(reul)_
▤ swim suit	수영복(을)	_su-yeong-bok(eul)_

▓ tee shirt	티샤쓰(를)	*t'i-shya-sseu(reul)*
▓ tie	넥타이(를)	*nek-t'a-i(reul)*
▓ undershirt	런닝샤쓰(를)	*reon-ning-shya-sseu(reul)*
▓ undershorts (men's)	팬티(를)	*p'aen-t'i(reul)*
▓ panty (women's)	팬티(를)	*p'aen-t'i(reul)*
▓ wallet	지갑(을)	*chi-gap(eul)*
▓ sweat suit	땀복(을)	*ttam-bok(eul)*

Is there a sale today? 오늘 할인 판매해요? *O-neul ha-rin p'an-mae-hae-yo?*

I'd like the one with <u>long</u> sleeves. 소매가 긴 것으로 주세요. *So-mae-ga kin keo-seu-ro chu-se-yo.*

▓ short 짧은 *jjal-beun*

Do you have anything <u>else</u>? <u>다른</u> 것 없어요? *Ta-reun keot eop-sseo-yo?*

▓ larger	더 큰	*teo k'eun*
▓ smaller	더 작은	*teo cha-geun*
▓ cheaper	더 싼	*teo ssan*
▓ of better quality	더 좋은	*teo cho-eun*
▓ longer	더 긴	*teo kin*
▓ shorter	더 짧은	*teo jjal-beun*

I'd prefer a different <u>color</u>. 색깔이 마음에 안 들어요. <u>*Saek-kkal-i*</u> *ma-eum-e an teu-reo-yo.*

▓ style	스타일	*seu-t'a-il*
▓ material	천	*ch'eon*

<u>Black</u> is fine. 검은색이 좋아요. <u>*Keo-meun-saek-i*</u> *cho-a-yo.*

▓ blue	파란색	*p'a-ran-saek*
▓ brown	갈색	*kal-saek*

■ gray	회색	*hoe-saek*
■ green	녹색	*nok-saek*
■ pink	분홍색	*pun-hong-saek*
■ purple	보라색	*po-ra-saek*
■ red	빨간색	*ppal-gan-saek*
■ white	흰색	*hin-saek*
■ yellow	노란색	*no-ran-saek*

I'd like <u>stripes</u>.   줄무늬로 주세요.   <u>*Chul-mu-ni-ro*</u> *chu-se-yo.*

■ a print	연속무늬	*yeon-sok-mu-ni*
■ a plaid	격자무늬	*kyeok-jja-mu-ni*
■ checks	체크무늬	*ch'e-k'eu-mu-ni*

I'd like a solid color.   무늬가 없는 것으로 주세요.   *Mu-ni-ga eom-neun keo-seu-ro chu-se-yo.*

Do you have anything to match this?   이것에 어울리는 것이 있어요 ?   *I-geo-se eo-ul-li-neun keo-shi i-sseo-yo?*

Do you have something in <u>cotton</u>?   면으로 된 것이 있어요 ?   <u>*Myeon-*</u> *eu-ro toen keo-shi i-sseo-yo?*

■ wool	모 (로)	*mo(ro)*
■ silk	실크 (로)	*shil-k'eu(ro)*
■ linen	마 (로)	*ma(ro)*
■ synthetic	합성 (으로)	*hap-seong(eu-ro)*
■ leather	가죽 (으로)	*ka-juk(eu-ro)*
■ vinyl	비닐 (로)	*pi-nil(ro)*
■ nylon	나일론 (으로)	*na-il-lon(eu-ro)*

SIZES

Be sure to try on any Korean clothing that you are thinking about buying. You can expect most things to fit, although some items may be short-waisted and sleeves may be too short for many Westerners. The following expressions will help you purchase what you need.

Please take my measurements.	재 주세요.	*Chae chu-se-yo.*
I don't know the Korean sizes.	한국 싸이즈는 모르겠어요.	*Han-guk ssa-i-jeu-neun mo-reu-ge-sseo-yo.*
My size is <u>small</u>.	제 싸이즈는 <u>스몰</u>이에요.	*Che ssa-i-jeu-neun <u>seu-mol</u>-i-e-yo.*
▥ medium	미디움	*mi-di-um*
▥ large	라지	*ra-ji*
▥ extra large	엑스라지	*ek-seu-ra-ji*
▥ 42	사십이	*sa-ship-i*
▥ 14½	십사 반	*ship-sa pan*
May I try it on?	입어 봐도 될까요 ?	*I-beo pwa-do toel-kka-yo?*
Where's the dressing room?	어디서 옷 갈아입어요 ?	*Eo-di-seo ot ka-ra-i-beo-yo?*
Do you have a mirror?	거울 있어요 ?	*Keo-ul i-sseo-yo?*
It's too <u>long</u>.	너무 <u>길어요</u>.	*Neo-mu <u>ki-reo-yo</u>.*
▥ short	짧아요	*jjal-ba-yo*
▥ tight	꼭 껴요	*kkok kkyeo-yo*
▥ loose	헐렁해요	*heol-leong-hae-yo*
Can you alter it?	고쳐 줄 수 있어요 ?	*Ko-ch'yeo chul su i-sseo-yo?*

The zipper doesn't work.	지퍼가 잘 안 돼요.	*Chi-p'eo-ga chal an twae-yo.*
There's a button missing.	단추가 하나 없어요.	*Tan-ch'u-ga ha-na eop-sseo-yo.*
It doesn't fit me.	잘 안 맞아요.	*Chal an ma-ja-yo.*
It fits very well.	잘 맞아요.	*Chal ma-ja-yo.*
It looks good on you.	잘 어울려요.	*Chal eo-ul-lyeo-yo.*
I'll take this one.	이것으로 주세요.	*I-geo-seu-ro chu-se-yo.*

SHOES

Shoes are widely available in Korea in various price ranges. Stores that cater to foreigners, such as those in Itaewon, may have larger selections. Dongdaemun and Namdaemun also offer Korean-made athletic shoes at reasonable prices.

Where can I buy a pair of <u>shoes</u>?	구두를 어디서 팔아요 ?	<u>*Ku-du-reul eo-di-seo p'a-ra-yo?*</u>
▓ boots	부츠(를)	*pu-ch'eu(reul)*
▓ casual shoes	신발(을)	*shin-bal(eul)*
▓ dressy shoes	고급 신발(을)	*ko-geup shin-bal(eul)*
▓ high-heeled shoes	굽이 높은 신발(을)	*ku-bi no-p'eun shin-bal(eul)*
▓ low-heeled shoes	굽이 낮은 신발(을)	*ku-bi na-jeun shin-bal(eul)*
▓ running shoes	조깅화(를)	*cho-ging-hwa(reul)*
▓ sandals	샌달(을)	*saen-dal(eul)*
▓ tennis shoes	테니스화(를)	*t'e-ni-seu-hwa(reul)*

There's a pair in the window that I like.

쇼윈도에 있는 것이 마음에 들어요.
Shyo-win-do-e in-neun keo-shi ma-eum-e teu-reo-yo.

Do they come in <u>another color</u>?

<u>다른 색</u>도 있어요 ? *Ta-reun saek-do i-sseo-yo?*

▓ black 검은색 *keom-eun-saek*

▓ white 흰색 *hin-saek*

▓ beige 베이지색 *pe-i-ji-saek*

▓ brown 갈색 *kal-saek*

Can you measure for my size?

발 좀 재 주시겠어요 ? *Pal chom chae chu-shi-ge-sseo-yo?*

These are too <u>narrow</u>.

볼이 너무 <u>좁아요</u>. *Po-ri neo-mu cho-ba-yo.*

▓ wide 넓어요 *neol-beo-yo*

▓ tight 꼭 껴요 *kkok kkyeo-yo*

▓ loose 헐렁해요 *heol-leong-hae-yo*

They fit fine.

잘 맞아요. *Chal ma-ja-yo.*

Do you have a <u>larger</u> size?

더 큰 싸이즈는 없어요 ? *<u>Teo k'eun</u> ssa-i-jeu-neun eop-sseo-yo?*

▓ smaller 더 작은 *teo cha-geun*

Are the prices fixed?

정찰제예요 ? *Cheong-ch'al-je-ye-yo?*

I'll take them.

그것으로 하겠어요. *Keu-geo-seu-ro ha-ge-sseo-yo.*

Do you have shoelaces here?

구두끈이 있어요 ? *Ku-du-kkeun-i i-sseo-yo?*

ELECTRICAL APPLIANCES

Korea is a major manufacturer of appliances, cell phones, computer-related products, cameras, electronic games and software, and CD/DVD players. You can purchase items in specialty shops, department stores, and large malls dedicated to electronics. If you plan to take an electronic product to Korea, you should make sure it works on 220 volts. If you don't have an adaptor for Korean electrical outlets, you can obtain one at your hotel or at a Korean store. Also, if you purchase an electronic product in Korea for use back home, you should be sure that it is compatible with electrical standards in North America or in whatever country you plan to use it. Two of the largest electronics stores are the Yongsan Electronics Market and Techno Mart.

Where can I buy electrical appliances?	가전제품을 어디서 팔아요?	_Ka-jeon-je-p'um-eul eo-di-seo p'a-ra-yo?_
Are they sold wholesale anywhere?	어디서 도매로 팔아요?	_Eo-di-seo to-mae-ro p'a-ra-yo?_
I want to buy <u>a battery</u>.	<u>건전지</u>를 사고 싶어요.	<u>_Keon-jeon-ji-reul_</u> _sa-go shi-p'eo-yo._
▪ a camcorder	캠코더(를)	_k'aem-k'o-deo(reul)_
▪ a CD player	씨디 플레이어(를)	_sshi-di p'eul-le-i-eo(reul)_
▪ a clock	시계(를)	_shi-gye(reul)_
▪ a DVD player	디비디 플레이어(를)	_ti-bi-di p'eul-le-i-eo(reul)_
▪ a calculator	계산기(를)	_kye-san-gi(reul)_
▪ a GPS (global positioning system)	네비게이션(을) or 지피에스(를)	_ne-bi-ge-i-shyeon(eul)_ or _chi-p'i-e-seu(reul)_
▪ a hair dryer	헤어 드라이어(를)	_he-eo teu-ra-i-eo(reul)_
▪ an iron	다리미(를)	_ta-ri-mi(reul)_

■ a radio   라디오(를)   *ra-di-o(reul)*

■ a shaver   전기 면도기(를)   *cheon-gi myeon-do-gi(reul)*

■ a television   텔레비전(을)   *t'el-le-bi-jeon(eul)*

Where can I buy a <u>desktop computer</u>?   어디에서 <u>데스크탑 컴퓨터를</u> 살 수 있을까요?   *Eo-di-e-seo <u>te-seu-k'eu-t'ap k'eom-p'yu-t'eo</u>-reul sal su i-sseul-kka-yo?*

■ notebook computer   노트북 컴퓨터   *no-t'eu-buk-k'eom-p'yu-t'eo*

■ computer game   컴퓨터 게임   *k'eom-p'yu-t'eo ke-im*

■ headphone   헤드폰   *he-deu-p'on*

■ headset   헤드셋   *he-deu-set*

■ keyboard   키보드   *k'i-bo-deu*

■ monitor   모니터   *mo-ni-t'eo*

■ mouse   마우스   *ma-u-seu*

■ portable hard drive   이동식 하드디스크   *i-dong-shik ha-deu-di-seu-k'eu*

■ USB flash drive   유에스비 메모리   *yu-e-seu-bi me-mo-ri*

■ Web cam   웹캠   *Web-k'em*

What voltage does this take?   이것은 몇 볼트 짜리예요?   *I-geo-seun myeot pol-t'eu jja-ri-ye-yo?*

Is this suitable for <u>110 volts</u>?   이것은 <u>110 볼트</u>에 맞아요?   *I-geo-seun <u>paek ship pol-t'eu</u>-e ma-ja-yo?*

■ 220 volts   220 볼트   *i-baek-i-ship pol-t'eu*

This is out of order/broken.   이것이 고장났어요.   *I-geo-shi ko-jang-na-sseo-yo.*

How much does it cost?   얼마입니까?   *Eol-ma-im-ni-kka?*

It costs <u>150,000</u> won.   십오만원이예요. *Ship-o-man weon-i-ye-yo.*

■ 200,000   이십만 *i-shim-man*

■ 1,000,000   백만 *paeng-man*

■ 1,500,000   백오십만 *paek-o-shim-man*

BUYING ITEMS IN MARKETS AND SUPERMARKETS

Most food items in Korean markets are sold by approximate measurement and packaged on the spot. It is therefore useful to know the appropriate term for counting and measuring when you purchase the items. In Korean supermarkets, most items are prepackaged and sold by exact measurements. The following phrases will help you with your purchases.

Is there a supermarket near here?   이 근처에 수퍼마켓이 있어요 ? *I keun-ch'eo-e su-p'eo-ma-k'e-shi i-sseo-yo?*

Please give me <u>a jar of mayonnaise</u>.   마요네즈 한 병 주세요. *<u>Ma-yo-ne-jeu han pyeong</u> chu-se-yo.*

■ a jar of instant coffee   인스탄트 커피 한 병 *in-seu-t'an-t'eu k'eo-p'i han pyeong*

■ a bottle of ketchup   케챂 한 병 *k'e-ch'ap han pyeong*

■ a can of tuna   참치 통조림 하나 *ch'am-ch'i t'ong-jo-rim ha-na*

■ a loaf of bread   식빵 하나 *shik-ppang ha-na*

■ a package of cookies   과자 한 봉지 *kwa-ja han pong-ji*

Shall we buy some food in the market?   시장에서 식품을 살까요 ? *Shi-jang-e-seo shik-p'um-eul sal-kka-yo?*

I'd like 1,000 won worth of <u>bean sprouts</u>.	콩나물 천원어치 주세요.	*K'ong-na-mul ch'eon weon-eo-ch'i chu-se-yo.*
■ lettuce	상치	*sang-ch'i*
The <u>apples</u> are 5 for 10,000 won.	사과가 만원에 다섯 개예요.	*Sa-gwa-ga man weon-e ta-seot kae-ye-yo.*
■ peaches	복숭아	*pok-sung-a*
I'd like a *mal* of rice. (1 *mal* is about 15 liters or 4 gallons)	쌀 한 말 주세요.	*Ssal han mal chu-se-yo.*
■ a *toe* of barley (a handful)	보리 한 되	*po-ri han toe*
■ a *keun* of beef (1 *keun* is about 1 pound or 500 grams)	쇠고기 한 근	*soe-go-gi han keun*
■ a half liter of sesame oil (about 18 fluid ounces)	참기름 반 리터	*ch'am-gi-reum pan ri-t'eo*
■ a bunch of bananas	바나나 한 다발	*ppa-na-na han ta-bal*
■ 300 grams of peanuts (about 10 ounces)	땅콩 삼백 그램	*ttang-k'ong sam-baek keu-raem*
■ 1 kilogram of rice cakes (about 2.2 pounds)	떡 일 킬로그램	*tteok il k'il-lo-geu-raem*

JEWELRY

Jewelry stores are everywhere in Korea. Native smoky topaz, amethyst, white jade, and gold are the best buys, and you can get the stones already set in a variety of ways. If possible, when buying jewelry, buy through a friend or at one of the major hotels. The price may be more expensive, but you can be more certain that you are buying the real thing.

I'd like to see **a bracelet**.

팔찌 좀 보여 주시겠어요 ? _P'al-jji chom po-yeo chu-shi-ge-sseo-yo?_

■ a brooch
브로치 _peu-ro-ch'i_

■ a chain
체인 _ch'e-in_

■ some cufflinks
커프스 단추 _k'eo-p'eu-seu tan-ch'u_

■ some earrings
귀고리 _kwi-go-ri_

■ a necklace
목걸이 _mok-kkeo-ri_

■ a pendant
펜단트 _p'en-dan-t'eu_

■ a pin
핀 _p'in_

■ a ring
반지 _pan-ji_

■ a tie-clip
넥타이 클립 _nek-t'a-i k'eul-lip_

■ a wristwatch
손목 시계 _son-mok shi-gye_

Is this **gold**?
이거 금이에요 ? _I-geo keum-i-e-yo?_

■ silver
은 _eun_

■ platinum
백금 _paek-kkeum_

■ stainless steel
스텐레스 _seu-t'en-re-seu_

How many karats is it? (for gold)
몇 케이 금이에요 ? _Myeot k'e-i keum-i-e-yo?_

It is 14 karat gold.
십사 케이예요. _Ship-sa k'e-i-ye-yo._

Is it real gold?
진짜 금이에요 ? _Chin-jja keum-i-e-yo?_

Is it solid gold?
순금이에요 ? _Sun-geum-i-e-yo?_

How much does it weigh?
몇 돈이에요 ? _Myeot ton-i-e-yo?_
(_ton_ is a unit for measuring gold; _1 ton_ = 3.75 grams or .13 ounces)

Is it gold plated?
금도금이에요 ? _Keum-do-geum-i-e-yo?_

What kind of stone is that?	저것은 무슨 보석이에요? *Cheo-geo-seun mu-seun po-seok-i-e-yo?*
How many karats is it? (for diamonds)	몇 캐럿이에요? *Myeot k'ae-reo-shi-ye-yo?*
I want to buy <u>an amethyst</u>.	<u>자수정</u>을 사고 싶어요. *Cha-su-jeong-eul sa-go shi-p'eo-yo.*
▨ coral	산호(를) *san-ho(reul)*
▨ a diamond	다이아몬드(를) *ta-i-a-mon-deu(reul)*
▨ an emerald	에메랄드(를) *e-me-ral-deu(reul)*
▨ a topaz	황옥(을) *hwang-ok(eul)*
▨ some white jade	흰 비취(를) *hin pi-ch'wi(reul)*
Will you sell only the stone?	보석만 파시겠어요? *Po-seong-man p'a-shi-ge-sseo-yo?*
Would you set this in a 14 karat gold ring?	이것을 십사 케이 반지에 박아 주시겠어요? *I-geo-seul ship-sa k'e-i pan-ji-e pa-ga chu-shi-ge-sseo-yo?*
How much is it?	얼마예요? *Eol-ma-ye-yo?*
When can I pick it up?	언제 찾을 수 있어요? *Eon-je ch'a-jeul su i-sseo-yo?*

WATCHES AND CLOCKS

I want to buy <u>a quartz</u> watch.	전지로 가는 손목시계를 사고 싶은데요. *Cheon-ji-ro ka-neun son-mok-shi-gye-reul sa-go ship-eun-de-yo.*
▨ an automatic	자동으로 가는 *cha-dong-eu-ro ka-neun*

▥ a light-powered	태양전지로 가는	*t'ae-yang-jeon-ji-ro ka-neun*
▥ a water-resistant	방수기능이 있는	*pang-su-gi-neung-i in-neun*

Do you have a watch with a <u>date function</u>?	날짜 기능이 있는 시계가 있습니까 ?	<u>*Nal-jja ki-neung-i in-neun*</u> *shi-gye-ga i-sseum-ni-kka?*
▥ second hand	초침이 있는	*ch'o-ch'im-i in-neun*
▥ stopwatch function	스톱워치 기능이 있는	*seu-t'op-weo-ch'i ki-neung-i in-neun*
▥ gold finish	금도금이 된	*keum-do-geum-i toen*
▥ silver finish	은도금이 된	*eun-do-geum-i toen*
▥ titanium finish	티타늄도금이 된	*t'i-t'a-nyum-do-geum-i toen*
▥ leather band	가죽줄이 있는	*ka-juk-jju-ri in-neun*
▥ rubber band	고무줄이 있는	*ko-mu-ju-ri in-neun*

I'd like a <u>sports</u> watch.	<u>스포츠</u> 시계를 사고 싶은데요.	<u>*Seu-p'o-ch'eu*</u> *shi-gye-reul sa-go ship-eun-de-yo.*
▥ digital	디지털	*ti-ji-t'eol*

I'd like a clock.	벽시계를 주세요.	*Pyeok-shi-gye-reul chu-se-yo.*

I want <u>an alarm clock</u>.	<u>알람시계</u>를 주세요.	<u>*Al-lam-shi-gye*</u>*-reul chu-se-yo.*
▥ a travel alarm clock	여행용 알람시계	*yeo-haeng-yong al-lam-shi-gye*

Can you repair this watch?	이 시계 좀 수리해 주시겠어요 ?	*I shi-gye chom su-ri-hae chu-shi-ge-sseo-yo?*

The glass is broken.	유리가 깨졌어요.	*Yu-ri-ga kkae-jyeo-sseo-yo.*

MUSIC, CDS, AND TAPES

Music is an integral part of Korean life. You can hear music of all types, from Korean traditional and popular styles to that of artists from throughout the world. You will have many opportunities to buy examples of Korean music in the form of CDs, DVDs, and downloads.

Where can I buy CDs?	어디에서 씨디를 살 수 있을까요 ? *Eo-di-e-seo sshi-di-reul sal su i-seul-kka-yo?*
■ DVDs	디비디 *di-bi-di*
■ i-PODs	아이팟 *a-i-p'at*
■ MP3 players	엠피쓰리 플레이어 *em-p'i-sseu-ri p'eul-le-i-eo*

NEWSPAPERS AND MAGAZINES

Do you carry newspapers in English?	영자 신문 있어요 ? *Yeong-jja shin-mun i-sseo-yo?*
■ magazines	잡지 *chap-jji*
I'd like an English-language newspaper.	영자 신문을 주세요. *Yeong-jja shin-mun-eul chu-se-yo.*
Do you have news magazines?	뉴스 잡지 있어요 ? *Nyu-seu chap-jji i-sseo-yo?*
■ picture postcards	그림 엽서 *keu-rim yeop-sseo*
■ stamps	우표 *u-p'yo*
I'd like these.	이것으로 주세요. *I-geo-seu-ro chu-se-yo.*
How much are they?	얼마예요 ? *Eol-ma-ye-yo?*

PHOTOGRAPHIC SUPPLIES

Where is there a camera shop?	카메라점이 어디 있어요 ? *K'a-me-ra-jeom-i eo-di i-sseo-yo?*
I want to buy a <u>digital camera</u>.	디지털 카메라를 사고 싶은데요. *Di-ji-t'eol k'a-me-ra-reul sa-go ship-eun-de-yo.*
▪ recharger	충전기 *ch'ung-jeon-gi*
▪ battery	건전지 *keon-jeon-ji*
▪ disposable camera	일회용 카메라 *il-hoe-yong k'a-me-ra*
I want to print photos from my digital camera.	제 디지털 카메라의 사진을 현상하고 싶은데요. *Che ti-ji-t'eol k'a-me-ra-eui sa-jin-eul hyeon-sang-ha-go ship-eun-de-yo.*
Do you develop film here?	여기서 사진 현상하세요 ? *Yeo-gi-seo sa-jin hyeon-sang-ha-se-yo?*
How much does it cost to develop a roll?	한 통에 얼마예요 ? *Han t'ong-e eol-ma-ye-yo?*
I have <u>one roll</u>.	한 통 있어요. *Han t'ong i-sseo-yo.*
▪ two rolls	두 통 *tu t'ong*
I want one print of each.	한 장씩 빼 주세요. *Han chang-sshik ppae chu-se-yo.*
I want an enlargement.	확대 좀 해 주세요. *Hwak-ttae chom hae chu-se-yo.*
I want a print with a <u>glossy</u> finish.	글로씨로 해 주세요. *Keul-lo-sshi-ro hae chu-se-yo.*
▪ matte	양피지 *yang-p'i-ji*

I'd like some film for this camera.	이 카메라에 맞는 필름을 주세요. *I k'a-me-ra-e man-neun p'il-leum-eul chu-se-yo.*
Do you have <u>an exposure meter</u>?	<u>노출계</u> 있어요 ? *<u>No-ch'ul-gye</u> i-sseo-yo?*

- ▧ a filter — 필터 *p'il-t'eo*
- ▧ a lens — 렌즈 *ren-jeu*
- ▧ a lens cap — 렌즈 두껑 *ren-jeu ttu-kkeong*
- ▧ a lens cleaner — 렌즈 닦개 *ren-jeu ttak-kkae*
- ▧ a telescopic lens — 망원 렌즈 *mang-weon ren-jeu*
- ▧ a tripod — 삼각대 *sam-gak-ttae*
- ▧ a wide angle lens — 광각 렌즈 *kwang-gak ren-jeu*
- ▧ a zoom lens — 줌 렌즈 *chum ren-jeu*

SOUVENIRS

Korea offers opportunities to purchase items that reveal its rich cultural heritage. From department stores and shopping malls to traditional markets and street-side push carts, you will marvel at the variety of souvenirs available in all price ranges.

Ginseng, a plant known for its medicinal value, is noted for its high quality in Korea. It is made into tea, wine, soap and other products, but can also be purchased in capsule, powder, or root form. Other traditional Korean products include ceramics and porcelain, scrolls, screens, antique furniture, brassware, costume dolls, and laquerware with inlaid mother-of-pearl. Handicrafts, such as knotting and embroidery, make excellent gifts for friends and family. Silk, one of the most elegant products of Korea, can be purchased in a multitude of colors and variety of forms. As you travel around Korea, you will want to keep your eyes open for unique, local products.

I'd like to buy a <u>nice gift</u>.	좋은 선물을 사고 싶어요.	*Cho-eun seon-mul-eul sa-go shi-p'eo-yo.*
▨ small gift	작은 선물	*cha-geun seon-mul*
▨ souvenir	기념품	*ki-nyeom-p'um*

Where are <u>baskets</u> sold?	바구니를 어디서 팔지요 ?	*Pa-gu-ni-reul eo-di-seo p'al-ji-yo?*
▨ antiques	골동품 (을)	*kol-ttong-p'um(eul)*
▨ antique furniture	고가구 (를)	*ko-ga-gu(reul)*
▨ medicine chests	약장 (을)	*yak-jjang(eul)*
▨ mirror and cosmetics boxes	좌경 (을)	*chwa-gyeong(eul)*
▨ rice chests	쌀뒤주 (를)	*ssal-dwi-ju(reul)*
▨ wedding boxes	결혼함 (을)	*kyeol-hon-ham(eul)*
▨ brassware products	놋쇠제품 (을) /유기 (를)	*not-ssoe-je-p'um(eul) / yu-gi(reul)*
▨ dolls	인형 (을)	*in-hyeong(eul)*
▨ fans	부채 (를)	*pu-ch'ae(reul)*
▨ ginseng products	인삼제품 (을)	*in-sam-je-p'um(eul)*
▨ handicrafts	수공예품 (을)	*su-gong-ye-p'um(eul)*
▨ *hanbok* (traditional Korean dresses)	한복 (을)	*han-bok(eul)*
▨ lacquerware products	나전칠기 (를)	*na-jeon-ch'il-gi(reul)*
▨ procelains	도자기 (를)	*to-ja-gi(reul)*
▨ screens	병풍 (을)	*pyeong-p'ung(eul)*
▨ scrolls	족자 (를)	*chok-jja(reul)*
▨ silk products	실크 제품 (을)	*shil-k'eu che-p'um(eul)*

You can buy ceramics in Insadong.	도자기를 인사동에서 살 수 있어요. *To-ja-gi-reul in-sa-dong-e-seo sal su i-sseo-yo.*

You can buy silk at Dongdaemun (East Gate) Market.

주단을 동대문 시장에서 살 수 있어요. *Chu-dan-eul Tong-dae-mun shi-jang-e-seo sal su i-sseo-yo.*

You can buy brassware at Namdaemun (South Gate) Market.

놋쇠를 남대문 시장에서 살 수 있어요. *Not-ssoe-reul Nam-dae-mun shi-jang-e-seo sal su i-sseo-yo.*

You can buy antique furniture in Insadong.

고가구를 인사동에서 살 수 있어요. *Ko-ga-gu-reul In-sa-dong-e-seo sal su i-sseo-yo.*

TOBACCO

A pack of cigarettes, please.

담배 한 갑 주세요. *Tam-bae han kap chu-se-yo.*

I'd like <u>Korean</u> cigarettes.

한국 담배를 주세요. *<u>Han-guk</u> tam-bae-reul chu-se-yo.*

■ American

양 *yang*

Please give me some matches.

성냥 좀 주세요. *Seong-nyang chom chu-se-yo.*

Do you sell <u>cigars</u>?

<u>시가</u> 팔아요? *<u>Shi-ga</u> p'a-ra-yo?*

■ pipe tobacco

파이프 담배 *p'a-i-p'eu tam-bae*

■ pipes

파이프 *p'a-i-p'eu*

■ lighters

라이터 *ra-i-t'eo*

■ lighter fluid

라이터 기름 *ra-i-t'eo ki-reum*

■ gas (for lighter)

까스 *kka-seu*

SMOKING

Would you like a cigarette?	담배 피우시겠어요 ? *Tam-bae p'i-u-shi-ge-sseo-yo?*
No, thanks. I don't smoke.	아니요. 못 피워요. *A-ni-yo. Mot p'i-weo-yo.*
I've given it up.	끊었어요. *Kkeun-eo-sseo-yo.*
May I trouble you for a cigarette?	실례지만 담배 한 대 빌릴까요 ? *Shil-lye-ji-man tam-bae han tae pil-lil-kka-yo?*
May I trouble you for a match?	성냥 좀 빌릴까요 ? *Seong-nyang chom pil-kka-yo?*
Is it all right if I smoke?	담배 좀 피워도 될까요 ? *Tam-bae chom p'i-weo-do toel-kka-yo?*
Yes, go ahead.	네, 피우세요. *Ne, p'i-u-se-yo.*

TOILETRIES

You can purchase toiletries from a variety of stores in Korea such as hotel gift shops, convenience stores, pharmacies, and department stores.

Is there a store that carries <u>American</u> toiletries?	미제 화장품 파는 데가 있어요 ? *<u>Mi-je</u> hwa-jang-p'um p'a-neun te-ga i-sseo-yo?*
■ European	유럽 *Yu-reop*
Do you have <u>bobby pins</u>?	머리핀 있어요 ? *<u>Meo-ri-p'in</u> i-sseo-yo?*
■ body lotion	바디 로션 *pa-di ro-shyeon*

▦ brushes	브러시	*peu-reo-shi*
▦ cleansing cream	클렌징 크림	*k'eul-len-jing k'eu-rim*
▦ cologne	콜론수	*k'ol-lon-su*
▦ combs	머리빗	*meo-ri-bit*
▦ condoms	콘돔	*k'on-dom*
▦ cream rinse	린스	*rin-seu*
▦ curlers	클립	*k'eul-lip*
▦ deodorant	방취제	*pang-ch'wi-je*
▦ emery boards	손톱줄	*son-t'op-jjul*
▦ eye liner	아이 라이너	*a-i ra-i-neo*
▦ eye pencil	아이 펜슬	*a-i p'en-seul*
▦ eye shadow	아이 섀도우	*a-i shyae-do-u*
▦ face powder	분	*pun*
▦ hair color	머리 염색약	*meo-ri yeom-sae-gyak*
▦ hair spray	헤어 스프레이	*he-eo seu-p'eu-re-i*
▦ hand lotion	핸드 로션	*haen-deu ro-shyeon*
▦ lipstick	립스틱	*rip-seu-t'ik*
▦ mascara	마스카라	*ma-seu-k'a-ra*
▦ mirrors	거울	*keo-ul*
▦ nail brushes	손톱 솔	*son-t'op sol*
▦ nail clippers	손톱 깎기	*son-t'op kka-kki*
▦ nail files	손톱 다듬는 줄	*son-t'op ta-deum-neun chul*
▦ nail polish	매니큐어	*mae-ni-k'yu-eo*
▦ nail polish remover	매니큐어 지우개	*mae-ni-k'yu-eo chi-u-gae*
▦ perfume	향수	*hyang-su*
▦ razors	면도칼	*myeon-do-k'al*
▦ razor blades	면도날	*myeon-do-nal*
▦ rouge, blush	루즈	*ru-jeu*

- safety pins · 안전핀 · *an-jeon-p'in*
- sanitary napkins · 생리대 · *saeng-ni-dae*
- scissors (nail) · 손톱 가위 · *son-t'op ka-wi*
- shampoo · 샴푸 · *shyam-p'u*
- shaving cream · 면도 크림 · *myeon-do k'eu-rim*
- soap · 비누 · *pi-nu*
- sponges · 스폰지 · *seu-p'on-ji*
- sunscreen · 선스크린 · *seon-seu-k'eu-rin*
- suntan lotion · 선탠 로션 · *seon-t'aen ro-shyeon*
- tampons · 탐폰 · *t'am-p'on*
- tissues · 티슈 · *t'i-shyu*
- toothbrushes · 치솔 · *ch'i-ssol*
- toothpaste · 치약 · *ch'i-yak*
- towels · 수건 · *su-geon*
- tweezers · 쪽집게 · *jjok-jjip-kke*

PACKING, SHIPPING, AND GIFT-WRAPPING

If you want to mail a parcel, a post office is usually nearby. The Gwanghwamun Post Office is conveniently located in downtown Seoul. You can purchase boxes and other packing materials at a post office or stationery store. Many post offices will wrap packages at your request. If you are staying at a hotel, ask staff for information about packing and mailing your items. If you simply want an item gift-wrapped, ask the clerk at the store where you purchased the item.

Where is the nearest post office? · 가장 가까운 우체국이 어디에 있어요 ? *Ka-jang ka-kka-un u-ch'e-guk-i eo-di-e i-sseo-yo?*

- stationery store · 문방구점 · *mun-bang-gu-jeom*

Where can I get this packaged for mailing?	어디에서 소포포장 할 수 있어요 ? *Eo-di-e-seo so-p'o-p'o-jang hal su i-sseo-yo?*
I need packing materials.	포장재료가 필요한데요. *P'o-jang-jae-ryo-ga p'il-yo-han-de-yo.*
Please package this for mailing.	이것을 소포포장해 주세요. *I-geo-seul so-p'o-p'o-jang-hae chu-se-yo.*
Please send it to this address.	이 주소로 보내주세요. *I chu-so-ro po-nae-ju-se-yo.*
Where can I get this gift-wrapped?	어디에서 선물포장 할 수 있어요 ? *Eo-di-e-seo seon-mul-p'o-jang hal su i-sseo-yo?*
Will you gift-wrap this for me?	선물포장해 주시겠어요 ? *Seon-mul-p'o-jang-hae chu-shi-ge-sseo-yo?*
Please send it by sea.	배로 부쳐 주세요. *Pae-ro pu-ch'yeo chu-se-yo.*
Please send it by air.	항공으로 부쳐 주세요. *Hang-gong-eu-ro pu-ch'yeo chu-se-yo.*
Thank you.	수고하셨어요. *Su-go-ha-shyeo-sseo-yo.*

PERSONAL CARE AND SERVICES

If you are unable to obtain these services where you are staying, check with personnel at your hotel for a recommendation.

BARBER SHOPS AND BEAUTY SALONS

Various services are available from barber shops and beauty salons. Typically, men go to barber shops for a haircut, a shave, or a massage. Women go to beauty salons to have their hair cut, permed, or colored as well as for manicures, pedicures, facials, and massages. Many men also use beauty salons to have their hair cut, styled, and colored.

Does this hotel have a <u>barber shop</u>?	이 호텔안에 <u>이발소</u>가 있어요 ? *I ho-t'el-an-e <u>i-bal-so</u>-ga i-sseo-yo?*
■ beauty salon	미장원(이) *mi-jang-weon(i)*
How much does a haircut cost there?	이발요금이 얼마예요 ? *I-bal yo-geum-i eol-ma-ye-yo?*
Do I have to wait long?	오래 기다려야 돼요 ? *O-rae ki-da-ryeo-ya twae-yo?*
I don't have much time.	시간이 별로 없어요. *Shi-gan-i pyeol-lo eop-sseo-yo.*
I want a haircut.	이발해 주세요. *I-bal-hae chu-se-yo.*
Don't cut it too short, please.	너무 짧게 깎지 마세요. *Neo-mu jjalp-kke kkak-jji ma-se-yo.*
Just a trim, please.	조금만 깎아 주세요. *Cho-geum-man kka-kka chu-se-yo.*

Short in back, long in front.	뒤는 짧게 앞은 길게 해 주세요. *Twi-neun jjalp-kke a-p'eun kil-ge hae chu-se-yo.*
I want it long.	길게 해 주세요. *Kil-ge hae chu-se-yo.*
I want it very short.	아주 짧게 해 주세요. *A-ju jjalp-kke hae chu-se-yo.*
You can cut a little <u>in back</u>.	<u>뒤는</u> 짧지 않게 깎아 주세요. *<u>Twi-neun</u> jjalp-jji an-k'e kka-kka chu-se-yo.*
▨ in front	앞은 *a-p'eun*
▨ on the top	위는 *wi-neun*
▨ on the sides	옆은 *yeo-p'eun*
Shall I give you a shave?	면도 해 드릴까요 ? *Myeon-do hae teu-ril-kka-yo?*
Yes, but please shave me lightly. My skin is sensitive.	네, 그런데 조심해서 면도해 주세요. 제 피부는 아주 약해요. *Ne, keu-reon-de cho-shim-hae-seo myeon-do-hae chu-se-yo. Che p'i-bu-neun a-ju yak-k'ae-yo.*
I part my hair <u>on the left</u>.	가르마를 <u>왼쪽으로</u> 해 주세요. *Ka-reu-ma-reul <u>weon-jjok-eu-ro</u> hae chu-se-yo.*
▨ on the right	오른쪽으로 *o-reun-jjok-eu-ro*
▨ in the middle	가운데로 *ka-un-de-ro*
Would you like a shampoo?	머리 감으실까요 ? *Meo-ri kam-eu-shil-kka-yo?*
I comb my hair straight back.	머리를 뒤로 넘겨 빗어요. *Meo-ri-reul twi-ro neom-gyeo pi-seo-yo.*

Cut a little more here.	여기를 좀 더 깎아 주세요. *Yeo-gi-reul chom teo kka-kka chu-se-yo.*
That's enough.	이제 됐어요. *I-je twae-sseo-yo.*
It's fine that way.	그대로 좋아요. *Keu-dae-ro cho-a-yo.*
Use the scissors only.	가위로 해 주세요. *Ka-wi-ro hae chu-se-yo.*
Please trim my <u>beard</u>.	<u>수염</u>을 좀 다듬어 주세요. <u>*Su-yeom*</u>*-eul chom ta-deum-eo chu-se-yo.*
▩ eyebrows	눈썹 *nun-sseop*
▩ mustache	코밑 수염 *k'o-mit su-yeom*
▩ sideburns	구레나룻 *k'u-re-na-reut*
How much do I owe you?	얼마예요? *Eol-ma-ye-yo?*
Thank you. Please come again.	감사합니다. 또 오세요. *Kam-sa-ham-ni-da. Tto o-se-yo.*
Is there a beauty salon <u>near</u> the hotel?	이 호텔 <u>근처에</u> 미장원이 있어요? *I ho-t'el <u>keun-ch'eo-e</u> mi-jang-weon-i i-sseo-yo?*
▩ in	안에 *an-e*
Do you know where a good beauty salon is?	잘하는 미장원을 아세요? *Chal-ha-neun mi-jang-weon-eul a-se-yo?*
What are the business hours?	영업 시간은 몇 시부터 몇 시까지예요? *Yeong-eop shi-gan-eun myeot shi-bu-t'eo myeot shi-kka-ji-ye-yo?*
Are they used to foreigners' hair?	외국 사람의 머리도 할 줄 알아요? *Woe-guk sa-ram-eui meo-ri-do hal jjul a-ra-yo?*

Is it an expensive place?	거기는 비싸요 ? *Keo-gi-neun pi-ssa-yo?*
Can you give me a <u>color tint</u>?	머리염색해 줄 수 있어요 ? *<u>Meo-ri-yeom-saek-hae chul su i-sseo-yo?</u>*
▓ facial massage	얼굴 맛사지 *eol-gul mas-sa-ji*
▓ massage	맛사지 *mas-sa-ji*
▓ haircut	커트 *k'eo-t'eu*
▓ manicure	매니큐어 *mae-ni-k'yu-eo*
▓ permanent	파마 *p'a-ma*
▓ shampoo	샴푸 *shyam-p'u*
▓ shampoo and blow dry	샴푸와 드라이 *shyam-p'u-wa teu-ra-i*
▓ wash and set	샴푸와 세트 *shyam-p'u-wa se-t'eu*

I want <u>auburn</u>.	다갈색으로 해 주세요. *<u>Ta-gal-saek-eu-ro</u> hae chu-se-yo.*
▓ blonde	금발(로) *keum-bal(ro)*
▓ brunette	갈색(으로) *kal-saek(eu-ro)*
▓ a darker color	더 진한 색(으로) *teo chin-han saek(eu-ro)*
▓ a lighter color	더 엷은 색(으로) *teo yeol-beun saek(eu-ro)*
▓ the same color	같은 색(으로) *ka-t'eun saek(eu-ro)*

| Don't apply any hair spray. | 스프레이는 하지 마세요. *Seu-p'eu-re-i-neun ha-ji ma-se-yo.* |
| Not too much hair spray. | 스프레이를 너무 많이 하지 마세요. *Seu-p'eu-re-i-reul neo-mu man-i ha-ji ma-se-yo.* |

| I want <u>bangs</u>. | <u>앞머리를 가지런하게</u> 해 주세요. *<u>Ap-meo-ri-reul ka-ji-reon-ha-ge</u> hae chu-se-yo.* |
| ▓ it curly | 곱슬 곱슬하게 *kop-seul kop-seul-ha-ge* |

▓ it straight	스트레이트로	*seu-t'eu-re-i-t'eu-ro*
▓ it wavy	웨이브지게	*we-i-beu-ji-ge*
Is it done?	다 됐어요?	*Ta twae-sseo-yo?*
Thank you very much. (said by customer)	수고하셨어요.	*Su-go-ha-shyeo-sseo-yo.*
How much do I owe you?	얼마예요?	*Eol-ma-ye-yo?*

PUBLIC BATHS AND HEALTH CLUBS

Koreans enjoy going to public bath houses for relaxation as well as for good health. The basic bath, or "sauna" as it is called in Korea, is divided into separate facilities for men and women. It offers a variety of services, such as showers, soaking tubs, sauna rooms, and resting areas. Upon entering and paying the initial fee, you will be given a key for a locker where you can store your clothes and shoes. The key will be on a rubber or elastic band that you can secure around your wrist or ankle during the bath. Once in the bath area, your first task is to shower, making sure your body is completely free of all traces of soap and dirt, before entering one of the soaking tubs or sauna areas. For an extra fee, you can also request a body scrub or massage.

Another type of public bath, called *jjim-jil-bang*, is similar to a spa. It has a communal as well as a segregated area. The communal area is where both men and women, as well as family members can enjoy some of the facilities together. There are sleeping areas, often on a heated, Korean-style floor; restaurants; and exercise rooms. In this area patrons are issued some type of clothing to wear, such as shorts and t-shirts or robes. The segregated area provides services similar to the basic bath houses: saunas, body scrubs, massages, showers, and soaking tubs. Clothes, including bathing suits, are not worn in the segregated areas.

Some spas also offer other recreation, such as board games, karaoke and video rooms, indoor golf ranges, and Internet rooms.

Health clubs are another popular way for Koreans to improve their overall health. They include an exercise area with treadmills, stationary bikes, and weight-training equipment as well as a place to relax, play sports, and get advice on nutrition. Your hotel can direct you to its own club or to other fitness centers you can use.

Is there a <u>bathhouse</u> near here?	이 근처에 <u>목욕탕</u>이 있어요 ? *I keun-ch'eo-e <u>mok-yok-t'ang</u>-i i-sseo-yo?*
▓ spa	찜질방 *jjim-jil-bang*
▓ health club	헬스클럽 *hel-seu-k'eul-leop*
What are the business hours?	영업 시간은 몇 시부터 몇 시까지예요 ? *Yeong-eop shi-gan-eun myeot shi-bu-t'eo myeot shi-kka-ji-ye-yo?*
Here's your key. Put your things inside your locker.	여기 열쇠가 있어요. 장에 옷가지를 넣으세요. *Yeo-gi yeol-soe-ga i-sseo-yo. Chang-e ot-kka-ji-reul neo-eu-se-yo.*
How much does it cost?	얼마예요 ? *Eol-ma-ye-yo?*
May I have <u>soap</u>?	<u>비누</u> 좀 주세요. *<u>Pi-nu</u> chom chu-se-yo.*
▓ shampoo	샴푸 *shyam-p'u*
▓ a scrub towel	이태리 타월 *i-t'ae-ri t'a-weol*
▓ a towel	타월/수건 *t'a-weol/su-geon*
Is there someone to give me a body scrub?	때 밀어 주는 사람이 있어요 ? *Ttae mi-reo chu-neun sa-ram-i i-sseo-yo?*

LAUNDRY AND DRY CLEANING

Do you have <u>laundry service</u> in this hotel?	이 호텔에서 세탁을 해 줘요 ? *I ho-t'e-re-seo se-t'ak-eul hae chweo-yo?*
▓ dry cleaning service	드라이클리닝 *teu-ra-i-k'eul-li-ning*
Where is the nearest laundry/dry cleaners?	제일 가까운 세탁소가 어디에요 ? *Che-il ka-kka-un se-t'ak-so-ga eo-di-e-yo?*
I want this <u>dry cleaned</u>.	이것을 드라이클리닝 해 주세요. *I-geo-seul <u>teu-ra-i-k'eul-li-ning hae</u> chu-se-yo.*
▓ ironed/pressed	다려 주세요 *ta-ryeo chu-se-yo*
▓ mended	기워 주세요 *ki-weo chu-se-yo*
▓ washed	빨아 주세요 *ppa-ra chu-se-yo*
When will it be ready?	언제 오면 될까요 ? *Eon-je o-myeon toel-kka-yo?*
I need it <u>tonight</u>.	<u>오늘 저녁에</u> 입어야 되는데요. <u>*O-neul cheo-nyeok-e i-beo-ya toe-neun-de-yo.*</u>
▓ tomorrow	내일 *nae-il*
▓ the day after tomorrow	모레 *mo-re*
Can you get the stain out?	이 얼룩을 뺄 수 있어요 ? *I eol-luk-eul ppael su i-sseo-yo?*
Please sew this button on.	이 단추를 좀 달아 주세요. *I tan-ch'u-reul chom ta-ra chu-se-yo.*

I want my shirts <u>stiffly</u> starched.	와이샤쓰를 빳빳하게 풀을 먹여 주세요. *Wa-i-shya-sseu-reul <u>ppat-ppat-ha-ge</u> p'u-reul meo-gyeo chu-se-yo.*
▦ lightly	가볍게 *ka-byeop-kke*
I don't want my shirts starched.	와이샤쓰를 풀기 없이 해 주세요. *Wa-i-shya-sseu-reul p'ul-kki eop-sshi hae chu-se-yo.*
When shall I come for them?	언제 찾으러 올까요? *Eon-je ch'a-jeu-reo ol-kka-yo?*

SHOE REPAIRS

This heel <u>came off</u>.	이 뒤축이 떨어졌어요. *I twi-ch'uk-i tteo-reo-jyeo-sseo-yo.*
▦ broke	부러졌어요 *pu-reo-jyeo-sseo-yo*
Can you fix it while I wait?	기다리는 동안 고칠 수 있어요? *Ki-da-ri-neun tong-an ko-ch'il su i-sseo-yo?*
I want these shoes repaired.	이 구두를 좀 고쳐 주세요. *I ku-du-reul chom ko-ch'yeo chu-se-yo.*
I need new <u>heels</u>.	굽을 좀 갈아 주세요. *Kup-eul chom ka-ra chu-se-yo.*
▦ soles	창 *ch'ang*
▦ heels and soles	뒤축과 창 *twi-ch'uk-kkwa ch'ang*
▦ shoelaces	구두 끈 *ku-du kkeun*
Would you polish them, too?	닦아도 주시겠어요? *Ta-kka-do chu-shi-ge-sseo-yo?*
When will they be ready?	언제 오면 될까요? *Eon-je o-myeon toel-kka-yo?*

WATCH REPAIRS

I need a new battery for this watch.

이 시계에 새 전지를 넣고 싶은데요.
I shi-gye-e sae cheon-ji-reul neo-k'o shi-p'eun-de-yo.

Can you fix this watch?

이 시계를 고칠 수 있어요 ? *I shi-gye-reul ko-ch'il su i-sseo-yo?*

Can you tell me what's wrong with it?

왜 고장났는지 아세요 ? *Wae ko-jang-nan-neun-ji a-se-yo?*

Can you clean it?

소제해 주시겠어요 ? *So-je-hae chu-shi-ge-sseo-yo?*

I dropped it.

떨어뜨렸어요. *Tteo-reo-tteu-ryeo-sseo-yo.*

It doesn't run well.

잘 안 가요. *Chal an ka-yo.*

It doesn't run.

안 가요. *An ka-yo.*

Please replace the <u>crystal</u>.

유리 좀 갈아 주세요. *Yu-ri chom ka-ra chu-se-yo.*

■ a screw

나사 *na-sa*

■ the band

시계줄 *shi-gye-jul*

Please replace the <u>hour hand</u>.

시침 좀 갈아 주세요. *Shi-ch'im chom ka-ra chu-se-yo.*

■ minute hand

분침 *pun-ch'im*

■ second hand

초침 *ch'o-ch'im*

When will it be ready?

언제 오면 될까요 ? *Eon-je o-myeon twoel-kka-yo?*

May I have a receipt?

영수증을 주세요. *Yeong-su-jeung-eul chu-se-yo.*

CAMERA REPAIRS

There's something wrong with this camera.	이 카메라가 고장났는데요. *I k'a-me-ra-ga ko-jang-nan-neun-de-yo.*
Can you fix it?	고칠 수 있어요 ? *Ko-ch'il su i-sseo-yo?*
There's a problem with the <u>zoom lens</u>.	<u>줌 렌즈</u>가 잘 안되요. *Chum ren-jeu-ga chal an-doe-yo.*
▓ memory card door	메모리카드 두껑 (이) *me-mo-ri-k'a-deu ttu-kkeong(i)*
▓ battery cover	배터리 두껑 (이) *pae-t'eo-ri ttu-kkeong(i)*
▓ LCD	엘씨디 (가) *el-sshi-di(ga)*
▓ recharger	충전기 (가) *ch'ung-jeon-gi(ga)*
It needs a new battery.	새 배터리가 필요합니다. *Sae pae-t'eo-ri-ga p'il-yo-ham-ni-da.*
How much will it cost to fix it?	고치는데 얼마예요 ? *Ko-ch'i-neun-de eol-ma-ye-yo?*
I'd like it as soon as possible.	가능한한 빨리 해 주세요. *Ka-neung-han-han ppal-li hae chu-se-yo.*
When will it be ready?	언제 오면 될까요 ? *Eon-je o-myeon toel-kka-yo?*

HEALTH AND MEDICAL CARE

THE PHARMACY

Medical services in Korea are provided by highly educated and knowledgeable professionals. Pharmacies are widely available where you can fill a prescription and purchase the usual medical supplies and medications for common ailments such as colds, flu, sunburn, indigestion, insect bites, and cuts. You can also buy condoms, contraceptives, and pregnancy tests. Pharmacies have a variety of energy drinks and some herbal remedies. The staff may know medical terminology in English, but it will be helpful if you write down your medical condition or the medications you need. You may also point to relevant phrases or vocabulary in this book.

You should consult with your physician well in advance of your trip to obtain information about any immunizations or health advisories that may be in effect. You should also have evidence of any medical insurance. If you have a preexisting medical condition or use prescription medications, you should take a summary of relevant medical records and prescriptions. After checking into your hotel, you may want to locate a nearby specialty clinic, hospital, or physician.

Here are some phrases you might need for the pharmacy.

Where's the nearest pharmacy?	이 근처에 약국이 어디 있어요 ? *I keun-ch'eo-e yak-kkuk-i eo-di i-sseo-yo?*
What time does the pharmacy <u>open</u>?	약국이 몇 시에 <u>열어요</u> ? *Yak-kkuk-i myeot shi-e <u>yeo-reo-yo</u>?*
■ close	닫아요 *ta-da-yo*

Please give me something for <u>a cold</u>.	감기약 좀 주세요. <u>*Kam-gi* yak</u> *chom chu-se-yo.*
▩ constipation	변비 *pyeon-bi*
▩ a cough	기침 *ki-ch'im*
▩ diarrhea	설사 멎는 *seol-sa meon-neun*
▩ hay fever	건초열 *keon-ch'o-yeol*
▩ headache	두통 *tu-t'ong*

Please give me something good for <u>a burn</u>.	화상(에) 좋은 약 좀 주세요. <u>*Hwa-sang(e)* cho-eun yak chom chu-se-yo.</u>
▩ a fever	열내리는 데 *yeol-nae-ri-neun te*
▩ an insect bite	벌레 물린 데 *peol-le mul-lin te*
▩ insomnia	불면증(에) *pul-myeon-jeung(e)*
▩ nausea	구토증(에) *ku-t'o-jjeung(e)*
▩ sinus congestion	코막힌 데 *k'o-ma-k'in te*
▩ a sore throat	편도선염(에) *p'yeon-do-seon-yeom(e)*
▩ a sunburn	햇볕에 탔을 때 *haet-ppyeo-t'e t'a-sseul ttae*
▩ a toothache	치통(에) *ch'i-t'ong(e)*
▩ an upset stomach	체했을 때 *ch'e-hae-sseul ttae*

How often should I take this medicine?	하루에 몇 번 먹을까요? *Ha-ru-e myeot ppeon meo-geul-kka-yo?*
Take two tablets every four hours.	두 알씩 네 시간마다 드세요. *Tu al-sshik ne shi-gan-ma-da teu-se-yo.*
Take two tablets three times a day.	두 알씩 하루에 세 번 드세요. *Tu al-sshik ha-ru-e se peon teu-se-yo.*
Is a prescription needed for the medicine?	약 사는데 처방이 필요해요? *Yak sa-neun-de ch'eo-bang-i p'i-ryo-hae-yo?*

Can you fill this prescription for me now?	이 처방대로 조제해 주시겠어요 ? *I ch'eo-bang-dae-ro cho-je-hae chu-shi-ge-sseo-yo?*
I need it right away.	금방 해 주세요. *Keum-bang hae chu-se-yo.*
Can I wait for it?	기다릴까요 ? *Ki-da-ril-kka-yo?*
How long will it take?	얼마나 걸릴까요 ? *Eol-ma-na keol-lil-kka-yo?*
When can I come for it?	언제 찾으러 올까요 ? *Eon-je ch'a-jeu-reo ol-kka-yo?*
Where can I get my hearing aid repaired?	보청기를 어디에서 수리할 수 있나요 ? *Po-ch'eong-gi-reul eo-di-e-seo su-ri-hal su in-na-yo?*
Do you have contact lens care products for <u>soft lenses</u>?	<u>소프트 렌즈</u> 세척제가 있어요 ? <u>*So-p'eu-t'eu ren-jeu*</u> *se-ch'eok-jje-ga i-sseo-yo?*
■ hard lenses	하드 렌즈 *ha-deu ren-jeu*
May I see what you have?	있는 것 좀 보여 주세요. *In-neun keot chom po-yeo chu-se-yo.*
I need a contact-lens case.	콘택트 렌즈 통을 주세요. *K'on-t'aek-t'eu ren-jeu t'ong-eul chu-se-yo.*
I would like <u>adhesive tape</u>.	접착 테이프 좀 주세요. <u>*Cheop-ch'ak t'e-i-p'eu*</u> *chom chu-se-yo.*
■ alcohol	알콜 *al-k'ol*
■ antacids	제산제 *che-san-je*
■ an antiseptic	방부제 *pang-bu-je*
■ aspirin	아스피린 *a-seu-p'i-rin*
■ aspirin-free pain killer	아스피린 성분이 없는 진통제 *a-seu-p'i-rin seong-bun-i eom-neun chin-t'ong-je*

- bandages — 붕대 *pung-dae*
- band-aids — 일회용 반창고 *il-hoe-yong pan-ch'ang-go*
- birth control pills — 피임약 *p'i-im-yak*
- contraceptives — 피임기구 *p'i-im-gi-gu*
- condoms — 콘돔 *k'on-dom*
- corn plasters — 티눈약 *t'i-nun-yak*
- cotton — 탈지면 *t'al-jji-myeon*
- cough syrup — 시럽으로 된 기침약 *shi-reop-eu-ro toen ki-ch'im-yak*
- decongestant — 소염제 *so-yeom-je*
- (disposable) diapers — 종이 기저귀 *chong-i ki-jeo-gwi*
- ear drops — 귀에 넣는약 *kwi-e neon-neun yak*
- eye drops — 안약 *an-yak*
- a first aid kit — 응급 처치함 *eung-geup ch'eo-ch'i-ham*
- gauze — 가아제 *ka-a-je*
- insect repellent — 방충제 *pang-ch'ung-je*
- iodine — 옥도정기 *ok-tto-jeong-kki*
- a laxative — 완하제/변비약 *wan-ha-je/pyeon-bi-yak*
- a pregnancy test — 임신 진단 테스트 *im-shin chin-dan t'e-seu-t'eu*
- sanitary napkins — 생리대 *saeng-ni-dae*
- sleeping pills — 수면제 *su-myeon-je*
- suppositories — 좌약 *chwa-yak*
- talcum powder — 분 *pun*
- tampons — 탐폰 *t'am-p'on*
- thermometer — 체온계 *ch'e-on-gye*
- facial tissues — 클리넥스 *k'eul-li-nek-seu*
- tranquilizers — 진정제 *chin-jeong-je*
- vitamins — 비타민 *pi-t'a-min*

ACCIDENTS AND EMERGENCIES

For the ambulance and fire department, dial 119; for police, 112. You can receive medical information and general travel help by dialing 1330 (add the area code if you use a cell phone). This service is available in English and other selected languages 24 hours a day.

Hello. It's an emergency!	여보세요. 위급해요.	*Yeo-bo-se-yo. Wi-geup-p'ae-yo.*
<u>I'm</u> hurt.	제가 다쳤어요.	*<u>Che-ga</u> ta-ch'yeo-sseo-yo.*
▓ My husband's	제 남편(이)	*che nam-p'yeon(i)*
▓ My wife's	제 아내(가)	*che a-nae(ga)*
▓ My child's	제 아이(가)	*che a-i(ga)*
▓ Somebody's	누가	*nu-ga*
Can you send an ambulance immediately?	구급차 좀 빨리 보내 주세요.	*Ku-geup-ch'a chom ppal-li po-nae chu-se-yo.*
We're located at _____.	여기는 _____ 이에요.	*Yeo-gi-neun _____ i-e-yo.*
Help!	도와 주세요 !	*To-wa chu-se-yo!*
Help me, somebody!	누가 좀 도와 주세요.	*Nu-ga chom to-wa chu-se-yo.*
Get a <u>doctor</u>, quick!	의사 좀 불러 주세요. 빨리 !	*<u>Eui-sa</u> chom pul-leo chu-se-yo. Ppal-li!*
▓ nurse	간호사	*kan-ho-sa*
Call an ambulance!	구급차 좀 불러 주세요 !	*Ku-geup-ch'a chom pul-leo chu-se-yo!*

I need first aid.	응급 처치를 받아야 돼요.	*Eung-geup ch'eo-ch'i-reul pa-da-ya twae-yo.*
I've fallen.	제가 넘어졌어요.	*Che-ga neom-eo-jyeo-sseo-yo.*
I was knocked down.	제가 얻어맞아 쓰러졌어요.	*Che-ga eo-deo-ma-ja sseu-reo-jyeo-sseo-yo.*
I've had a heart attack.	심장마비가 났어요.	*Shim-jang-ma-bi-ga na-sseo-yo.*
I burned myself.	불에 데었어요.	*Pu-re te-eo-sseo-yo.*
I cut myself.	칼에 베었어요.	*K'a-re pe-eo-sseo-yo.*
I'm bleeding.	피가 나요.	*P'i-ga na-yo.*
I've lost a lot of blood.	출혈이 심해요.	*Ch'ul-hyeo-ri shim-hae-yo.*
My <u>wrist</u> is sprained.	손목을 삐었어요.	*Son-mok-eul ppi-eo-sseo-yo.*
▨ ankle	발목	*pal-mok*
I can't bend my <u>elbow</u>.	팔꿈치를 구부릴 수가 없어요.	*P'al-kkum-ch'i-reul ku-bu-ril su-ga eop-sseo-yo.*
▨ knee	무릎	*mu-reup*
I can't move my <u>arm</u>.	팔을 움직일 수가 없어요.	*P'al-eul um-jig-il su-ga eop-sseo-yo.*
▨ leg	다리(를)	*ta-ri(reul)*
I think the bone is <u>broken</u>.	뼈가 부러진 것 같아요.	*Ppyeo-ga pu-reo-jin keot ka-t'a-yo.*
▨ dislocated	탈골된	*t'al-gol-doen*
The leg is swollen.	다리가 부었어요.	*Ta-ri-ga pu-eo-sseo-yo.*

FINDING A DOCTOR

Korea maintains high standards for medical care. Hotel staff or Korean associates can help you find doctors and hospitals with experience in serving international patients. The following expressions will help you find assistance.

Do you know a doctor who speaks English?	영어할 줄 아는 의사를 아세요 ? *Yeong-eo-hal jjul a-neun eui-sa-reul a-se-yo?*
Where is the <u>doctor's office</u>?	병원이 어디 있어요 ? *Pyeong-weon-i eo-di i-sseo-yo?*
▓ hospital	종합 병원 *chong-hap pyeong-weon*

Note: In Korea, a doctor's office or specialty clinic is called *pyeong-weon*, which is often translated "hospital" in English. The Korean equivalent of the Western hospital may also be translated as *pyeong-weon* or sometimes *chong-hap pyeong-weon*.

What are the hours of operation?	진료 시간은 몇 시부터 몇 시까지예요 ? *Chil-lyo shi-gan-eun myeot shi-bu-t'eo myeot shi-kka-ji-ye-yo?*
Can I just walk in?	예약 없이 가도 돼요 ? *Ye-yak eop-sshi ka-do twae-yo?*
Do I need to make an appointment?	예약해야 돼요 ? *Ye-yak-hae-ya twae-yo?*
What's the telephone number?	전화 번호가 어떻게 되지요 ? *Cheon-hwa peon-ho-ga eo-tteo-k'e toe-ji-yo?*
I want to see an <u>internist</u>.	내과 의사한테 진찰을 받고 싶은데요. *Nae-kkwa eui-sa-han-t'e chin-ch'a-reul pat-kko shi-p'eun-de-yo.*

■ a cosmetic surgeon　성형외과 의사　*seong-hyeong-oe-kkwa eui-sa*

■ an ear, nose and throat specialist　이비인후과 의사　*i-bi-in-hu-kkwa eui-sa*

■ a dermatologist　피부과 의사　*p'i-bu-kkwa eui-sa*

■ a gynecologist　부인과 의사　*pu-in-kkwa eui-sa*

■ an obstetrician　산부인과 의사　*san-bu-in-kkwa eui-sa*

■ an ophthalmologist　안과 의사　*an-kkwa eui-sa*

■ an orthopedist　정형외과 의사　*cheong-hyeong-oe-kkwa eui-sa*

■ a surgeon　외과의사　*oe-kkwa-eui-sa*

Note : To refer to the specialty, drop *eui-sa* (doctor). For example, *cheon-hyeong-oe-kkwa* is used for "orthopedics."

| I want a general check-up. | 종합 진찰을 받고 싶어요. *Chong-hap chin-ch'a-reul pat-kko shi-p'eo-yo.* |

WITH THE DOCTOR

There are two parts in this section: "Telling the Doctor" and "What the Doctor Says." The expressions under "Telling the Doctor" are for you to use. Give the book to the doctor so he or she can point to expressions that are apropos under "What the Doctor Says."

| Please point to the phrase in this book. | 이 책에서 그 말을 찾아 주세요. *I ch'aek-e-seo keu ma-reul ch'a-ja chu-se-yo.* |

TELLING THE DOCTOR

| I don't feel well. | 몸이 아파요. *Mom-i a-p'a-yo.* |

| I'm dizzy. | 현기증이 나요. *Hyeon-gi-jjeung-i na-yo.* |

I feel weak.	기운이 없어요.	*Ki-un-i eop-sseo-yo.*
It hurts me here.	여기가 아파요.	*Yeo-gi-ga a-p'a-yo.*
My whole body hurts.	온 몸이 아파요.	*On mom-i a-p'a-yo.*
I feel faint.	어지러워요.	*Eo-ji-reo-weo-yo.*
I feel nauseated.	메스꺼워요.	*Me-seu-kkeo-weo-yo.*
I feel a chill.	오한이 나요.	*O-han-i na-yo.*
I've been vomiting.	토했어요.	*T'o-hae-sseo-yo.*
I'm pregnant.	임신중이에요.	*Im-shin-jung-i-e-yo.*
I want to sit down for a while.	잠시 앉았으면 좋겠어요.	*Cham-shi an-ja-sseu-myeon cho-k'e-sseo-yo.*
My temperature is normal. (98.6°F, 37°C)	체온은 정상이에요.	*Ch'e-on-eun cheong-sang-i-e-yo.*
I feel all right now.	지금은 괜찮아요.	*Chi-geum-eun kwaen-ch'an-a-yo.*
I feel better.	좀 나았어요.	*Chom na-a-sseo-yo.*
I feel worse.	더 안 좋아요.	*Teo an cho-a-yo.*
My <u>ankle</u> hurts.	<u>발목</u>이 아파요.	*<u>Pal-mok</u>-i a-p'a-yo.*
▨ arm	팔(이)	*p'al(i)*
▨ back	등(이)	*teung(i)*
▨ chest	가슴(이)	*ka-seum(i)*
▨ ear	귀(가)	*kwi(ga)*
▨ elbow	팔꿈치(가)	*p'al-kkum-ch'i(ga)*
▨ eye	눈(이)	*nun(i)*
▨ face	얼굴(이)	*eol-gul(i)*

▧ finger	손가락(이)	*son-kka-rak(i)*
▧ foot	발(이)	*pal(i)*
▧ hand	손(이)	*son(i)*
▧ head	머리(가)	*meo-ri(ga)*
▧ heel	뒤꿈치(가)	*twi-kkum-ch'i(ga)*
▧ joint	관절(이)	*kwan-jeol(i)*
▧ knee	무릎(이)	*mu-reup(i)*
▧ leg	다리(가)	*ta-ri(ga)*
▧ muscle	근육(이)	*keun-yuk(i)*
▧ neck	목(이)	*mok(i)*
▧ nose	코(가)	*k'o(ga)*
▧ rib	갈비뼈(가)	*kal-bi-ppyeo(ga)*
▧ shoulder	어깨(가)	*eo-kkae(ga)*
▧ skin	피부(가)	*p'i-bu(ga)*
▧ spine	척추(가)	*ch'eok-ch'u(ga)*
▧ stomach	배(가)	*pae(ga)*
▧ thigh	넓적다리(가)	*neolp-jjeok-tta-ri(ga)*
▧ throat	목구멍(이)	*mok-kku-meong(i)*
▧ thumb	엄지손가락(이)	*eom-ji-son-kka-rak(i)*
▧ toe	발가락(이)	*pal-kka-rak(i)*
▧ tongue	혀(가)	*hyeo(ga)*
▧ wrist	손목(이)	*son-mok(i)*

I have an abscess. 종기가 났어요. *Chong-gi-ga na-sseo-yo.*

I have a bee sting. 벌에 쏘였어요. *Peo-re sso-yeo-sseo-yo.*

I have a bruise. 타박상을 입었어요. *T'a-bak-sang-eul i-beo-sseo-yo.*

I have a burn.	불에 데었어요. *Pu-re te-eo-sseo-yo.*
I have the chills.	오한이 나요. *O-han-i na-yo.*
I have <u>a cold</u>.	<u>감기</u>에 걸렸어요. *<u>Kam-gi</u>-e keol-lyeo-sseo-yo.*
▧ a chest cold	기침 감기 *ki-ch'im kam-gi*
▧ a head cold	두통 감기 *tu-t'ong kam-gi*
I'm constipated.	변비에 걸렸어요. *Pyeon-bi-e keol-lyeo-sseo-yo.*
I have cramps.	복통이 나요. *Pok-t'ong-i na-yo.*
I have a cut.	베었어요. *Pe-eo-sseo-yo.*
I have diarrhea.	설사가 나요. *Seol-sa-ga na-yo.*
I have a fever.	열이 있어요. *Yeo-ri i-sseo-yo.*
I have a headache.	머리가 아파요. *Meo-ri-ga a-p'a-yo.*
I have indigestion.	소화불량이에요. *So-hwa-pul-lyang-i-e-yo.*
I have acid indigestion.	위산과다예요. *Wi-san-gwa-da-ye-yo.*
I have an infection.	곪았어요. *Kol-ma-sseo-yo.*
I have an insect bite.	벌레에 물렸어요. *Peol-le-e mul-lyeo-sseo-yo.*
I have a lump.	혹이 났어요. *Hok-i na-sseo-yo.*
I have a sore throat.	목이 따끔따끔해요. *Mok-i tta-kkeum-tta-kkeum-hae-yo.*
I have a stomachache.	배가 아파요. *Pae-ga a-p'a-yo.*

I have swelling.	부어 올랐어요. *Pu-eo ol-la-sseo-yo.*
I think I have <u>a broken bone</u>.	뼈가 부러진 것 같아요. *Ppyeo-ga pu-reo-jin keot ka-t'a-yo.*
▧ dysentery	이질(인) *i-jil(in)*
▧ the flu	몸살(인) *mom-sal(in)*
▧ a stomach ulcer	위궤양(인) *wi-gwe-yang(in)*
I've had pain since <u>this morning</u>.	오늘 아침부터 아파요. *O-neul a-ch'im-bu-t'eo a-p'a-yo.*
▧ last night	어제 저녁 *eo-je cheo-nyeok*
▧ yesterday	어제 *eo-je*
▧ the day before yesterday	그저께 *keu-jeo-kke*
▧ last week	지난주 *chi-nan-ju*
I'm having chest pain.	가슴이 아파요. *Ka-seum-i a-p'a-yo.*
I had a heart attack five years ago.	오년 전에 심장마비가 있었어요. *O-nyeon cheon-e shim-jang-ma-bi-ga i-sseo-sseo-yo.*
I'm a diabetic.	당뇨병이 있어요. *Tang-nyo-byeong-i i-sseo-yo.*
I'm taking <u>this medicine</u>.	이 약을 먹고 있어요. *I yak-eul meok-kko i-sseo-yo.*
▧ insulin	인슐린 *in-syul-lin*
I'm allergic to <u>antibiotics</u>.	항생제에 알레르기가 있어요. *Hang-saeng-je-e al-le-reu-gi-ga i-sseo-yo.*
▧ aspirin	아스피린 *a-seu-p'i-rin*
▧ penicillin	페니실린 *p'e-ni-shil-lin*
There's a history of _____ in my family.	가족중에 _____ (을/를) 앓은 사람이 있어요. *Ka-jok-jjung-e _____(eul/reul) a-reun sa-ram-i i-sseo-yo.*

There's no history of _____ in my family.	가족중에 아무도 _____(을/를) 앓은 사람이 없어요. *Ka-jok-jjung-e a-mu-do _____(eul/reul) a-reun sa-ram-i eop-sseo-yo.*
Do you know what's wrong with me?	제가 무슨 병에 걸렸어요? *Che-ga mu-seun pyeong-e keol-lyeo-sseo-yo?*
Am I overweight?	제가 과체중인가요? *Che-ga kwa-ch'e-jung-in-ga-yo?*
Do I have _____?	제가 _____에 걸렸어요? *Che-ga _____-e keol-lyeo-sseo-yo?*

[See next page, under "What the Doctor Says," for a list of medical ailments.]

Is it serious?	심해요? *Shim-hae-yo?*
Is it contagious?	전염이 돼요? *Cheon-yeom-i twae-yo?*
Do I have to stay in bed?	집에서 누워 있어야 돼요? *Chip-e-seo nu-weo i-sseo-ya twae-yo?*
How long do I have to stay in bed?	얼마나 오래 누워 있어야 돼요? *Eol-ma-na o-rae nu-weo i-sseo-ya twae-yo?*
Do I have to go to the hospital?	병원에 가야 돼요? *Pyeong-weon-e ka-ya twae-yo?*
Are you going to give me a prescription?	처방해 주실 거예요? *Ch'eo-bang-hae chu-shil kkeo-ye-yo?*
What kind of medicine is it?	이것은 무슨 약이에요? *I-geo-seun mu-seun yak-i-e-yo?*
Will it make me sleepy?	이 약을 먹으면 졸려요? *I yak-eul meo-geu-myeon chol-lyeo-yo?*

How often must I take this medicine?	하루에 몇 번 먹을까요 ? *Ha-ru-e myeot ppeon meo-geul-kka-yo?*
When can I continue my trip?	언제 여행을 계속할 수 있을까요 ? *Eon-je yeo-haeng-eul kye-sok-k'al su i-sseul-kka-yo?*
Thank you very much.	대단히 감사합니다. *Tae-dan-i kam-sa-ham-ni-da.*
Where do I pay?	계산은 어디서 하지요 ? *Kye-san-eun eo-di-seo ha-ji-yo?*

WHAT THE DOCTOR SAYS

Where were you before you came to Korea?	한국에 오기 전에 어디에 계셨어요 ? *Han-guk-e o-gi cheon-e eo-di-e kye-shyeo-sseo-yo?*
I'm going to take your temperature.	열 좀 재겠어요. *Yeol chom chae-ge-sseo-yo.*
I'm going to take your blood pressure.	혈압 좀 재겠어요. *Hyeo-rap chom chae-ge-sseo-yo.*
I am going to check your weight.	몸무게 좀 재겠어요. *Mom-mu-ge chom chae-ge-sseo-yo.*
Open your mouth, please.	입 좀 벌려 보세요. *Ip chom peol-lyeo po-se-yo.*
Stick out your tongue.	혀 좀 내밀어 보세요. *Hyeo chom nae-mi-reo po-se-yo.*
Cough, please.	기침해 보세요. *Ki-ch'im-hae po-se-yo.*
Breathe deeply, please.	숨을 크게 쉬세요. *Sum-eul k'eu-ge shwi-se-yo.*

Roll up your sleeve, please.	소매 좀 걷어 주세요. *So-mae chom keo-deo chu-se-yo.*
Take off your clothing to the waist, please.	웃옷 좀 벗으세요. *U-dot chom peo-seu-se-yo.*
Remove your trousers and underwear, please.	바지와 속옷을 벗으세요. *Pa-ji-wa so-go-seul peo-seu-se-yo.*
Remove your skirt and underwear, please.	치마와 속옷을 벗으세요. *Ch'i-ma-wa so-go-seul peo-seu-se-yo.*
Lie down, please.	누우세요. *Nu-u-se-yo.*
Does it hurt when I press here?	여기를 누르면 아파요 ? *Yeo-gi-reul nu-reu-myeon a-p'a-yo?*
Stand up, please.	일어나세요. *I-reo-na-se-yo.*
Get dressed, please.	옷을 입으세요. *O-seul i-beu-se-yo.*
Have you ever had this before?	전에도 이런 증상이 있었어요 ? *Cheon-e-do i-reon cheung-sang-i i-sseo-sseo-yo?*
Are you having shortness of breath?	숨이 차지 않으세요 ? *Sum-i ch'a-ji an-eu-se-yo?*
Do you have any numbness here?	여기 감각이 없으세요 ? *Yeo-gi kam-gak-i eop-sseu-se-yo?*
What medicine have you been taking?	어떤 약을 드시고 계세요 ? *Eo-tteon yak-eul teu-shi-go kye-se-yo?*
What dosage of insulin do you take?	어떤 인슐린을 맞으세요 ? *Eo-tteon in-syul-lin-eul ma-jeu-se-yo?*

Is it by injection or oral?	주사 맞나요, 아니면 약을 복용해요 ? *Chu-sa man-na-yo, a-ni-myeon yak-eul po-gyong-hae-yo?*
What treatment have you been having?	어떤 치료를 받고 계세요 ? *Eo-tteon ch'i-ryo-reul pat-kko kye-se-yo?*
Is there a history of _____ in your family?	가족중에 _____ (을/를) 앓은 사람이 있어요 ? *Ka-jok-jjung-e _____ (eul/reul) a-reun sa-ram-i i-sseo-yo?*
When is your baby due?	해산 예정일이 언제예요 ? *Hae-san ye-jeong-i-ri eon-je-ye-yo?*
I want a <u>urine</u> sample.	<u>소변</u> 쌤플이 필요한데요. *<u>So-byeon</u> ssaem-p'eu-ri p'i-ryo-han-de-yo.*
■ stool	대변 *tae-byeon*
■ blood	혈액 *hyeo-raek*
I want you to have an X-ray.	엑스레이를 찍어 보세요. *Ek-sseu-re-i-reul jji-geo po-se-yo.*
When was your last tetanus shot?	마지막으로 파상풍 주사를 맞은 게 언제예요 ? *Ma-ji-mak-eu-ro p'a-sang-p'ung chu-sa-reul ma-jeun ke eon-je-ye-yo?*
It's minor.	대단치 않아요. *Tae-dan-ch'i an-a-yo.*
It's acute.	심각해요. *Shim-gak-k'ae-yo.*
It's infected.	감염됐어요. *Kam-yeom-dwae-sseo-yo.*
It's broken.	부러졌어요. *Pu-reo-jyeo-sseo-yo.*
It's sprained.	삐었어요. *Ppi-eo-sseo-yo.*
It's dislocated.	탈골되었어요. *T'al-gol-doe-eo-sseo-yo.*

It's inflamed.	염증이 생겼어요. *Yeom-jjeung-i saeng-gyeo-sseo-yo.*
I'll have to take stitches.	꿰매야 되겠어요. *Kkwe-mae-ya toe-ge-sseo-yo.*
I'll have to lance it.	절개해야 되겠어요. *Cheol-gae-hae-ya toe-ge-sseo-yo.*
You can't travel until _____.	_____까지 여행할 수 없어요. *_____-kka-ji yeo-haeng-hal su eop-sseo-yo.*
I want you to go to the hospital for some tests.	몇 가지 검사를 받으러 병원에 가 보시면 좋겠어요. *Myeot kka-ji keom-sa-reul pa-deu-reo pyeong-weon-e ka po-shi-myeon cho-k'e-sseo-yo.*
You need <u>a blood</u> test.	<u>혈액검사</u>를 하셔야겠어요. *<u>Hyeo-raek-kkeom-sa-reul</u> ha-shyeo-ya-ge-sseo-yo.*
▦ an HIV	에이치아이브이 *e-i-ch'i-a-i-beu-i*
▦ a urine	소변 *so-byeon*
I want you to go to the hospital for treatment.	치료를 받으러 입원하시는 것이 좋겠어요. *Ch'i-ryo-reul pa-deu-reo i-bweon-ha-shi-neun keo-shi cho-k'e-sseo-yo.*
I want you to go to the hospital for surgery.	수술받으러 입원하시는 것이 좋겠어요. *Su-sul-ba-deu-reo i-bweon-ha-shi-neun keo-shi cho-k'e-sseo-yo.*
Shall I make the arrangements for you to go to the hospital?	입원 수속을 해 드릴까요? *I-bweon su-sok-eul hae teu-ril-kka-yo?*

Do you have medical insurance?	의료보험이 있으세요 ? *Eui-ryo-bo-heom-i i-sseu-se-yo?*
You've had a mild heart attack.	심장마비 증세가 약간 있어요. *Shim-jang-ma-bi cheung-se-ga yak-kkan i-sseo-yo.*
You are overweight.	과체중이시네요. *Kwa-ch'e-jung-i-shi-ne-yo.*
Are you allergic to _____?	_____에 알레르기가 있어요 ? *_____-e al-le-reu-gi-ga i-sseo-yo?*
Are you allergic to any medicines?	아무 약에나 알레르기가 있어요 ? *A-mu yak-e-na al-le-reu-gi-ga i-sseo-yo?*
I'm prescribing an antibiotic.	항생제를 처방해 드리지요. *Hang-saeng-je-reul ch'eo-bang-hae teu-ri-ji-yo.*
I'm writing a prescription for you.	처방을 해 드리지요. *Ch'eo-bang-eul hae teu-ri-ji-yo.*
We don't use _____ in Korea.	한국에서는 _____(을/를) 쓰지 않아요. *Han-guk-e-seo-neun _____(eul/reul) sseu-ji an-a-yo.*
This is quite similar to _____.	_____하고 아주 비슷해요. *_____-ha-go a-ju pi-seut-t'ae-yo.*
Take two teaspoons of this medicine at a time.	이 약을 두 스푼씩 드세요. *I yak-eul tu seu-p'un-sshik teu-se-yo.*
Take it every four hours.	네 시간마다 드세요. *Ne shi-gan-ma-da teu-se-yo.*
Take two tablets with a glass of water.	두 알을 물 한 컵과 같이 드세요. *Tu a-reul mul han k'eop-gwa ka-ch'i teu-se-yo.*

Take it three times a day.	하루에 세 번 드세요.	*Ha-ru-e se peon teu-se-yo.*
Take it after meals.	식후에 드세요.	*Shik-k'u-e teu-se-yo.*
Take it before meals.	식전에 드세요.	*Shik-jjeon-e teu-se-yo.*
Take it in the morning.	아침에 드세요.	*A-ch'im-e teu-se-yo.*
Take it at night.	밤에 드세요.	*Pam-e teu-se-yo.*
Use a cold pack.	냉찜질 하세요.	*Naeng-jjim-jil ha-se-yo.*
Use a hot pack.	뜨겁게 찜질하세요.	*Tteu-geop-kke jjim-jil-ha-se-yo.*
I want you to come back after six days.	육일 후에 다시 오세요.	*Yuk-il hu-e ta-shi o-se-yo.*
I think it's _____.	_____인 것 같아요.	*_____-in keot ka-t'a-yo.*

- an allergy　알레르기　*al-le-reu-gi*
- appendicitis　맹장염　*maeng-jang-yeom*
- a bacterial infection　박테리아 감염　*pak-t'e-ri-a kam-yeom*
- a bladder infection　방광염　*pang-gwang-yeom*
- bronchitis　기관지염　*ki-gwan-ji-yeom*
- a common cold　감기　*kam-gi*
- conjunctivitis　결막염　*kyeol-ma-gyeom*
- dysentery　이질　*i-jil*
- food poisoning　식중독　*shik-jjung-dok*
- gastroenteritis　위산과다증　*wi-san-gwa-da-jeung*
- hepatitis　간염　*kan-yeom*

▓ high cholesterol	높은 콜레스테롤	*no-p'eun k'ol-le-seu-t'e-rol*
▓ influenza	인플루엔자	*in-p'eul-lu-en-ja*
▓ a muscle spasm	근육경련	*keun-yuk-kkyeong-nyeon*
▓ muscular	근육통	*keun-yuk-t'ong*
▓ pneumonia	폐렴	*p'ye-ryeom*
▓ tonsillitis	편도선염	*p'yeon-do-seon-yeom*
▓ an ulcer	위궤양	*wi-gwe-yang*
▓ a urinary infection	요도염	*yo-do-yeom*
▓ a virus infection	바이러스 감염	*pa-i-reo-seu kam-yeom*

AT THE DENTIST

There are two parts in this section: "Patient" and "Dentist." You can use the expressions under "Patient," and the dentist can point to appropriate expressions under "Dentist."

Please point to the phrase in the book.	이 책에서 그 말을 찾아 주세요. *I ch'aek-e-seo keu ma-reul ch'a-ja chu-se-yo.*

PATIENT

I have to go to a dentist.	치과에 가야 돼요. *Ch'i-kkwa-e ka-ya twae-yo.*
Can you recommend a dentist?	잘하는 치과 의사를 소개해 주세요. *Chal-ha-neun ch'i-kkwa eui-sa-reul so-gae-hae chu-se-yo.*
I'd like an appointment with the dentist.	그 치과에 예약을 하고 싶은데요. *Keu ch'i-kkwa-e ye-yak-eul ha-go shi-p'eun-de-yo.*

I need to see the dentist immediately.	의사한테 당장 가야 돼요. *Eui-sa-han-t'e tang-jang ka-ya twae-yo.*
I have a really bad toothache.	이가 심하게 아파요. *I-ga shim-ha-ge a-p'a-yo.*
I think I have a cavity.	충치가 있는 것 같아요. *Ch'ung-ch'i-ga in-neun keot ka-t'a-yo.*
■ an abscess	농양(이) *nong-yang(i)*
I've lost a filling.	뽕이 빠졌어요. *Ppong-i ppa-jyeo-sseo-yo.*
I've broken a tooth.	이가 부러졌어요. *I-ga pu-reo-jyeo-sseo-yo.*
I can't chew.	씹을 수가 없어요. *Sship-eul su-ga eop-sseo-yo.*
My gums hurt.	잇몸이 아파요. *In-mom-i a-p'a-yo.*
Can you give me a temporary filling?	임시로 뽕을 박아 주시겠어요 ? *Im-shi-ro ppong-eul pa-ga chu-shi-ge-sseo-yo?*
■ composite/resin	레진(으로) *re-jin(eu-ro)*
■ silver	은(으로) *eun(eu-ro)*
Can you fix this bridge?	이 브릿지를 고쳐 주시겠어요 ? *I peu-rit-jji-reul ko-ch'yeo chu-shi-ge-sseo-yo?*
■ crown	치관(을) *ch'i-kkwan(eul)*
■ denture	틀니/의치(를) *t'eul-li/eui-ch'i(reul)*
Can you adjust my braces?	치아 교정기 좀 조절해 주시겠어요 ? *Ch'i-a kyo-jeong-gi chom cho-jeol-hae chu-shi-ge-sseo-yo?*

Can you whiten my teeth?	치아미백해 주시겠어요 ? *Ch'i-a-mi-baek-hae chu-shi-ge-sseo-yo?*

DENTIST

I see the problem.	원인을 알겠어요. *Weon-in-eul al-ge-sseo-yo.*
I want to take an X-ray.	엑스레이를 찍어야겠어요. *Ek-sseu-re-i-reul jji-geo-ya-ge-sseo-yo.*
We should do it now.	지금 해야겠어요. *Chi-geum hae-ya-ge-sseo-yo.*
It can wait until you return to your country.	귀국하신 다음에 해도 되겠어요. *Kwi-guk-k'a-shin ta-eum-e hae-do toe-ge-sseo-yo.*
I'm going to give you a <u>temporary</u> filling.	임시로 뽕을 박아 드리겠어요. *Im-shi-ro ppong-eul pa-ga teu-ri-ge-seo-yo.*
■ composite/resin	레진(으로) *re-jin(eu-ro)*
■ silver	은(으로) *eun(eu-ro)*
You need a <u>crown</u>.	크라운을 하셔야겠어요. *K'eu-ra-un-eul ha-shyeo-ya-ge-sseo-yo.*
■ an implant	임플란트(를) *im-p'eul-lan-t'eu(reul)*
Do you want a <u>gold</u> crown?	금 크라운을 하시겠어요 ? *Keum k'eu-ra-un-eul ha-shi-ge-sseo-yo?*
■ porcelain/ceramic	세라믹 *se-ra-mik*
Would you like a <u>local</u> anesthetic?	국부마취를 하시겠어요 ? *Kuk-bbu-ma-ch'wi-reul ha-shi-ge-sseo-yo?*
■ general	전신 *cheon-shin*
Does this hurt?	여기가 아파요 ? *Yeo-gi-ga a-p'a-yo?*
I'm giving you a prescription.	약을 처방해 드리지요. *Yak-eul ch'eo-bang-hae teu-ri-ji-yo.*

Rinse with this four times daily.	하루에 네 번 이것으로 씻으세요. *Ha-ru-e ne peon i-geo-seu-ro sshi-seu-se-yo.*
This is <u>an antibiotic</u>.	이것은 항생제예요. *I-geo-seun hang-saeng-je-ye-yo.*
■ a pain killer	진통제 *chin-t'ong-je*
Take two tablets at a time.	한 번에 두 알씩 드세요. *Han peon-e tu al-sshik teu-se-yo.*
Take them every 12 hours.	열두 시간마다 드세요. *Yeol-ttu shi-gan-ma-da teu-se-yo.*

TRADITIONAL TREATMENTS

Koreans' use of Western medicine is complemented by a history of traditional treatments including acupressure, acupuncture, and herbal remedies. Traditional treatments made from plants and other natural medications are designed to address everything from skin disease and depression to cancer. Herbal medicine clinics and shops are widely available in every city. Koreans who are skilled in acupressure and acupuncture are also easily accessible. Check with hotel staff or Korean associates if you are interested in exploring these aspects of Korean medicine.

Where can I find an herbal medicine shop?	한의원이 어디 있어요? *Han-eui-weon-i eo-di i-sseo-yo?*
I need herbal medicine for my <u>cold</u>.	감기에 좋은 한약을 지어주세요. *<u>Kam-gi</u>-e cho-eun han-yak-eul chi-eo-ju-se-yo.*
■ arthritis	관절염 (에) *kwan-jeol-yeom(e)*
■ fatigue	피곤한 데 *p'i-gon-han te*
■ allergies	알레르기 (에) *al-le-reu-ki(e)*

■ skin problem	피부 트러블(에)	*p'i-bu t'eu-reo-beul(e)*
Where can I get <u>acupressure</u>?	어디서 지압을 받을 수 있을까요?	*Eo-di-seo <u>chi-ap-eul</u> pa-deul su i-sseul-kka-yo?*
■ acupuncture	침치료(를)	*ch'im-ch'i-ryo(reul)*
Do you know a good <u>acupressurist</u>?	잘하는 지압사를 아세요?	*Chal-ha-neun <u>chi-ap-sa</u>-reul a-se-yo?*
■ acupuncturist	침술사	*ch'im-sul-sa*
Does he/she come to my place?	그 사람이 이곳까지 와요?	*Keu sa-ram-i i-got-kka-ji wa-yo?*
How much is it for an hour?	한 시간에 얼마예요?	*Han shi-gan-e eol-ma-ye-yo?*
Do I need to make an appointment?	예약을 해야 될까요?	*Ye-yak-eul hae-ya toel-kka-yo?*
Could you get me one?	한 사람 불러 주시겠어요?	*Han sa-ram pul-leo chu-shi-ge-sseo-yo?*

WITH THE ACUPRESSURIST OR ACUPUNCTURIST

My problem is here.	여기가 아파요.	*Yeo-gi-ga a-p'a-yo.*
My <u>neck</u> is stiff.	목이 뻣뻣해요.	*<u>Mok</u>-i ppeot-ppeot-t'ae-yo.*
■ shoulders (are)	어깨(가)	*eo-kkae(ga)*
■ back (is)	등(이)	*teung(i)*
My <u>head</u> ache(s).	머리가 아파요.	*<u>Meo-ri</u>-ga a-p'a-yo.*
■ arms	팔(이)	*p'al(i)*
■ lower back	허리(가)	*heo-ri(ga)*

▨ stomach   배(가)   *pae(ga)*

▨ legs   다리(가)   *ta-ri(ga)*

WITH THE ACUPRESSURIST

You're pressing too hard.	지압이 너무 아파요. *Chi-ap-i neo-mu a-p'a-yo.*
Can you do it more gently?	좀 부드럽게 해 주세요. *Chom pu-deu-reop-kke hae chu-se-yo.*
Please apply more pressure.	세게 해 주세요. *Se-ge hae chu-se-yo.*

WITH THE OPTICIAN

Can you repair these glasses for me?	이 안경을 고쳐 주세요. *I an-gyeong-eul ko-ch'yeo chu-se-yo.*
I've broken a lens.	안경알이 깨졌어요. *An-gyeong-a-ri kkae-jyeo-sseo-yo.*
I've broken the frame.	안경테가 부러졌어요. *An-gyeong-t'e-ga pu-reo-jyeo-sseo-yo.*
Would you put in a new lens?	새 알을 끼워 주세요. *Sae a-reul kki-weo chu-se-yo.*
Can you get a prescription from the old lens?	저번 알의 도수를 알 수 있어요? *Cheo-beon a-reui tot-ssu-reul al su i-sseo-yo?*
Will you tighten the screw?	나사를 꽉 죄어 주세요. *Na-sa-reul kkwak choe-eo chu-se-yo.*

I need the glasses as soon as possible.

가능한한 안경을 빨리 좀 해 주세요. *Ka-neung-han-han an-gyeong-eul ppal-li chom hae chu-se-yo.*

I don't have any others.

여벌이 없어요. *Yeo-beo-ri eop-sseo-yo.*

I'd like a new pair of eyeglasses.

안경을 새로 하고 싶은데요. *An-gyeong-eul sae-ro ha-go shi-p'eun-de-yo.*

Can you give me a new prescription?

새로 도수를 재 주시겠어요? *Sae-ro tot-ssu-reul chae chu-shi-ge-sseo-yo?*

I'd like the lenses tinted.

알에 연한 색을 넣고 싶어요. *A-re yeon-han saek-eul neo-k'o shi-p'eo-yo.*

Do you sell <u>contact lenses</u>?

콘택트 렌즈를 파세요? *K'on-t'aek-t'eu ren-jeu-reul p'a-se-yo?*

▧ soft contact lenses

소프트 콘택트 렌즈 *so-p'eu-t'eu k'on-t'aek-t'eu ren-jeu*

▧ sunglasses

선글라스 *sseon-geul-la-seu*

COMMUNICATIONS

POST OFFICE

Korean post offices are easily recognized by their red signs and distinctive logo, an image of three swallows symbolizing speedy, reliable, and safe postal delivery. The Gwangwhamun Post Office, conveniently located in downtown Seoul, offers a full range of services. At any post office, you can take advantage of the international mail counter, where you can have your items weighed and mailed. Most post offices sell packing materials and wrap packages at your request. Postal charges for domestic and international mail are based on weight in grams. Aerograms, cards, and letters may be dropped in any mailbox, as long as they have the correct postage. You may also ask staff at your hotel to mail items for you.

I want to mail a letter.	편지를 부치고 싶은데요. *P'yeon-ji-reul pu-ch'i-go shi-p'eun-de-yo.*
Where is a <u>mailbox</u>?	우체통이 어디 있어요 ? *U-ch'e-t'ong-i eo-di i-sseo-yo?*
■ post office	우체국 *u-ch'e-guk*
How much is <u>an airmail letter</u> to the U.S.?	미국까지 항공 우편요금이 얼마예요 ? *Mi-guk-kka-ji hang-gong u-p'yeon yo-geum-i eol-ma-ye-yo?*
■ a registered letter	등기우편 *teung-gi u-p'yeon*
■ express mail	속달우편 *sok-ttal u-p'yeon*
■ a postcard	엽서 *yeop-sseo*
I'd like five aerograms.	항공 엽서 다섯 장 주세요. *Hang-gong yeop-sseo ta-seot chang chu-se-yo.*

Please give me five 250 won stamps.	이백오십원짜리 우표 다섯 장 주세요. *I-baek-o-ship-weon-jja-ri u-p'yo ta-seot chang chu-se-yo.*
I want pretty stamps.	예쁜 우표로 주세요. *Ye-ppeun u-p'yo-ro chu-se-yo.*
Where can I get this wrapped?	포장하는 데가 어디 있어요 ? *P'o-jang-ha-neun te-ga eo-di i-sseo-yo?*
I'd like to send this parcel.	이 소포를 부치고 싶은데요. *I so-p'o-reul pu-ch'i-go shi-p'eun-de-yo.*
Can I purchase insurance?	보험에 들 수 있을까요 ? *Po-heom-e teul su i-sseul-kka-yo?*
The contents are fragile.	내용물이 깨지기 쉬워요. *Nae-yong-mul-i kkae-ji-gi shwi-weo-yo.*
What is the postal code?	우편번호가 어떻게 되나요 ? *U-p'yeon-beon-ho-ga eo-tteo-k'e toe-na-yo?*
Please send it registered.	등기로 부쳐 주세요. *Teung-gi-ro pu-ch'yeo chu-se-yo.*
How much does it cost <u>by air</u>?	<u>항공편</u>으로 얼마예요 ? *<u>Hang-gong-p'yeon</u>-eu-ro eol-ma-ye-yo?*
■ by sea	선박편 *seon-bak-p'yeon*
Please send this by air.	항공편으로 부쳐 주세요. *Hang-gong-p'yeon-eu-ro pu-ch'yeo chu-se-yo.*
Do I need to fill out a customs declaration form?	세관 신고용지에 기입해야 돼요 ? *Se-gwan shin-go-yong-ji-e ki-ip-p'ae-ya twae-yo?*
Thank you.	수고하셨어요. *Su-go-ha-shyeo-sseo-yo.*

INTERNET

Korean's widespread use of the Internet makes electronic communication easy and convenient for visitors to the country. Internet cafés can be found throughout Seoul and other cities. Koreans use the cafés for Internet surfing, checking e-mail, and gaming. You may toggle between English and Korean on the keyboards. If you need to fax printed documents, go to a stationery store or have it done at your hotel.

Does my hotel room have <u>Internet</u> access?	제 호텔방이 인터넷이 되나요 ? *Che ho-t'el-bang-i <u>In-t'eo-ne-shi</u> toe-na-yo?*
■ wireless	무선 인터넷 *mu-seon in-t'eo-net*
Where is <u>the business center</u>?	비지니스 센터가 어디에 있지요 ? <u>*Pi-ji-ni-seu sen-t'eo-ga*</u> *eo-di-e i-jji-yo?*
■ an Internet café	인터넷 까페 *In-t'eo-net kka-p'e*
How do I log in?	어떻게 로그인 하지요 ? *Eo-tteo-k'e ro-geu-in ha-ji-yo?*
What's the charge?	요금이 얼마인가요 ? *Yo-geum-i eol-ma-in-ga-yo?*
I need to <u>check e-mail</u>.	이메일을 체크해야 하는데요. <u>*I-me-i-reul ch'e-k'eu-hae-ya*</u> *ha-neun-de-yo.*
■ print my document	서류를 프린트해야 *seo-ryu-reul p'eu-rin-t'eu-hae-ya*
■ scan my document	서류를 스캔해야 *seo-ryu-reul seu-k'aen-hae-ya*
I think the <u>PC has crashed</u>.	컴퓨터가 안되는 것 같은데요. <u>*K'eom-p'yu-t'eo-ga an-doe-neun keot*</u> *kat-eun-de-yo.*

■ USB port is not working 유에스비가 안되는 것 *yu-e-seu-bi-ga an-doe-neun keot*

TELEPHONE

Public telephones are difficult to find as almost everyone has a cell phone (*haen-deu-p'on*). You may consider renting a cell phone. Check at the airport upon arrival or with staff at your hotel. Most public phones require cards, although there are a few that will accept coins. Card phones are good for local, long-distance, or international calls and are the most economical way to call outside Korea. International cards can be purchased in convenience stores and special phone card shops. You may want to compare cards from different companies for the most favorable rate. In case you have an emergency and you need a phone quickly, a passing stranger will happily let you use his or her cell phone.

Can I rent a cell phone?	핸드폰 대여를 할 수 있을까요 ? *Haen-deu-p'on tae-yeo-reul hal su i-sseul-kka-yo?*
What are the rates?	요금이 어떻게 되지요 ? *Yo-geum-i eo-tteo-k'e toe-ji-yo?*
Where is a public telephone?	공중 전화가 어디 있어요 ? *Kong-jung cheon-hwa-ga eo-di i-sseo-yo?*
Is there an English telephone directory?	영어로 된 전화부가 있어요 ? *Yeong-eo-ro toen cheon-hwa-bu-ga i-sseo-yo?*
Please give me change for the telephone.	잔돈 좀 바꿔 주세요. *Chan-don chom pa-kkweo chu-se-yo.*
May I use your <u>phone</u>?	전화 좀 써도 될까요 ? <u>*Cheon-hwa chom sseo-do toel-kka-yo?*</u>

■ cell phone
핸드폰 *haen-deu-p'on*

I want to make a/an local call.
시내 전화를 하고 싶은데요. *Shi-nae cheon-hwa-reul ha-go shi-p'eun-de-yo.*

■ long distance call
시외 전화 *shi-woe cheon-hwa*

■ international call
국제 전화 *kuk-jje cheon-hwa*

■ collect call
수신인 지불 전화 *su-shin-in chi-bul cheon-hwa*

Please tell me how to call this number.
이 번호로 어떻게 전화하지요 ? *I peon-ho-ro eo-tteo-k'e cheon-hwa-ha-ji-yo?*

My phone number is 123-4567.
제 전화 번호는 일이삼에 사오육칠입니다. *Che cheon-hwa peon-ho-neun il-i-sam-e sa-o-yuk-ch'il-im-ni-da.*

What's the area code?
지역 번호는 뭐예요 ? *Chi-yeok peon-ho-neun mweo-ye-yo?*

Do I need an operator's assistance?
교환을 통해야 돼요 ? *Kyo-hwan-eul t'ong-hae-ya twae-yo?*

Is there an operator who speaks English?
영어 하는 교환이 있어요 ? *Yeong-eo ha-neun kyo-hwan-i i-sseo-yo?*

What's the number for the operator?
교환 번호는 뭐예요 ? *Kyo-hwan peon-ho-neun mweo-ye-yo?*

How do I call Busan information?
부산 전화안내를 어떻게 호출하지요 ? *Pu-san cheon-hwa-an-nae-reul eo-tteo-k'e ho-ch'ul-ha-ji-yo?*

WITH THE OTHER PARTY

Hello.	여보세요. *Yeo-bo-se-yo.*
Hello. Is this Mr./Mrs./Ms. (<u>full name</u>) residence?	네,여보세요. _____씨댁이에요 ? *Ne, yeo-bo-se-yo. _____-sshi-daek-i-e-yo?*

Note: "*sshi*" is an appropriate title to use when asking for someone by phone. Be sure to use the full name of the person. If the party is Korean, give the last name first, followed by the given name; for example: "*Kim, Yong-Hae-sshi-daek i-e-yo?*"

May I speak to _____? Mr./Mrs./Ms. (<u>full name</u>)	_____씨 좀 바꿔 주세요. *_____-sshi chom pa-kkweo chu-se-yo.*
You have the wrong number.	전화 잘못 거셨어요. *Cheon-hwa chal-mot keo-shyeo-sseo-yo.*
Is this (<u>company name</u>)?	_____ 이에요 ? *_____ i-e-yo?*
I want extension 20.	교환 내선 이십 번 좀 부탁해요. *Kyo-hwan nae-seon i-ship ppeon chom pu-t'ak-k'ae-yo.*
Is Mr./Mrs./Miss/ Ms. (<u>full name</u>) in?	_____씨 계세요 ? *_____-sshi kye-se-yo?*
Excuse me, but could you please talk more <u>slowly</u>.	실례지만 좀 더 <u>천천히</u> 말씀해 주세요. *Shil-lye-ji-man chom teo ch'eon-ch'eon-hi mal-sseum-hae chu-se-yo.*
■ loudly	크게 *k'eu-ge*
Excuse me, but who's calling?	실례지만 누구시지요 ? *Shil-lye-ji-man nu-gu-shi-ji-yo?*
This is (<u>full name</u>).	저는 _____ 인데요. *Cheo-neun ___ in-de-yo.*

When using Western names, say the given name first, followed by the family name; for example, "*Cheo-neun* Jane Smith *in-de-yo.*"

Hello! Is this (<u>full name</u>)?	여보세요 ? _____ 씨세요 ?	*Yeo-bo-se-yo ? _____-sshi-se-yo?*
Yes, speaking.	네, 그렇습니다.	*Ne, keu-reo-seum-ni-da.*
I'm busy now. Can I call you later?	지금 바쁜데, 나중에 전화해 드릴까요 ?	*Chi-geum pa-ppeun-de, na-jung-e cheon-hwa-hae teu-ril-kka-yo?*
Sure. That's fine.	네. 그렇게 하세요.	*Ne. Keu-reo-k'e ha-se-yo.*

IF THE PERSON ISN'T THERE

He/She's not here now.	지금 안 계신데요.	*Chi-geum an kye-shin-de-yo.*
When will he/she be back?	언제 돌아오시지요 ?	*Eon-je to-ra-o-shi-ji-yo?*
Well, I'm not sure.	글쎄요, 잘 모르겠는데요.	*Keul-sse-yo, chal mo-reu-gen-neun-de-yo.*
Will you tell him/her that I called?	제가 전화했다고 좀 전해 주시겠어요 ?	*Che-ga cheon-hwa-haet-tta-go chom cheon-hae chu-shi-ge-sseo-yo?*
Would you tell him/her to call me?	저한테 전화해 달라고 전해 주시겠어요 ?	*Cheo-han-t'e cheon-hwa-hae tal-la-go cheon-hae chu-shi-ge-sseo-yo?*

My phone number is _____.	제 전화 번호는 _____ 이에요. *Che cheon-hwa peon-ho-neun _____ i-e-yo.*
My extension is _____.	교환 _____번이에요. *Kyo-hwan _____-beon-i-e-yo.*
Please tell him/her to leave a message if I'm not here.	제가 없으면 메시지를 남겨 놓으라고 전해 주세요. *Che-ga eop-sseu-myeon me-sshi-ji-reul nam-gyeo no-eu-ra-go cheon-hae chu-se-yo.*
I'll call again.	다시 전화 걸겠어요. *Ta-shi cheon-hwa keol-ge-sseo-yo.*
Thank you very much.	고맙습니다. *Ko-map-sseum-ni-da.*
I'm going to hang up.	끊겠어요. *Kkeun-k'e-sseo-yo.*
Good-bye.	안녕히 계세요. *An-nyeong-i kye-se-yo.*

DRIVING A CAR

Driving in Korea can be a challenging experience. Roadways are crowded with vehicles and pedestrians, and you may be unfamiliar with the formal and informal rules of driving there. Driving is done on the right side of the road, with the driver sitting on the left side of the car. If you want to drive, rental cars are available. If you would rather not drive, you can hire a driver along with your rental. If you choose to drive, you must have a valid license from your country and an International Driving Permit (IDP). In the U.S. before departure, you should obtain an IDP at a local office of the American Automobile Association or the National Automobile Club. IDPs are not issued in Korea to foreigners. When driving, you must carry the IDP and your valid driver's license with you at all times. You may also wish to check your auto and medical insurance to determine coverage when traveling abroad. You should consider having extensive liability coverage. The penalties in Korea for driving while intoxicated are severe. If you find yourself unable to drive, you can hire a driver to take you in your car to your destination.

RENTING A CAR

Where can I rent a car?	차를 어디에서 빌릴 수 있어요 ? *Ch'a-reul eo-di-e-seo pil-lil su i-sseo-yo?*
I'd like to rent a car.	차를 빌리고 싶은데요. *Ch'a-reul pil-li-go shi-p'eun-de-yo.*
Do you have a <u>small car</u>?	소형차가 있어요 ? <u>*So-hyeong-ch'a-ga i-sseo-yo?*</u>
■ mid-size car	중형차 *chung-hyeong-ch'a*
■ large car	대형차 *tae-hyeong-ch'a*

- sports car   스포츠카   *seu-p'o-ch'eu-k'a*
- minivan   봉고   *pong-go*
- SUV (sports utility vehicle)   에스유브이   *e-seu-yu-beu-i*

I want one with <u>automatic transmission</u>.   <u>오토매틱으로</u> 주세요.   <u>*O-t'o-mae-t'ik-eu-ro*</u> *chu-se-yo.*

- standard transmission   스틱/매뉴얼   *seu-t'ik/mae-nyu-eol*
- a GPS (global positioning system)   네비게이션 or 지피에스   *ne-bi-ge-i-shyeon* or *chi-p'i-e-seu*

May I see your list of rates?   요금표를 보여 주시겠어요?   *Yo-geum-p'yo-reul po-yeo chu-shi-ge-sseo-yo?*

I'd like it for <u>a day</u>.   <u>하루</u> 필요한데요.   <u>*Ha-ru*</u> *p'i-ryo-han-de-yo.*

- a week   일주일   *il-jju-il*

Does the rate include <u>mileage</u>?   계산에 <u>주행 거리</u>가 포함돼요?   *Kye-san-e <u>chu-haeng keo-ri</u>-ga p'o-ham-dwae-yo?*

- gas   휘발유(가)   *hwi-bal-lyu(ga)*
- insurance   보험(이)   *po-heom(i)*

How much is the insurance?   보험료가 얼마예요?   *Po-heom-ryo-ga eol-ma-ye-yo?*

Do you provide a driver?   운전수를 구할 수 있어요?   *Un-jeon-su-reul ku-hal su i-sseo-yo?*

What's the charge?   운전수비는 얼마예요?   *Un-jeon-su-bi-neun eol-ma-ye-yo?*

Do I have to leave a deposit?   선금을 내야 돼요?   *Seon-geum-eul nae-ya twae-yo?*

How much is it?	얼마예요 ? *Eol-ma-ye-yo?*
Do you take credit cards?	크레딧 카드를 받아요 ? *K'eu-re-dit k'a-deu-reul pa-da-yo?*
Can you deliver it to <u>my hotel</u>?	차를 제 호텔로 보내 줄 수 있어요 ? *Ch'a-reul che ho-t'el-ro po-nae chul su i-sseo-yo?*
■ this address	이 주소 *i chu-so*
Here's my <u>International Driving Permit</u>.	여기 제 국제 운전 면허증이 있어요. *Yeo-gi che kuk-jje un-jeon myeon-heo-jjeung-i i-sseo-yo.*
■ driver's license	운전 면허증 *un-jeon myeon-heo-jjeung*
Please give me some emergency telephone numbers.	비상 전화 번호를 좀 가르쳐 주세요. *Pi-sang cheon-hwa peon-ho-reul chom ka-reu-ch'yeo chu-se-yo.*
Could I have a road map?	도로 지도를 주시겠어요 ? *To-ro chi-do-reul chu-shi-ge-sseo-yo?*

INFORMATION AND DIRECTIONS

Excuse me, but I'd like to ask you a question.	실례지만, 말씀 좀 묻겠는데요. *Shil-lye-ji-man, mal-sseum chom mut-kken-neun-de-yo.*
How do I get to _____?	_____에 어떻게 가지요 ? *_____-e eo-tteo-k'e ka-ji-yo?*
Is this the road to _____?	이 길이 _____ 가는 길이에요 ? *I ki-ri _____ ka-neun ki-ri-e-yo?*

Could you show me where _____ is on the map?	_____(이/가)이 지도에 어디 있는지 가리켜 주세요. _____(i/ga) i chi-do-e eo-di in-neun-ji ka-ri-k'yeo chu-se-yo.
Could you show me where I am on the map?	제가 있는 지점을 이 지도에서 가리켜 주세요. Che-ga in-neun chi-jeom-eul i chi-do-e-seo ka-ri-k'yeo chu-se-yo.
Do I go straight?	똑바로 가요 ? Ttok-ppa-ro ka-yo?
Do I turn <u>to the right</u>?	<u>오른쪽</u>으로 가요 ? <u>O-reun-jjok</u>-eu-ro ka-yo?
■ to the left	왼쪽 woen-jjok
Where is the <u>entrance to the highway</u>?	<u>고속도로 진입구</u>가 어디 있어요 ? <u>Ko-sok-tto-ro chin-ip-kku</u>-ga eo-di i-sseo-yo?
■ tourist information center	관광 안내소 kwan-gwang an-nae-so
■ gas station	주유소 chu-yu-so

AT THE HIGHWAY TOLL PLAZA

Tolls are required on most of Korea's major highways. As you enter the highway, tell the attendant at the toll plaza your destination, and your toll will be computed accordingly.

How far are you going?	어디까지 가세요 ? Eo-di-kka-ji ka-se-yo?
I am going as far as _____.	_____까지 가요. _____-kka-ji ka-yo.
That will be _____ won.	_____원 주세요. _____ weon chu-se-yo.

THE SERVICE STATION

In Korea gasoline is sold by the liter, and it may be confusing for the driver who wishes to calculate miles per gallon (kilometer per liter). Below are two tables to help with making conversions.

LIQUID MEASURES (APPROXIMATE)		
LITERS	U.S. GALLONS	IMPERIAL GALLONS
30	8	6
40	10	8
50	13	11
60	15	13
70	18	15
80	21	17

Where is there a gas station?   주유소는 어디 있어요 ? *Chu-yu-so-neun eo-di i-sseo-yo?*

DISTANCE MEASURES (APPROXIMATE)	
KILOMETERS	MILES
1	.75
5	3
10	6
20	12
50	31
100	62

I need to buy some gas.   휘발유를 사야겠는데요. *Hwi-bal-lyu-reul sa-ya-gen-neun-de-yo.*

Fill it up with <u>diesel</u>.   경유를 가득 넣어 주세요. *Kyeong-yu-reul ka-deuk neo-eo chu-se-yo.*

- ■ regular   보통휘발유   *po-t'ong-hwi-bal-lyu*
- ■ premium   고급휘발유   *ko-geup-hwi-bal-lyu*

Give me 25 liters.	이십오 리터를 넣어 주세요. *I-ship-o ri-t'eo-reul neo-eo chu-se-yo.*
Please give me 25,000 won worth of gasoline.	휘발유 이만 오천원어치 넣어주세요. *Hwi-bal-lyu i-man o-ch'eon-weon-eo-ch'i neo-eo-ju-se-yo.*
Please fill it up.	가득 넣어주세요. *Ka-deuk neo-eo-ju-se-yo.*
Please check the <u>battery</u>.	<u>배터리</u> 좀 점검해 주세요. *Pae-t'eo-ri chom cheom-geom-hae chu-se-yo.*
■ the brakes	브레이크 *peu-re-i-k'eu*
■ the carburetor	카뷰레터 *k'a-byu-re-t'eo*
■ the oil	오일 *o-il*
■ the spark plugs	점화전/스파크 플러그 *cheom-hwa-jeon/seu-p'a-k'eu p'eul-leo-geu*
■ the tires	타이어 *t'a-i-eo*
■ the water	물 *mul*
Change the oil.	오일을 바꿔 주세요. *O-il-eul pa-kkweo chu-se-yo.*
Charge the battery.	배터리를 충전해 주세요. *Pae-t'eo-ri-reul ch'ung-jeon-hae chu-se-yo.*
Change this tire.	타이어를 갈아 주세요. *T'a-i-eo-reul ka-ra chu-se-yo.*
Where are the restrooms?	화장실이 어디에요? *Hwa-jang-shi-ri eo-di-e-yo?*

PARKING

Parking can be difficult in the larger cities like Seoul and Busan. Street parking is almost nonexistent, and finding

a parking lot may be difficult. Some hotels offer parking
facilities for their guests.

Excuse me, can I park here?	실례합니다.여기서 주차해도 될까요 ? *Shil-lye-ham-ni-da. Yeo-gi-seo chu-ch'a-hae-do toel-kka-yo?*
Is there any street parking nearby?	이 근처에 주차시킬 도로가 있어요 ? *I keun-ch'eo-e chu-ch'a-shi-k'il to-ro-ga i-sseo-yo?*
Is there a parking lot nearby?	이 근처에 주차장이 있어요 ? *I keun-ch'eo-e chu-ch'a-jang-i i-sseo-yo?*
When does the parking lot <u>open</u>?	주차장은 몇 시에 <u>열어요</u> ? *Chu-ch'a-jang-eun myeot shi-e yeo-reo-yo?*
■ close	닫아요 *ta-da-yo*
What's the parking fee?	주차요금이 얼마예요 ? *Chu-ch'a yo-geum-i eol-ma-ye-yo?*
I'd like to park <u>for one hour</u>.	<u>한 시간</u> 주차하고 싶은데요. *<u>Han shi-gan</u> chu-ch'a-ha-go shi-p'eun-de-yo.*
■ for two hours	두 시간 *tu shi-gan*
■ until noon	열두 시까지 *yeol-ttu shi-kka-ji*
■ until 5:00	다섯 시까지 *ta-seot shi-kka-ji*
■ overnight	하룻밤 *ha-ru-ppam*
■ for a day	하루 *ha-ru*
■ for two days	이틀 *i-t'eul*
Do I leave the key in the car?	열쇠를 차에 놓고 갈까요 ? *Yeol-soe-reul ch'a-e no-k'o kal-kka-yo?*

ACCIDENTS AND REPAIRS

Can you help me?	좀 도와 주시겠어요 ?	*Chom to-wa chu-shi-ge-sseo-yo?*
The engine is overheating.	엔진이 과열되어서요.	*En-jin-i kwa-yeol-doe-eo-sseo-yo.*
It doesn't start.	시동이 걸리지 않아요.	*Shi-dong-i keol-li-ji an-a-yo.*
I have a flat tire.	타이어가 빵꾸났어요.	*T'a-i-eo-ga ppang-kku-na-sseo-yo.*
My car has broken down.	차가 고장났어요.	*Ch'a-ga ko-jang-na-sseo-yo.*
The radiator is leaking.	냉각기가 새요.	*Naeng-gak-kki-ga sae-yo.*
The battery is dead.	배터리가 고장났어요.	*Pae-t'eo-ri-ga ko-jang-na-sseo-yo.*
The keys are locked inside the car.	열쇠를 차안에 놓고 문을 걸었어요.	*Yeol-soe-reul ch'a-an-e no-k'o mun-eul keo-reo-sseo-yo.*
Is there a car repair shop near here?	이 근처에 자동차 정비소가 있어요 ?	*I keun-ch'eo-e cha-dong-ch'a cheong-bi-so-ga i-sseo-yo?*
I need a <u>mechanic</u>.	정비공이 필요한데요.	<u>*Cheong-bi-gong-i*</u> *p'i-ryo-han-de-yo.*
■ tow truck	견인차(가)	*kyeon-in-ch'a(ga)*
Can you <u>push</u> me?	좀 밀어 주시겠어요 ?	*Chom <u>mi-reo</u> chu-shi-ge-sseo-yo?*
■ tow	끌어	*kkeu-reo*

I don't have any tools.	도구가 없어요. *To-gu-ga eop-sseo-yo.*
Can you lend me <u>a flashlight</u>?	플래시 좀 빌려 주시겠어요 ? <u>*P'eul-lae-sshi*</u> *chom pil-lyeo chu-shi-ge-sseo-yo?*
■ a hammer	망치 *mang-ch'i*
■ a jack	잭 *chaek*
■ a wrench	스패너 / 렌치 *seu-p'ae-neo / ren-ch'i*
■ pliers	펜찌 *p'en-jji*
■ a screwdriver	드라이버 *teu-ra-i-beo*
Can you fix my car?	제 차 좀 고쳐 주시겠어요 ? *Che ch'a chom ko-ch'yeo chu-shi-ge-sseo-yo?*
Can you repair it temporarily?	임시로 고칠 수 있어요 ? *Im-shi-ro ko-ch'il su i-sseo-yo?*
Do you have the part?	부품이 있어요 ? *Pu-p'um-i i-sseo-yo?*
I think that there is something wrong with the <u>directional signal</u>.	깜박이가 고장난 것 같아요. <u>*Kkam-ppak-i*</u>*-ga ko-jang-nan keot ka-t'a-yo.*
■ clutch	클러치 (가) *k'eul-leo-ch'i(ga)*
■ electrical system	전기 장치 (가) *cheon-gi chang-ch'i(ga)*
■ engine	엔진 (이) *en-jin(i)*
■ fan	팬 (이) *p'aen(i)*
■ fan belt	팬 벨트 (가) *p'aen pel-t'eu(ga)*
■ fuel pump	연료펌프 (가) *yeol-lyo p'eom-p'eu(ga)*

■ gear shift 변속 기어 (가) *pyeon-sok ki-eo(ga)*

■ headlight 헤드라이트 (가) *he-deu-ra-i-t'eu(ga)*

■ horn 크락션 (이) *k'eu-rak-shyeon(i)*

■ ignition 점화 (가) *cheom-hwa(ga)*

■ radio 라디오 (가) *ra-di-o(ga)*

■ starter 시동 (이) *shi-dong(i)*

■ steering wheel 핸들 (이) *haen-deul(i)*

■ tail light 미등 (이) *mi-deung(i)*

■ transmission 트랜스미션/미션 (이) *t'eu-raen-seu-mi- shyeon/mi-shyeon(i)*

■ water pump 물 펌프 (가) *mul p'eom-p'eu(ga)*

■ windshield wipers 와이퍼 (가) *wa-i-p'eo(ga)*

Is it possible to fix it today? 오늘중으로 수리할 수 있어요 ? *O-neul-jung-eu-ro su-ri-hal su i-sseo-yo?*

How long will it take? 시간이 얼마나 걸릴까요 ? *Shi-gan-i eol-ma-na keol-lil-kka-yo?*

Is everything O.K. now? 이제 다 됐어요 ? *I-je ta twae-sseo-yo?*

How much do I owe you? 얼마지요 ? *Eol-ma-ji-yo?*

ROAD SIGNS IN KOREAN

Most road signs use symbols. You may see some with Korean writing. This list can help you recognize the sign and understand the meaning. Remember that numbers refer to kilometers, not miles.

Road Closed

 No Bicycles

 No Entry

 No Automobiles

 No Right Turn

 No U Turn

 No Passing

No Vehicles Carrying Inflammables

 Minimum Speed

 Maximum Speed

 No Stopping

 No Parking

 Stop

 Slow Down

Crossing by Pedestrians Prohibited

 School Crossing

 Straight or Right Turn

 Left Turn

 Traffic Circle

 Vehicles Only

 Go Straight

Pedestrian Crossing

One Way

Road Divides

Bicycles Only

Pedestrian Path

Snow Tires or Chains

Keep Right

Parking

 Safety Zone

GENERAL INFORMATION

Koreans use two numbering systems, one purely native and one borrowed from Chinese. Pure Korean numbers are used to count objects such as people, countries, months, and one's age. Koreans use Chinese-based numbers mainly when referring to prices, money, and large sums. Korean numbers go only to ninety-nine, after which Chinese numbers must be used.

TELLING TIME

A.M.	오전	*o-jeon*
P.M.	오후	*o-hu*
o'clock	시	*shi*

The following is a list of hours which are read with native Korean numbers. Minutes are read with Chinese-derived numbers.

HOURS

1 o'clock	한시	*han-shi*
2 o'clock	두시	*tu-shi*
3 o'clock	세시	*se-shi*
4 o'clock	네시	*ne-shi*
5 o'clock	다섯시	*ta-seot-shi*
6 o'clock	여섯시	*yeo-seot-shi*

7 o'clock	일곱시	*il-gop-shi*
8 o'clock	여덟시	*yeo-deol-shi*
9 o'clock	아홉시	*a-hop-shi*
10 o'clock	열시	*yeol-shi*
11 o'clock	열한시	*yeol-han-shi*
12 o'clock	열두시	*yeol-ttu-shi*

MINUTES

1 minute	일분	*il-bun*
2 minutes	이분	*i-bun*
3 minutes	삼분	*sam-bun*
4 minutes	사분	*sa-bun*
5 minutes	오분	*o-bun*
6 minutes	육분	*yuk-ppun*
7 minutes	칠분	*ch'il-bun*
8 minutes	팔분	*p'al-bun*
9 minutes	구분	*ku-bun*
10 minutes	십분	*ship-ppun*
11 minutes	십일분	*ship-il-bun*
12 minutes	십이분	*ship-i-bun*
13 minutes	십삼분	*ship-sam-bun*

14 minutes	십사분	*ship-sa-bun*
15 minutes	십오분	*ship-o-bun*
16 minutes	십육분	*shim-nyuk-ppun*
17 minutes	십칠분	*ship-ch'il-bun*
18 minutes	십팔분	*ship-p'al-bun*
19 minutes	십구분	*ship-kku-bun*
20 minutes	이십분	*i-ship-ppun*
21 minutes	이십일분	*i-ship-il-bun*
22 minutes	이십이분	*i-ship-i-bun*
23 minutes	이십삼분	*i-ship-sam-bun*
24 minutes	이십사분	*i-ship-sa-bun*
25 minutes	이십오분	*i-ship-o-bun*
26 minutes	이십육분	*i-shim-nyuk-ppun*
27 minutes	이십칠분	*i-ship-ch'il-bun*
28 minutes	이십팔분	*i-ship-p'al-bun*
29 minutes	이십구분	*i-ship-kku-bun*
30 minutes	삼십분	*sam-ship-ppun*
31 minutes	삼십일분	*sam-ship-il-bun*
32 minutes	삼십이분	*sam-ship-i-bun*
33 minutes	삼십삼분	*sam-ship-sam-bun*
34 minutes	삼십사분	*sam-ship-sa-bun*

35 minutes	삼십오분	*sam-ship-o-bun*
36 minutes	삼십육분	*sam-shim-nyuk-ppun*
37 minutes	삼십칠분	*sam-ship-ch'il-bun*
38 minutes	삼십팔분	*sam-ship-p'al-bun*
39 minutes	삼십구분	*sam-ship-kku-bun*
40 minutes	사십분	*sa-ship-ppun*
41 minutes	사십일분	*sa-ship-il-bun*
42 minutes	사십이분	*sa-ship-i-bun*
43 minutes	사십삼분	*sa-ship-sam-bun*
44 minutes	사십사분	*sa-ship-sa-bun*
45 minutes	사십오분	*sa-ship-o-bun*
46 minutes	사십육분	*sa-shim-nyuk-ppun*
47 minutes	사십칠분	*sa-ship-ch'il-bun*
48 minutes	사십팔분	*sa-ship-p'al-bun*
49 minutes	사십구분	*sa-ship-kku-bun*
50 minutes	오십분	*o-ship-ppun*
51 minutes	오십일분	*o-ship-il-bun*
52 minutes	오십이분	*o-ship-i-bun*
53 minutes	오십삼분	*o-ship-sam-bun*
54 minutes	오십사분	*o-ship-sa-bun*
55 minutes	오십오분	*o-ship-o-bun*

56 minutes	오십육분	*o-shim-nyuk-ppun*
57 minutes	오십칠분	*o-ship-ch'il-bun*
58 minutes	오십팔분	*o-ship-p'al-bun*
59 minutes	오십구분	*o-ship-kku-bun*

COMBINING HOURS AND MINUTES

a quarter after ten	열시 십오분	*yeol-shi ship-o-bun*
a quarter to ten	아홉시 사십오분	*a-hop-shi sa-ship-o-bun*
	or	
	열시 십오분 전	*yeol-shi ship-o-bun cheon*
half past ten	열시 반	*yeol-shi pan*
What time is it?	몇 시예요 ?	*Myeot shi-ye-yo?*
It's 4 o'clock.	네시예요.	*Ne-shi-ye-yo.*

- ■ 4:05 네시 오분 *ne-shi o-bun*
- ■ 4:10 네시 십분 *ne-shi ship-ppun*
- ■ 4:15 네시 십오분 *ne-shi ship-o-bun*
- ■ 4:20 네시 이십분 *ne-shi i-ship-ppun*
- ■ 4:25 네시 이십오분 *ne-shi i-ship-o-bun*

In the following, note that *pan* means *half* and is used as an alternative to *sam-ship-ppun* (thirty minutes). As in English, after 31 minutes past the hour, time may be expressed in two ways. For example, 4:35 is *ne-shi sam-ship-o-bun* (four thirty-five) or *ta-seot-shi i-ship-o-bun cheon* (twenty-five minutes before five).

- ■ 4:30 네시 반 *ne-shi pan*
- ■ 4:35 네시 삼십오분 *ne-shi sam-ship-o-bun*

- 4:40 네시 사십분 *ne-shi sa-ship-ppun*
- 4:45/quarter to five 다섯시 십오분 전 *ta-seot-shi ship-o-bun cheon*
- 4:50/ten to five 다섯시 십분 전 *ta-seot-shi ship-ppun cheon*
- 4:55/five to five 다섯시 오분 전 *ta-seot-shi o-bun cheon*

When discussing airline or railroad timetables, numbers 1 to 59 are used for minutes, not "a quarter to" or "twenty before" the hour. Times are usually posted according to a 24-hour clock; for example, "2:25 p.m." is written "14:25."

The train leaves at 5:50.	기차가 다섯시 오십분에 출발해요. *Ki-ch'a-ga ta-seot-shi o-ship-ppun-e ch'ul-bal-hae-yo.*
The plane arrives at 10:45.	비행기가 열시 사십오분에 도착해요. *Pi-haeng-gi-ga yeol-shi sa-ship-o-bun-e to-ch'ak-k'ae-yo.*

DAYS OF THE WEEK

Sunday	일요일	*i-ryo-il*
Monday	월요일	*weo-ryo-il*
Tuesday	화요일	*hwa-yo-il*
Wednesday	수요일	*su-yo-il*
Thursday	목요일	*mo-gyo-il*
Friday	금요일	*keum-yo-il*
Saturday	토요일	*t'o-yo-il*

MONTHS OF THE YEAR

January	일월	*i-rweol*
February	이월	*i-weol*
March	삼월	*sam-weol*
April	사월	*sa-weol*
May	오월	*o-weol*
June	유월	*yu-weol*
July	칠월	*ch'i-rweol*
August	팔월	*p'a-rweol*
September	구월	*ku-weol*
October	시월	*shi-weol*
November	십일월	*ship-i-rweol*
December	십이월	*ship-i-weol*

THE FOUR SEASONS

spring	봄	*pom*
summer	여름	*yeo-reum*
fall	가을	*ka-eul*
winter	겨울	*kyeo-ul*

TIME PHRASES

today	오늘	*o-neul*
yesterday	어제	*eo-je*
the day before yesterday	그저께	*keu-jeo-kke*
tomorrow	내일	*nae-il*
the day after tomorrow	모레	*mo-re*
two days after tomorrow	글피	*keul-p'i*
this week	이번주	*i-beon-jju*
last week	지난주	*chi-nan-ju*
next week	다음주	*tae-um-jju*
for one week	일주일간	*il-jju-il-gan*
for two weeks	이주일간	*i-ju-il-gan*
for one day	하루	*ha-ru*
for two days	이틀간	*i-t'eul-gan*
three days ago	삼일 전	*sam-il cheon*
four months ago	사개월 전	*sa-gae-weol cheon*
five years ago	오년 전	*o-nyeon cheon*
this year	금년	*keum-nyeon*

last year	작년	*chang-nyeon*
next year	내년	*nae-nyeon*
at night	밤에	*pam-e*
in summer	여름에	*yeo-reum-e*
in winter	겨울에	*kyeo-u-re*
by Tuesday	화요일까지	*hwa-yo-il-kka-ji*
by June	유월까지	*yu-weol-kka-ji*
by morning	아침까지	*a-ch'im-kka-ji*
this morning	오늘 아침	*o-neul a-ch'im*
this afternoon	오늘 오후	*o-neul o-hu*
this evening	오늘 저녁	*o-neul cheon-yeok*
tonight	오늘 밤	*o-neul ppam*
tomorrow night	내일 밤	*nae-il ppam*
for six years	육년간	*yung-nyeon-gan*
for seven months	칠개월간	*ch'il-gae-weol-gan*
in the morning	아침에	*a-ch'im-e*
in the afternoon	오후에	*o-hu-e*
in the evening	저녁에	*cheon-yeok-e*
What's today's date?	오늘은 며칠이에요 ?	*O-neu-reun myeo-ch'il-i-e-yo?*
It's _____.	_____이에요.	*_____-i-e-yo.*

Note: In Korea, the full date is usually written with the year first, followed by the month and then the day. For example, August 8, 2009 would be written:

2009년 8월 8일

The date would be read: *i-ch'eon-gu-nyeon* (2009); *p'a-rweol* (August); *p'a-ril* (8th)

What day is today?	오늘은 무슨 요일이에요 ?	*O-neu-reun mu-seun yo-il-i-e-yo?*
It's _____.	_____ 이에요.	_____ *-i-e-yo.*

DAYS OF THE MONTH

The days of the month are usually named with Chinese-derived numerals. These numerals can also be used for counting days (e.g., five days 오일/*o-il*; 12 days 십이일/*ship-i-il*, etc.).

1st	일일	*i-ril*
2nd	이일	*i-il*
3rd	삼일	*sam-il*
4th	사일	*sa-il*
5th	오일	*o-il*
6th	육일	*yuk-il*
7th	칠일	*ch'i-ril*
8th	팔일	*p'a-ril*
9th	구일	*ku-il*
10th	십일	*ship-il*

11th	십일일	*ship-i-ril*
12th	십이일	*ship-i-il*
13th	십삼일	*ship-sam-il*
14th	십사일	*ship-sa-il*
15th	십오일	*ship-o-il*
16th	십육일	*shim-nyuk-il*
17th	십칠일	*ship-ch'i-ril*
18th	십팔일	*ship-p'a-ril*
19th	십구일	*ship-kku-il*
20th	이십일	*i-ship-il*
21st	이십일일	*i-ship-i-ril*
22nd	이십이일	*i-ship-i-il*
23rd	이십삼일	*i-ship-sam-il*
24th	이십사일	*i-ship-sa-il*
25th	이십오일	*i-ship-o-il*
26th	이십육일	*i-shim-nyuk-il*
27th	이십칠일	*i-ship-ch'i-ril*
28th	이십팔일	*i-ship-p'a-ril*
29th	이십구일	*i-ship-kku-il*
30th	삼십일	*sam-ship-il*
31st	삼십일일	*sam-ship-i-ril*

COUNTING YEARS

one year	일년	*il-lyeon*
two years	이년	*i-nyeon*
three years	삼년	*sam-nyeon*
four years	사년	*sa-nyeon*
five years	오년	*o-nyeon*
six years	육년	*yung-nyeon*
seven years	칠년	*ch'il-lyeon*
eight years	팔년	*p'al-lyeon*
nine years	구년	*ku-nyeon*
ten years	십년	*shim-nyeon*

COUNTING DAYS

Chinese-derived numerals, which are listed above under "Days of the Month," are usually used for counting days. The native Korean words listed below may-also be used for counting a small number of days.

one day	하루	*ha-ru*
two days	이틀	*i-t'eul*
three days	사흘	*sa-heul*
four days	나흘	*na-heul*

five days	닷새	*tat-sae*
six days	엿새	*yeot-sae*
seven days	이레	*i-re*
eight days	여드레	*yeo-deu-re*
nine days	아흐레	*a-heu-re*
ten days	열흘	*yeo-reul*

COUNTING WEEKS

one week	일 주일	*il jju-il*
two weeks	이 주일	*i chu-il*
three weeks	삼 주일	*sam chu-il*
four weeks	사 주일	*sa chu-il*
five weeks	오 주일	*o chu-il*
six weeks	육 주일	*yuk jju-il*
seven weeks	칠 주일	*ch'il jju-il*
eight weeks	팔 주일	*p'al jju-il*
nine weeks	구 주일	*ku chu-il*
ten weeks	십 주일	*ship jju-il*

COUNTING TIMES

once	한 번	*han peon*
twice	두 번	*tu peon*
three times	세 번	*se peon*
four times	네 번	*ne peon*
five times	다섯 번	*ta-seot ppeon*
the first time	첫 번째	*ch'eot ppeon-jjae*
the second time	두 번째	*tu peon-jjae*
the third time	세 번째	*se peon-jjae*
the fourth time	네 번째	*ne peon-jjae*
the fifth time	다섯 번째	*ta-seot ppeon-jjae*

COUNTING DIFFERENT KINDS OF THINGS

When counting things, the number normally follows what is being counted, followed by a special classifier. Korean numbers are usually used, although some require the Chinese-derived numerals.

Please give me three sheets of paper.	종이 세 장 주세요.	*Chong-i se chang chu-se-yo.* (*se* is "three"; *chang* is the classifier for thin, flat objects)

The table below lists some of the most common classifiers.

	1	**2**	**3**
people	한 사람 *han sa-ram*	두 사람 *tu sa-ram*	세 사람 *se sa-ram*
honored people	한 분 *han pun*	두 분 *tu pun*	세 분 *se pun*
pencils sticks brushes	한 자루 *han cha-ru*	두 자루 *tu cha-ru*	세 자루 *se cha-ru*
paper bills tickets	한 장 *han chang*	두 장 *tu chang*	세 장 *se chang*
notebooks magazines books	한 권 *han kweon*	두 권 *tu kweon*	세 권 *se kweon*
vehicles machines	한 대 *han tae*	두 대 *tu tae*	세 대 *se tae*
packages boxes	한 갑 *han kap*	두 갑 *tu kap*	세 갑 *se kap*
buildings houses	한 채 *han ch'ae*	두 채 *tu ch'ae*	세 채 *se ch'ae*
bottles	한 병 *han pyeong*	두 병 *tu pyeong*	세 병 *se pyeong*
animals fish	한 마리 *han ma-ri*	두 마리 *tu ma-ri*	세 마리 *se ma-ri*
floors of a building	일 층 *il ch'eung*	이 층 *i ch'eung*	삼 층 *sam ch'eung*

Note: For many items and objects not listed above, *kae* is used. You will also be understood if you use it for items above when you cannot remember the appropriate classifier.

한 개	두 개	세 개
han kae	*tu kae*	*se kae*

NATIONAL HOLIDAYS AND SPECIAL DAYS

January 1
New Year's Day
신정/설날 *Shin-jeong/Seol-lal*

Lunar New Year
구정/설날 *Ku-jeong/Seol-lal*

Depending on the family's preferences, New Year's Day is celebrated according to either the solar or lunar calendar. It is an important holiday for Koreans, with family members getting together for festive meals.

March 1
Independence Day
삼일절 *Sam-il-jeol*

Commemoration of the March 1, 1919 independence movement against the Japanese occupation of Korea.

Eighth Day, Fourth
Lunar Month
Buddha's Birthday
사월 초파일 *Sa-weol ch'o-p'a-il*

Ceremonies are conducted in Buddhist temples across the country to celebrate the event.

May 1
Labor Day
노동절 *No-dong-jeol*

Although Labor Day is not a national holiday, some establishments are closed, and many people enjoy a day off.

May 5   어린이날   *Eo-rin-i-nal*
Children's Day

A day to celebrate the youth of Korea.

May 8   어버이 날   *Eo-beo-i nal*
Parents' Day

A day of recognition for parents.

June 6   현충일   *Hyeon-ch'ung-il*
Memorial Day

A tribute to those who died in war.

July 17   제헌절   *Che-heon-jeol*
Constitution Day

Observance of the proclamation of the Constitution on
July 17, 1948.

August 15   광복절   *Kwang-bok-jjeol*
Liberation Day

Commemoration of the Japanese acceptance of Allied
terms of surrender in 1945, which included the liberation of
Korea.

Fifteenth Day,   추석   *Ch'u-seok*
Eighth Lunar Month
Chuseok

A very important holiday in Korea, *Chuseok* is a
thanksgiving celebration in early fall marked with visiting
family members and paying respect to ancestors.

October 1   국군의 날   *Kuk-kkun-eui nal*
Armed Forces Day

This day is celebrated with colorful parades and military
ceremonies.

October 3 National Foundation Day	개천절	*Kae-ch'eon-jeol*

The commemoration of the founding of Korea by the legendary *Dangun*, who is said to have established the kingdom of Choson in 2333 B.C.

October 9 Hangeul Day	한글날	*Han-geul-lal*

The anniversary of the promulgation of *Hangeul*, the Korean script developed in 1443 during the reign of King Sejong.

December 25 Christmas Day	성탄절/크리스마스날	*Seong-t'an-jeol/K'eu-ri-seu-ma-seu-nal*

COUNTRIES

Argentina	아르헨티나	*A-reu-hen-t'i-na*
Australia	호주	*Ho-ju*
Austria	오스트리아	*O-seu-t'eu-ri-a*
Belgium	벨기에	*Pel-gi-e*
Bolivia	볼리비아	*Pol-li-bi-a*
Brazil	브라질	*Peu-ra-jil*
Burma (Myanmar)	버마	*Peo-ma*
Canada	캐나다	*K'ae-na-da*
Chile	칠레	*Ch'il-le*
People's Republic of China	중화 인민 공화국/중공	*Chung-hwa in-min kong-hwa-guk/Chung-gong*

Republic of China (Taiwan)	중화 민국/대만	*Chung-hwa min-guk/Tae-man*
Colombia	콜롬비아	*K'ol-lom-bi-a*
The Democratic People's Republic of Korea (North Korea)	조선 민주주의 인민공화국(북한)	*Cho-seon min-ju-ju-eu-i in-min-gong-hwa-guk(Puk-han)*
Denmark	덴마크	*Den-ma-k'eu*
Ecuador	에콰도르	*E-k'wa-do-reu*
Egypt	이집트	*I-jip-t'eu*
England	영국	*Yeong-guk*
Finland	핀란드	*P'il-lan-deu*
France	프랑스/불란서	*P'eu-rang-seu/Pul-lan-seo*
Germany	독일	*To-gil*
Greece	그리이스	*Keu-ri-i-seu*
India	인도	*In-do*
Indonesia	인도네시아	*In-do-ne-shi-a*
Iran	이란	*I-ran*
Iraq	이라크	*I-ra-k'eu*
Ireland	아일랜드	*A-il-laen-deu*
Israel	이스라엘	*I-seu-ra-el*
Italy	이탈리아/이태리	*I-t'al-li-a/I-t'ae-ri*

Japan	일본 *Il-bon*
Jordan	요르단 *Yo-reu-dan*
Kuwait	쿠웨이트 *K'u-we-i-t'eu*
Lebanon	레바논 *Re-ba-non*
Malaysia	말레이지아 *Mal-le-i-j-i-a*
Mexico	멕시코 *Mek-shi-k'o*
Netherlands	네덜란드 *Ne-deol-lan-deu*
New Zealand	뉴질랜드 *Nyu-jil-laen-deu*
Norway	노르웨이 *No-reu-we-i*
Pakistan	파키스탄 *P'a-k'i-seu-t'an*
Peru	페루 *P'e-ru*
Philippines	필리핀 *P'il-li-p'in*
Poland	폴란드 *P'ol-lan-deu*
Portugal	포르투갈 *P'o-reu-t'u-gal*
Russia	소련/러시아 *So-ryeon/Reo-shi-a*
Saudi Arabia	사우디 아라비아 *Sa-u-di a-ra-bi-a*
Singapore	싱가포르 *Shing-ga-p'o-reu*
South Africa	남 아프리카 공화국 *Nam a-p'eu-ri-k'a kong-hwa-guk*
Spain	스페인 *Seu-p'e-in*
Sweden	스웨덴 *Seu-we-den*

Switzerland	스위스	*Seu-wi-seu*
Thailand	타이/태국	*T'a-i/T'ae-guk*
Turkey	터어키	*T'eo-eo-k'i*
United States	미국	*Mi-guk*
Uruguay	우루과이	*U-ru-gwa-i*
Venezuela	베네수엘라	*Pe-ne-su-el-la*
Vietnam	베트남	*Pe-t'eu-nam*

NATIONALITIES

Nationalities are commonly expressed by adding *sa-ram* to the name of the country. Thus, "American" becomes *Mi-guk sa-ram.* When inquiring as to a person's nationality, you may say *Han-guk sa-ram-i-se-yo?* (Are you Korean?)

SIGNS

The following signs are presented so that you can associate them with their meaning.

입구	Entrance
출구	Exit
비상구	Emergency Exit
입장금지	No Entrance
화장실	Toilet
여자용/숙녀용	Women

남자용/신사용	Men
위험	Danger
출입금지	Keep Out
소화기	Fire Extinguisher
안내	Information
열렸음	Open
닫혔음	Closed
금연	No Smoking
병원	Hospital
미시오	Push
당기시오	Pull
개조심	Beware of Dog
둠/주차	Parking
출납계	Cashier
정지	Stop
판매	For Sale
품절/매진	Sold Out
낚시금지	No Fishing
수영금지	No Swimming

METRIC CONVERSIONS

Here are some tables and conversion charts that will be useful during your visit to Korea.

SOME CONVENIENT ROUGH EQUIVALENTS

These rough equivalents will help you deal with the metric system when you are not able to make exact calculations.

3 kilometers	= 2 miles
30 grams	= 1 ounce
100 grams	= 3.5 ounces
1 kilogram	= 2 pounds
1 liter	= 1 quart
1 hectare	= 1 acre

CENTIMETERS/INCHES

For an idea of how inches and centimeters compare, look at the guide below.

To convert centimeters into inches, multiply by .39.
To convert inches into centimeters, multiply by 2.54.

CENTIMETERS

INCHES

METERS/FEET

1 meter = 39.37 inches   1 foot = 0.3 meters
      = 3.28 feet   1 yard = 0.9 meters
      = 1.09 yards

Check your height in meters.

FEET/INCHES	METERS/CENTIMETERS
5	1.52
5.1	1.545
5.2	1.57
5.3	1.59
5.4	1.62
5.5	1.645
5.6	1.68
5.7	1.705
5.8	1.73
5.9	1.755
5.10	1.78
5.11	1.805
6	1.83
6.1	1.855

LIQUID MEASUREMENTS

1 liter = 1.06 quarts
4 liters = 1.06 gallons

A fast way to get an approximation: multiply the number of gallons by 4 to get liters; divide the number of liters by 4 to get gallons.

WHEN YOU WEIGH YOURSELF

1 kilogram	= 2.2 pounds
1 pound	= 0.45 kilograms

KILOGRAMS	POUNDS
40	88
45	99
50	110
55	121
60	132
65	143
70	154
75	165
80	176
85	187
90	198
95	209
100	220

QUICK GRAMMAR GUIDE

The following grammatical descriptions are provided to give you a deeper understanding of how the Korean language works.

LANGUAGE FAMILY

It is generally believed that Korean belongs to the Altaic language family, along with Turkish, Tungusic, and Mongolian. These languages share such common features as an absence of gender, articles, inflection and relative pronouns. One of the most striking similarities among these languages is the agglutinative process, whereby linguistic units are formed by putting together single elements, each with a distinct meaning.

For example, the Korean phrase, 가시겠어요 / *ka-shi-ge-sseo-yo*, has the elements 가 (to go), 시 (honorific marker), 겠 (future tense marker), and 요 (politeness marker and sentence conclusion).

In addition to developing an extensive collection of native words, Korean has borrowed heavily from Chinese, and more recently, English.

WORD ORDER

The basic word order of a Korean sentence is subject-object verb.

제가	한국어를	공부해요.
I	Korean	study
Che-ga	*Han-guk-eo-reul*	*kong-bu-hae-yo.*

The key element of a Korean sentence is the verb. It usually comes at the end of the sentence and is preceded by the subject, object, as well as any time or place words.

어제	제가	학교에서	한국어를	공부했어요.
yesterday	I	at school	Korean	studied
Eo-je	*che-ga*	*hak-kkyo-e-seo*	*Han-guk-eo-reul*	*kong-bu-hae-sseo-yo.*

PARTICLES

Particles are used in Korean to establish the relationship between words in the sentence. Some of the most important particles are listed below.

한국어<u>가</u> 재미있어요.
Han-guk-eo-<u>ga</u> chae-mi-i-sseo-yo.

Korean is interesting.

In this sentence, *ga* (가) is the subject particle. When a subject ends in a consonant, *i* (이) is used. *Eun* (은) and *neun* (는) are also subject particles.

제가 한국어<u>를</u> 공부하고 있어요.
Che-ga Han-guk-eo-<u>reul</u> kong-bu-ha-go i-sseo-yo.

I study Korean.

Reul is the object marker. When objects end in a consonant, *eul* is used.

한국어를 공부하고 계<u>세</u>요 ?
Han-guk-eo-reul kong-bu-ha-go kye-<u>se</u>-yo?

Do you study Korean?

Se is the contraction of *shi* (honorific marker) and *eo*, which is part of the ending *-i-eo-yo*. *Se* is used to show respect to the person to whom the question is asked.

학교<u>에서</u> 공부하세요 ?
Hak-kkyo-<u>e-seo</u> kong-bu-ha-se-yo?

Do you study at school?

In this sentence, the particle *e-seo* is used to mean "at."

서울<u>에</u> 가세요 ?
Seo-ul-<u>e</u> ka-se-yo?

Are you going to Seoul?

In this sentence, the particle *e* is used to mean "to."

LEVELS OF FORMALITY

Koreans use a variety of levels of formality, depending on the relationship between speakers. The following are five different ways of saying "I will eat." Relative differences in age, gender, social status, and length of acquaintance are some of the factors considered by Koreans when deciding which of the levels to use.

먹겠습니다. *Meok-kke-sseum-ni-da.* (I will eat.)	formal, polite
먹겠어요. *Meok-kke-sseo-yo.*	informal, polite
먹겠어. *Meok-kke-sseo.*	intimate, with a younger sibling or close friend
먹겠다. *Meok-kket-tta.*	plain, to a child or close friend
먹겠소. *Meok-kke-sso.*	authoritative, with a subordinate

This book uses the informal, yet polite *yo* form and occasionally the formal, polite *im-ni-da* form. Use of the other levels will take some careful study of both Korean language and culture, but once mastered will enable you not only to convey more of what you mean, but also what you feel to the listener.

PRONOUNS

Subject and object pronouns may be omitted when the context makes them unnecessary. Thus, in the sentence, "I enjoyed the meal," Koreans omit "I" since it can be inferred from the context.

잘　　　　　　　　　　　　먹었어요.
Chal　　　　　　　　　　*meo-geo-sseo-yo.*
well　　　　　　　　　　　　ate
(literally, "I ate well.")

On the other hand, if you are insisting to your friend that you want to pay the bill in a restaurant, you would include "I" in the sentence, "I will pay."

제가　　　　　　　　　　　내겠어요.
Che-ga　　　　　　　　　*nae-ge-sseo-yo.*
I　　　　　　　　　　　　　will pay.

Similarly, the object pronoun "me" can be omitted when it is clear from the context, as in:

담배　　　　　　한 갑　　　　　　주세요.
Tam-bae　　　*han kap*　　　*chu-se-yo.*
cigarettes　　　one pack　　　give
(Give me a pack of cigarettes.)

TYPES OF VERBS

Verbs in Korean can be classified into three types:

DESCRIPTIVE VERBS

These words are used like adjectives in English, but are inflected as verbs in Korean.

한국어가 어려워요.　　　　　　Korean is difficult.
Han-guk-eo-ga eo-ryeo-weo-yo.

We can also put the linking verb in this category since it links the subject with its descriptor.

그 분은 선생님이에요.　　　　　He is a teacher.
Keu pun-eun seon-saeng-nim-i-e-yo.

그 사람은 학생이 아니에요.　　　He is not a student.
Keu sa-ram-eun hak-ssaeng-i a-ni-e-yo.

VERBS OF EXISTENCE

The following verbs are used to indicate when someone or something exists or does not exist.

지도가 있어요.　　　　　　　　　　I have a map.
Chi-do-ga i-sseo-yo.

돈이 없어요.　　　　　　　　　　　I have no money.
Ton-i eop-sseo-yo.

ACTION VERBS

This type of Korean verb expresses an action.

그 사람이 공부해요.　　　　He is studying.
Keu sa-ram-i kong-bu-hae-yo.

저는 부산에 안 가요.　　　I'm not going to Busan.
Cheo-neun Pu-san-e an ka-yo.

VERB TENSES

The following are examples of how action verbs can be used to express the present, past, and future tenses.

집에 가요.
Chip-e ka-yo.

I'm (We're, He's, They're) going home. (This form may also be used to express future time, as well as first and third person singular and plural.)

그는 집에 갔어요.
Keu-neun chip-e ka-sseo-yo.

He went home.

집에 가겠어요.
Chip-e ka-ge-sseo-yo.

I intend to go home.

More complex expressions, such as presumption, immediate present, probability, and so forth, are formed by adding various infixes to the verb phrase.

NOUN MODIFIERS

In the Korean language, verbs are used to modify nouns in the way other languages use adjectives and relative clauses. For example, to form the construction, "a small house," the descriptive verb, 작다/*chak-tta*, is attached to "house" by adding 은/*eun* to the stem:

작은	집
Chak-eun	*chip*
small	house

Similarly, to make the phrase, "the man whom I met yesterday," the action verb, 만나다/*man-na-da*, is connected to "man" by adding ㄴ/*n* to the stem.

제가	어제	만난 사람
Che-ga	*eo-je*	*man-nan sa-ram*
I	yesterday	met man

WRITING SYSTEM

Koreans are deservedly proud of their phonetic writing system called *Hangeul*. Developed by King Sejong of the Yi Dynasty in 1443, it was designed to make Korean easy to read. Until *Hangeul* was invented, Koreans relied on Chinese characters for reading and writing their language.

With the advent of *Hangeul*, the literacy rate in Korea improved dramatically to what is now one of the highest in the world. One of the most remarkable aspects of the system is the way in which the shape of the consonants resembles the shape of the mouth and tongue as they form the corresponding sounds. Koreans continue to celebrate the development of this original invention on *Hangeul* Day, October 9.

THE HANGEUL ALPHABET

Vowels / Consonants	ㅏ	ㅑ	ㅓ	ㅕ	ㅗ	ㅛ	ㅜ	ㅠ	ㅡ	ㅣ
ㄱ	가	갸	거	겨	고	교	구	규	그	기
ㄴ	나	냐	너	녀	노	뇨	누	뉴	느	니
ㄷ	다	댜	더	뎌	도	됴	두	듀	드	디
ㄹ	라	랴	러	려	로	료	루	류	르	리
ㅁ	마	먀	머	며	모	묘	무	뮤	므	미
ㅂ	바	뱌	버	벼	보	뵤	부	뷰	브	비
ㅅ	사	샤	서	셔	소	쇼	수	슈	스	시
ㅇ	아	야	어	여	오	요	우	유	으	이
ㅈ	자	쟈	저	져	조	죠	주	쥬	즈	지
ㅊ	차	챠	처	쳐	초	쵸	추	츄	츠	치
ㅋ	카	캬	커	켜	코	쿄	쿠	큐	크	키
ㅌ	타	탸	터	텨	토	툐	투	튜	트	티
ㅍ	파	퍄	퍼	펴	포	표	푸	퓨	프	피
ㅎ	하	햐	허	혀	호	효	후	휴	흐	히

NOTES ABOUT KOREAN LANGUAGE AND CULTURE

GENERAL NOTES

1. Tipping is generally not required.

2. As when traveling in any country, protect your valuables.

3. For major purchases, shop at places recommended by a friend or acquaintance and compare prices.

4. Bargain seriously with the merchant only if you intend to buy and only if the price difference is sizable.

5. When eating or drinking with a Korean, don't suggest splitting the bill. One or the other person should pay for the entire bill. If you do not pay, try to reciprocate at a later date.

6. Be prepared to sing a song, preferably a Korean one, during social events.

7. Ask before photographing someone.

8. Ask for someone to write your destinations in Korean. Keep the business card of your hotel in case you need help in relocating it.

9. Koreans enjoy getting to know you, so do not be surprised if they ask you personal questions, such as your age, marital status, or salary.

10. For more information on tourism in Korea, contact the Korea Tourism Organization.

LEARNING KOREAN ON YOUR OWN

Congratulations! You have decided to learn Korean. You have recognized the many advantages that will result from learning one of the important languages of the Far East. *Korean at a Glance* will be very helpful in giving you the language needed for basic survival. It also provides a great deal of cultural information to help you connect the language with the Korean people and their country.

How much Korean you actually learn depends on many factors, such as the length of time you study, your own motivation, and the amount of exposure you have to the language. A lot depends on you and how you approach the task. The information provided below is designed to help you put *Korean at a Glance* to best use.

1. The romanized words and phrases in *Korean at a Glance* will help you get started, but it is important for you to listen carefully to the pronunciation of native speakers. It may be useful to ask a Korean to make an audio tape of parts of *Korean at a Glance* so that you can listen to the language as you work on your pronunciation and intonation.

2. Establish a relationship with a Korean who can help you work your way into the language. This person may not become your teacher in a formal sense; but he or she may be simply your informant, available to answer questions or check your pronunciation. You should take care to try to speak as much Korean as possible with this person. If you end up just speaking English, you will not learn much Korean.

3. Learn to read Korean as soon as possible. *Hangeul* can make you literate in Korean, just as it has thousands of Koreans over the centuries. It is a marvelously phonetic system and not too difficult to master. By learning to read it, you will be able to read the Korean in this book and elsewhere, as well as improve your pronunciation.

4. If you pick up a word or phrase, try it in a sentence. The pronunciation of words often changes when they are

placed with other words. Learning the entire sentence will also help you remember the word and expressions.

5. As you learn new expressions, remember to check their appropriateness. You should determine if the expressions are used in formal or informal situations, with adults or children, friends or strangers, etc. This is especially important with words you find in the dictionary.

6. When you learn something new, try to fit it into something you already know. If you know how to say, "This is my passport," and you learn "driver's license" later, try to make the sentence, "This is my driver's license." By recycling the expressions in this way, you will remember both the old and new things more easily.

7. Choose a few words and expressions that you will try to use each day. Look through *Korean at a Glance* and select a few expressions that you want to try. Note them in the book, or write them on a small piece of paper, for easy reference. During the day, look for situations where you can try out the expressions. Each time you make the effort to use them, you will improve. By limiting each day what you try, you will concentrate on what you *do* know and not be frustrated about what you *don't* know.

8. In general, Koreans will be impressed with your effort to learn their language. They do not expect accomplished perfection among those foreigners who are studying their language. Most of the Koreans you meet have studied English for several years and know well the frustrations of the language learner. Therefore, rather than worrying about making a mistake, think about making a positive impression! You will, if you keep trying even the most elementary Korean in your associations with the Korean people.

KOREAN PROVERBS

Koreans add color and clarity to their language through the use of proverbs. By studying them you can gain valuable insight into Korean culture. They will also give you something simple to say in those situations where more complicated language is beyond your ability. The literal translation is in quotation marks followed by an explanation.

금강산도 식후경.   *Keum-gang-san-do shik-k'u-gyeong.*

"Even Diamond Mountain should be seen after eating."
When one is deciding on whether to eat or do something else, eating should take priority.

둘이 먹다가 한 사람 죽어도 모른다.   *Tu-ri meok-tta-ga han sa-ram chu-geo-do mo-reun-da.*

"While two are eating, one could die and the other wouldn't know."
When eating a delicious meal, we are not conscious of anything else.

남의 떡이 더 크게 보인다.   *Nam-eui tteok-i teo k'eu-ge po-in-da.*

"The other person's rice cake looks bigger."
Someone else's situation always looks better.

그림의 떡이다.   *Keu-rim-eui tteok-i-da.*

"Rice cakes in a picture."
To long for something, but be unable to have it.

시작이 반이다.   *Shi-jak-i pan-i-da.*

"Starting is half."
A job begun is half completed.

수박 겉 핥기.   *Su-bak keot hal-kki.*

"Licking the outside of a watermelon."
Just scratching the surface, not dealing with something in depth.

고생한 보람 있다.　*Ko-saeng-han po-ram it-tta.*

"There are rewards for hard times."
We will be rewarded for enduring hard times.

눈코 뜰새가 없다.　*Nun-k'o tteul-ssae-ga eop-tta.*

"No time to open the eyes or the nose."
Too much to do, too little time to do it.

등잔 밑이 어둡다.　*Teung-jan mi-ch'i eo-dup-tta.*

"It is dark at the base of a lamp."
A lost item is most difficult to find when it is right in front of
us. A related meaning is that we tend not to know about the
affairs in our own immediate surroundings.

소 잃고 외양간 고친다.　*So il-kko woe-yang-kkan ko-ch'in-da.*

"Fixing the stable door after losing the ox."
Used to describe a belated effort to overcome a mistake.

눈치코치도 없다.　*Nun-ch'i-k'o-ch'i-do eop-tta.*

"Not only no eye sense, no nose sense."
Used about someone who has no ability to read the feelings
or sense the needs of others.

빈 수레가 더 요란하다.　*Pin su-re-ga teo yo-ran-ha-da.*

"An empty pushcart makes more noise."
The most talkative people are often those who know the
least.

우이독경.　*U-i-dok-kkyeong.*

"Reading into an ox's ear."
Used to describe the futility of trying to influence someone who
is too stubborn or otherwise unable to benefit from our effort.

동문서답.　*Tong-mun-seo-dap.*

"East question, west answer."
When someone gives an answer which is unrelated to the
question.

우물안 개구리.　*U-mul-an kae-gu-ri.*

"A frog in a well."
Used to describe someone who lacks vision or a broad
perspective.

개천에서 용 난다.　*Kae-ch'eon-e-seo yong nan-da.*

"A dragon emerges from a ditch."
Used to describe a situation where a person from a poor
background attains a privileged position. (The dragon
symbolizes a person in the highest position, such as a king or
ruler.)

고래 싸움에 새우등 터진다.　*Ko-rae ssa-um-e sae-u-
deung t'eo-jin-da.*

"Shrimps' backs are broken in a whale fight."
Small people are hurt when large people fight. For example,
small countries suffer when super powers are at war.

작은 고추가 맵다.　*Cha-geun ko-ch'u-ga maep-tta.*

"A small pepper is hot."
Small people have the fortitude and toughness to accomplish
things.

호랑이도 제말하면 온다.　*Ho-rang-i-do che-mal-ha-
myeon on-da.*

"A tiger comes when spoken about."
When someone walks into a room where he/she has just been
the topic of conversation.

오는 정이 있어야 가는 정이 있다.　*O-neun cheong-i i-
sseo-ya ka-neun cheong-i it-tta.*

"Love must come before it can go."
Before love can be given, it must be received.

KOREAN FOLK SONG

"Arirang" may be Korea's most widely recognized folk song. There are many versions of "Arirang." The basic version presented here is the story of a jilted lover who hopes that the one who is departing will develop sore feet before going ten *ri* (about two and a half miles) and therefore be forced to return.

A – ri- rang – a – ri- rang – a – ra – ri – yo.
A – ri- rang – ko – gae – ro – neo – meo – gan da.
Na – reul peo – – ri – go – ka – shi-neu-ni – meun
Shim – ni-do – mot – kka – seo – pal – byeong-nan da.

Arirang, Arirang, Arari, O—
Crossing over Arirang Pass
The lover who has left me and gone away
Will not go ten ri before his feet will hurt.

DICTIONARY

HOW TO USE THIS DICTIONARY

The following are most of the important words found in *Korean at a Glance*, plus some other useful vocabulary items. To help you use verbs in actual conversation, the dictionary provides the simple present tense form, as well as the basic form of the verb.

For example, with the English verb "to borrow," the dictionary gives you the basic form, followed by the simple present tense form in parentheses.

to borrow   *pil-li-da(pil-lyeo-yo)*   빌리다(빌려요)

Since adjectives in Korean are inflected like verbs, the inflection is provided in parentheses, as shown below. The inflection is used in conversation, while the basic form will help you in making other constructions with the word.

to be cheap   *ssa-da(ssa-yo)*   싸다(싸요)

Parentheses are also used to indicate when something is optional in a Korean expression. For example, the Korean word for "electric light" may be either *ppul* or *cheon-gi ppul*. This option is indicated as *(cheon-gi) ppul* in the dictionary. Parentheses are also used to clarify meanings, such as "to be hot (spicy)" or "football (American)."

A slash is used when alternative meanings are provided. Depending on the context, for example, the Korean word for "what kind" is either of the following: *mu-seun/eo-tteon*. Similarly, since two choices are given for the English equivalent of the Korean word, *ip-jjang-nyo*, they are written in the dictionary as "admission fee/cover charge."

ENGLISH-KOREAN
DICTIONARY

A

abalone *cheon-bok* 전복

abscess (to have an) *chong-gi-ga na-da(na-yo)* 종기가 나다(나요)

accident *sa-go* 사고

activity *haeng-sa* 행사

actor *pae-u* 배우

acupressure *chi-ap* 지압

acupressurist *chi-ap-sa* 지압사

acupuncture *ch'im-ch'i-ryo* 침치료

acupuncturist *ch'im-sul-sa* 침술사

address *chu-so* 주소

adhesive tape *cheop-ch'ak t'e-i-p'eu* 접착 테이프

admission fee *ip-jjang-nyo* 입장료

in advance *mi-ri* 미리

aerogram *hang-gong yeop-seo* 항공 엽서

Africa *A-p'eu-ri-k'a* 아프리카

after *hu-e* 후에

afternoon *o-hu* 오후

again *ta-shi* 다시

age *na-i* 나이

age (honorific) *yeon-se* 연세

air conditioner *e-eo-k'on* 에어콘

air mail *hang-gong-p'yeon* 항공편

air mattress *ko-mu-ch'im-dae* 고무침대

airplane *pi-haeng-gi* 비행기

airport *kong-hang* 공항

aisle *t'ong-no* 통로

alcohol *al-k'ol* 알콜

allergy *al-le-reu-gi* 알레르기

alley *kol-mok* 골목

to be all right to _____ _____-do toe-da(twae-yo) _____도 되다(돼요)

alone *hon-ja* 혼자

also *to* 도

to alter *ko-ch'i-da(ko-ch'yeo-yo)* 고치다(고쳐요)

always *hang-sang* 항상

ambulance *ku-geup-ch'a* 구급차

America *Mi-guk* 미국

American (person) *Mi-guk sa-ram* 미국 사람

American Embassy *Mi-guk tae-sa-gwan* 미국 대사관

amethyst *cha-su-jeong* 자수정

anchovies (stir-fried) *myeol-ch'i-bo-kkeum* 멸치볶음

and *wa/gwa* 와/과

ankle *pal-mok* 발목

antacid *che-san-je* 제산제

antibiotic *hang-saeng-je* 항생제

antique *kol-ttong-p'um* 골동품

antique furniture *ko-ga-gu* 고가구

antiseptic *pang-bu-je* 방부제

appendicitis *maeng-jang-yeom* 맹장염

appetizer *an-ju* 안주

apple *sa-gwa* 사과

to apply (lotion, medication) *pa-reu-da(pal-la-yo)* 바르다 (발라요)

appointment *yak-sok/ye-yak* 약속/예약

to be appropriate *cheok-ttang-ha-da(hae-yo)* 적당하다(해요)

April *sa-weol* 사월
archery *yang-gung* 양궁
architect *keon-ch'uk ki-sa* 건축 기사
architecture *keon-ch'uk* 건축
arm *p'al* 팔
arrival gate *to-ch'ak-kku* 도착구
to **arrive** *to-ch'ak-k'a-da(k'ae-yo)* 도착하다(해요)
art (painting) *mi-sul* 미술
art gallery *hwa-rang* 화랑
ashtray *chae-tteo-ri* 재떨이
aspirin *a-seu-p'i-rin* 아스피린
as soon as possible *ka-neung-han-han ppal-li* 가능한한 빨리
at *e-seo* 에서
athlete *un-dong seon-su* 운동 선수
ATM *hyeon-geum-ja-dong-ch'ul-nap-kki* 현금자동출납기
atmosphere *pun-wi-gi* 분위기
August *p'a-rweol* 팔월
Australia *Ho-ju* 호주
Australian (person) *Ho-ju sa-ram* 호주 사람
author *cheo-ja* 저자
automatic transmission *o-t'o-mae-t'ik* 오토매틱
to be **available** *it-tta(i-sseo-yo)* 있다(있어요)

B

baby *ae-gi* 애기
back (body) *teung* 등
to be **bad** *na-ppeu-da(na-ppa-yo)* 나쁘다(나빠요)
bag *ka-bang* 가방
baggage *chim* 짐
baggage claim *su-ha-mul(shin-go)* 수하물(신고)
bakery *ppang-jjip* 빵집
ballet *pal-le* 발레

bamboo *tae-na-mu* 대나무
banana *ppa-na-na* 바나나
bandage *pung-dae* 붕대
Band-aid® *il-hoe-yong pan-ch'ang-go* 일회용 반창고
bank *eun-haeng* 은행
bar *ppa* 빠
barber shop *i-bal-so* 이발소
barley tea *po-ri-ch'a* 보리차
baseball *ya-gu* 야구
basketball *nong-gu* 농구
baskets (straw) *pa-gu-ni* 바구니
to **take a bath** *mok-yok-k'a-da(k'ae-yo)* 목욕하다(해요)
bathhouse (public) *mok-yok-t'ang* 목욕탕
bathroom *hwa-jang-shil* 화장실
bathtub *mok-yok-t'ong* 목욕통
battery *keon-jeon-ji* 건전지
battery (car) *pae-t'eo-ri* 배터리
beach *hae-su-yok-jjang* 해수욕장
bean curd *tu-bu* 두부
bean sprouts *k'ong-na-mul* 콩나물
beard *su-yeom* 수염
to be **beautiful** *a-reum-dap-tta(a-reum-da-wo-yo)* 아름답다(아름다워요)
beauty salon *mi-jang-weon* 미장원
to **become/be ready** *toe-da(twae-yo)* 되다(돼요)
bed *ch'im-dae* 침대
beef (grilled) *pul-go-gi* 불고기
beef ribs (grilled) *pul-gal-bi* 불갈비
beer *maek-jju* 맥주
beer hall *pi-eo-hol* 비어홀
before *cheon-e* 전에
to **begin** *shi-jak-k'a-da(k'ae-yo)* 시작하다(해요)
behind *twi-e* 뒤에
bellflower root *to-ra-ji* 도라지

bellhop *bel-bo-i* 벨보이
belt *hyeok-ttae* 혁대
beside *yeo-p'e* 옆에
to be **better** *teo cho-t'a(cho-a-yo)* 더 좋다(좋아요)
between *sa-i-e* 사이에
beverage *eum-nyo-su* 음료수
bicycle *cha-jeon-geo* 자전거
to be **big** *k'eu-da(k'eo-yo)* 크다(커요)
to (ride a) **bike** *cha-jeon-geo t'a-da(t'a-yo)* 자전거 타다(타요)
bills (currency) *chi-p'ye* 지폐
bird *sae* 새
birthday *saeng-il* 생일
black *keom-jeong/keom-eun-saek* 검정/검은색
to be **bland** *shing-geop-tta(shing-geo-weo-yo)* 싱겁다(싱거워요)
blanket/quilt (Korean–style) *i-bul* 이불
blood *p'i/hyeo-raek* 피/혈액
blood pressure *hyeo-rap* 혈압
blouse *peul-la-u-seu* 블라우스
blue *p'a-rang/p'a-ran-saek* 파랑/파란색
boat *pae* 배
body lotion *pa-di ro-shyeon* 바디 로션
to **boil** *sam-tta(sal-ma-yo)* 삶다(삶아요)
bone *ppyeo* 뼈
book *ch'aek* 책
bookstore *seo-jeom* 서점
to **borrow** *pil-li-da(pil-lyeo-yo)* 빌리다(빌려요)
bottle *pyeong* 병
bowl *sa-bal/tae-jeop* 사발/대접
boxing *kweon-t'u* 권투
box lunch (Korean-style) *to-shi-rak* 도시락
boy *nam-ja a-i* 남자 아이
bra *peu-rae-ji-eo* 브래지어
bracelet *p'al-jji* 팔찌

brakes *peu-re-i-k'eu* 브레이크
brass *not-ssoe* 놋쇠
Brazil *Peu-ra-jil* 브라질
bread *ppang* 빵
to **break** (bone) *pu-reo-ji-da(pu-reo-jyeo-yo)* 부러지다 (부러져요)
to **break** (glass) *kkae-ji-da(kkae-jyeo-yo)* 깨지다 (깨져요)
breakfast *a-ch'im shik-sa* 아침 식사
bridge *ta-ri* 다리
briefcase *ka-bang* 가방
to be **bright** *palk-tta(pal-ga-yo)* 밝다(밝아요)
to **bring/take** *ka-jyeo-o-da/ka-jyeo-ka-da* 가져오다/가져가다
British (person) *Yeong-guk sa-ram* 영국 사람
British Embassy *Yeong-guk tae-sa-gwan* 영국 대사관
to **broil/grill** *kup-tta(ku-weo-yo)* 굽다(구워요)
brown *kal-saek* 갈색
bruise *t'a-bak-sang* 타박상
brush *peu-reo-shi* 브러시
to **build** *chit-tta(chi-eo-yo)* 짓다(지어요)
burgundy (color) *cha-ju-saek* 자주색
burn *hwa-sang* 화상
bus *ppeo-seu* 버스
business *sa-eop* 사업
business center *pi-ji-ni-seu sen-t'eo* 비지니스 센터
business hours *yeong-eop shi-gan* 영업 시간
businessperson *sa-eop-kka* 사업가
bus (express) *ko-sok-ppeo-seu* 고속버스
bus (shuttle) *shyeo-t'eul-beo-seu* 셔틀버스
bus stop *ppeo-seu cheong-nyu-jang* 버스 정류장
bus terminal *peo-seu t'eo-mi-neol* 버스 터미널

to be **busy** *pa-ppeu-da(pa-ppa-yo)* 바쁘다 (바빠요)

but *keu-reon-de* 그런데

butter *peo-t'eo* 버터

C

cabaret *k'ya-ba-re* 캬바레

cabbage *pae-ch'u* 배추

cafe *kka-p'e* 까페

cake *k'e-i-k'eu* 케이크

calculator *kye-san-gi* 계산기

calligraphy *seo-ye* 서예

camcorder *k'aem-k'o-deo* 캠코더

camera *k'a-me-ra* 카메라

camera shop *k'a-me-ra-jeom* 카메라점

to **camp** *k'aem-p'ing-ha-da(hae-yo)* 캠핑하다 (해요)

can (be able to) _____ *hal su-it-tta(i-sseo-yo)* _____ 할 수 있다 (있어요)

Canada *K'ae-na-da* 캐나다

Canadian (person) *K'ae-na-da sa-ram* 캐나다 사람

candy *sa-t'ang* 사탕

canoeing *k'a-nu* 카누

capital *su-do* 수도

car *ch'a* 차

carburetor *k'a-byu-re-t'eo* 카뷰레터

card (business, personal) *myeong-ham* 명함

card game (Korean) *hwa-t'u* 화투

to be **careful** *cho-shim-ha-da(hae-yo)* 조심하다 (해요)

to **carry** *teul-da(teu-reo-yo)* 들다 (들어요)

cavity *ch'ung-ch'i* 충치

CD player *sshi-di p'eul-le-i-eo* 씨디 플레이어

cell phone *haen-deeu-p'on* 핸드폰

center *ka-un-de/ssen-t'eo* 가운데/쎈터

ceramics *to-ja-gi* 도자기

chain *ch'e-in* 체인

champagne *shyam-p'e-in* 샴페인

champion *u-seung-ja* 우승자

change (coins) *chan-don* 잔돈

to **change** (clothes) *ot ka-ra-ip-tta(ka-ra-i-beo-yo)* 옷 갈아입다 (갈아입어요)

to **change/exchange** *pa-kku-da(pa-kkweo-yo)* 바꾸다 (바꿔요)

to be **cheap** *ssa-da(ssa-yo)* 싸다 (싸요)

check (bill) *kye-san-seo* 계산서

check (money) *su-p'yo* 수표

check (pattern) *ch'e-k'eu mu-ni* 체크 무늬

to **check/examine** *keom-t'o-ha-da(hae-yo)* 검토하다 (해요)

check-in (flight) *t'ap-seung su-sok* 탑승 수속

cherries *aeng-du* 앵두

chess (Korean-style) *chang-gi* 장기

chest (body) *ka-seum* 가슴

chestnuts *pam* 밤

chicken *tak-kko-gi* 닭고기

child *a-i/eo-rin-i* 아이/어린이

children *a-i-deul/eo-rin-i-deul* 아이들/어린이들

to **chill** (shiver) *o-han-i na-da(na-yo)* 오한이 나다 (나요)

China *Chung-guk* 중국

Chinese (lang.) *Chung-gu-keo* 중국어

Chinese (person) *Chung-guk sa-ram* 중국 사람

chocolate *ch'o-k'ol-let* 초콜렛

to **choose** *ko-reu-da(kol-la-yo)* 고르다 (골라요)

chopsticks *cheo-kka-rak* 젓가락

church *kyo-hoe* 교회

cigar *shi-ga* 시가

cigarette *tam-bae* 담배

city *to-shi* 도시
classical music *ko-jeon eum-ak* 고전 음악
to **clean** *ch'i-u-da(ch'i-weo-yo)* 치우다(치워요)
to **clean** (room) *ch'eong-so-ha-da(hae-yo)* 청소하다(해요)
cleansing cream *k'eul-len-jing k'eu-rim* 클렌징 크림
to be **clear** *mal-tta(mal-ga-yo)* 맑다(맑아요)
climate *ki-hu* 기후
clock/watch *shi-gye* 시계
alarm clock *al-lam-shi-gye* 알람시계
travel alarm clock *yeo-haeng-yong al-lam-shi-gye* 여행용 알람시계
cloisonne *ch'il-bo* 칠보
to **close** *tat-tta(ta-da-yo)* 닫다(닫아요)
closing ceremony *p'ye-mak-shik* 폐막식
clothes *ot* 옷
clothing (children's) *a-dong-bok* 아동복
clothing (made-to-order) *ma-ch'um-bok* 마춤복
clothing (ready-to-wear) *ki-seong-bok* 기성복
cloud *ku-reum* 구름
coast *hae-an* 해안
cocktail *k'ak-t'e-il* 칵테일
coffee *k'eo-p'i* 커피
coffee shop *k'eo-p'i shyop* 커피 숍
cola *k'ol-la* 콜라
to be **cold** *ch'up-tta(ch'u-weo-yo)* 춥다(추워요)
to catch **cold** *kam-gi-e keol-li-da(keol-lyeo-yo)* 감기에 걸리다(걸려요)
chest cold *ki-ch'im kam-gi* 기침 감기
head cold *tu-t'ong kam-gi* 두통 감기
cologne *k'ol-lon-su* 콜론수
color *saek-kkal* 색깔

color (tint) *yeom-saek* 염색
comb *meo-ri-bit* 머리빗
to **comb** *pit-tta(pi-seo-yo)* 빗다(빗어요)
to **come** *o-da(wa-yo)* 오다(와요)
comedy *k'o-mi-di* 코미디
to **come in** *teu-reo o-da(teu-reo wa-yo)* 들어 오다 (들어와요)
to **come out** *na-o-da(na-wa-yo)* 나오다(나와요)
compact discs *k'om-p'aek-t'eu ti-seu-k'eu* 콤팩트 디스크
computer *k'eom-p'yu-t'eo* 컴퓨터
desktop computer *te-seu-k'eu-t'ap k'eom-p'yu-t'eo* 데스크탑 컴퓨터
notebook computer *no-t'eu-buk k'eom-p'yu-t'eo* 노트북 컴퓨터
concert *yeon-ju-hoe* 연주회
concerto *hyeop-jju-gok* 협주곡
condom *k'on-dom* 콘돔
to **confirm** *hwa-gin-ha-da(hae-yo)* 확인하다(해요)
confirmation *hwa-gin-seo* 확인서
to be **constipated** *pyeon-bi-e keol-li-da(keol-lyeo-yo)* 변비에 걸리다(걸려요)
to **contact** (communicate) *yeol-lak-k'a-da(k'ae-yo)* 연락하다(해요)
contact lens *k'on-t'aek-t'eu ren-jeu* 콘택트 렌즈
soft contact lens *so-p'eu-t'eu k'on-t'aek-t'eu ren-jeu* 소프트 콘택트 렌즈
to **continue** *kye-sok-k'a-da(k'ae-yo)* 계속하다 (해요)
contraceptive *p'i-im-gi-gu* 피임기구
convenience store *p'yeon-eui-jeom* 편의점

to **cook** (v.t.) *yo-ri-ha-da(hae-yo)* 요리하다(해요)

to **cook** (v.i.) *ik-tta(i-geo-yo)* 익다(익어요)

cookie *kwa-ja* 과자

to be **cool** *ssal-ssal-ha-da(hae-yo)* 쌀쌀하다(해요)

corn *ok-ssu-su* 옥수수

corn plasters *t'i-nun-yak* 티눈약

cotton *t'al-jji-myeon* 탈지면

cotton (fabric) *myeon* 면

to **cough** *ki-ch'im-ha-da(hae-yo)* 기침하다(해요)

cough syrup *shi-reop-eu-ro toen ki-ch'im-yak* 시럽으로 된 기침약

country *na-ra* 나라

country music *k'an-ch'yu-ri myu-jik* 칸츄리 뮤직

countryside *shi-gol* 시골

courtyard *tteul* 뜰

cover charge *ip-jjang-nyo* 입장료

crab *ke* 게

to **cramp** *pok-t'ong-i na-da (na-yo)* 복통이 나다(나요)

crane dance *hak-ch'um* 학춤

cream rinse *rin-seu* 린스

credit card *k'eu-re-dit k'a-deu* 크레딧 카드

to **cross** *keon-neo-da(keon-neo-yo)* 건너다(건너요)

to be **crowded** *pok-jjap-ha-da(hae-yo)* 복잡하다(해요)

cucumber *o-i* 오이

cufflinks *k'eo-p'eu-seu-dan-ch'u* 커프스단추

cup *k'eop* 컵

curfew *t'ong-haeng-geum-ji* 통행금지

curlers *k'eul-lip* 클립

to be **curly** *kop-seul-ha-da (hae-yo)* 곱슬하다(해요)

currency (Korean) *weon(won)* 원

customs declaration form *se-gwan shin-go-seo* 세관 신고서

customs inspection *t'ong-gwan* 통관

to **cut** *kkak-tta(kka-kka-yo)* 깎다(깎아요)

to **cut the price** *kap-seul kka-kka chu-da(kka-kka chweo-yo)* 값을 깎아 주다 (깎아 줘요)

to **cut** (with a sharp object) *pe-da(pe-eo-yo)* 베다(베어요)

cycling *ssa-i-k'eul* 싸이클

D

to **dance** *ch'um-ch'u-da(ch'um-ch'weo-yo)* 춤추다 (춤춰요)

to **dance** (performance) *mu-yong-ha-da(hae-yo)* 무용하다(해요)

to be **dark** *eo-dup-tta(eo-du-weo-yo)* 어둡다(어두워요)

date *nal-jja* 날짜

daughter *ttal* 딸

day *il/nal* 일/날

  one day *ha-ru* 하루

  a few days *myeo-ch'il* 며칠

  the day after tomorrow *mo-re* 모레

December *ship-i-weol* 십이월

to **decide** *kyeol-jjeong-ha-da(hae-yo)* 결정하다(해요)

decongestant *so-yeom-je* 소염제

to be **delicious** *ma-shi it-tta(i-sseo-yo)* 맛이 있다 (있어요)

  not delicious *ma-shi eop-tta(eop-sseo-yo)* 맛이 없다(없어요)

to **deliver** *pae-dal-ha-da(hae-yo)* 배달하다(해요)

dentist *ch'i-kkwa eui-sa* 치과 의사

deodorant *pang-ch'wi-je* 방취제

to **depart** *ch'ul-bal-ha-da(hae-yo)* 출발하다(해요)

department store *paek-k'wa-jeom* 백화점

departure gate *ch'ul-bal-gu* 출발구

deposit *seon-geum/po-jeung-geum* 선금/보증금

dessert *ti-jeo-t'eu* 디저트

to **develop** (film) *hyeon-sang-ha-da(hae-yo)* 현상하다 (해요)

diamond *ta-i-a-mon-deu* 다이아몬드

diapers (disposable) *chong-i ki-jeo-gwi* 종이 기저귀

diarrhea (to have) *seol-sa na-da(na-yo)* 설사 나다 (나요)

dictionary *sa-jeon* 사전

　English-Korean dictionary *Yeong-han sa-jeon* 영한 사전

to **die** *chuk-tta(chu-geo-yo)* 죽다(죽어요)

to **die** (honorific) *to-ra-ga-shi-da(ga-sheo-yo)* 돌아가시다 (가셔요)

diesel *ti-jel/kyeong-yu* 디젤/경유

to be **different** *ta-reu-da(tal-la-yo)* 다르다(달라요)

to be **difficult** *eo-ryeop-tta(eo-ryeo-weo-yo)* 어렵다 (어려워요)

dining car *shik-ttang-ch'a* 식당차

dinner *cheo-nyeok(shik-sa)* 저녁(식사)

direct (route) *chik-k'aeng* 직행

to be **dirty** *teo-reop-tta(teo-reo-weo-yo)* 더럽다 (더러워요)

to **discount** *ha-rin-ha-da(hae-yo)* 할인하다(해요)

distance *keo-ri* 거리

diving *ta-i-bing* 다이빙

to **do** *ha-da(hae-yo)* 하다 (해요)

doctor *eui-sa* 의사

documents *seo-ryu* 서류

doll *in-hyeong* 인형

dollar *ttal-leo* 달러

door *mun* 문

down *a-rae* 아래

downtown *shi-nae* 시내

dramatic song (traditional Korean) *p'an-sso-ri* 판소리

to **draw** *keu-ri-da(keu-ryeo-yo)* 그리다(그려요)

dress *teu-re-sseu* 드레스

dress (traditional Korean) *han-bok* 한복

to **drink** *ma-shi-da(ma-shyeo-yo)* 마시다(마셔요)

driver *un-jeon-su* 운전수

driver's license *un-jeon myeon-heo-jeung* 운전 면허증

to **drop** *tteo-reo-tteu-ri-da(tteo-reo-tteu-ryeo-yo)* 떨어뜨리다 (떨어뜨려요)

drum dance (traditional Korean) *chang-go-ch'um* 장고춤

to be **dry** *ma-reu-da(mal-la-yo)* 마르다(말라요)

dry cleaning *teu-ra-i-k'eul-li-ning* 드라이클리닝

duck *o-ri* 오리

DVD player *ti-bi-di p'eul-le-i-eo* 디비디 플레이어

DVD room *ti-bi-di pang* 디비디 방

E

ear *kwi* 귀

ear drops *kwi-e neo-neun yak* 귀에 넣는약

early *il-jjik* 일찍

earrings *kwi-geo-ri* 귀걸이

earthquake *chi-jin* 지진

east *tong-jjok* 동쪽

to be **easy** *shwip-tta(shwi-weo-yo)* 쉽다 (쉬워요)

to **eat** *meok-tta(meo-geo-yo)* 먹다 (먹어요)

to **eat** (honorific) *chap-su-shi-da(chap-su-shyeo-yo)* 잡수시다 (잡수셔요)

egg *kye-ran* 계란

elbow *p'al-kkum-ch'i* 팔꿈치

electrical appliances *ka-jeon che-p'um* 가전 제품

electrical appliance store *cheon-ja-je-p'um-jeom* 전자제품점

electric fan *seon-p'ung-gi* 선풍기

electricity *cheon-gi* 전기

electric light *(cheon-gi)pul* (전기)불

electric razor *myeon-do-gi* 면도기

elevator *el-li-be-i-t'eo* 엘리베이터

embassy *tae-sa-gwan* 대사관

emergency *eung-geup* 응급

emery boards *son-t'op-jjul* 손톱줄

to **end/finish** (v.i.) *kkeun-na-da(kkeun-na-yo)* 끝나다 (끝나요)

engine *en-jin* 엔진

engineer *ki-sul-jja* 기술자

England *Yeong-guk* 영국

English (lang.) *Yeong-eo* 영어

to **enjoy** *cheul-geop-tta(cheul-geo-weo-yo)* 즐겁다 (즐거워요)

to be **enough** *ch'ung-bun-ha-da(hae-yo)* 충분하다 (해요)

entertainment guide *kong-yeon an-nae-seo* 공연 안내서

entrance *ip-kku* 입구

envelope *pong-t'u* 봉투

equestrian *seung-ma* 승마

equipment *yong-gu/ki-gu* 용구/기구

eraser *chi-u-gae* 지우개

escalator *e-seu-k'eol-le-i-t'eo* 에스컬레이터

evening *cheo-nyeok* 저녁

everyday *mae-il* 매일

to **exchange** *pa-kku-da(pa-kkweo-yo)* 바꾸다 (바뀌요)

exchange rate *hwan-yul* 환율

Excuse me. *Shil-lye-ham-ni-da.* 실례합니다.

executive *hoe-sa kan-bu* 회사 간부

to **exhibit** *cheon-shi-ha-da(hae-yo)* 전시하다 (해요)

exit *ch'ul-gu* 출구

to be **expensive** *pi-ssa-da(pi-ssa-yo)* 비싸다 (비싸요)

to **explain** *seol-myeong-ha-da(hae-yo)* 설명하다 (해요)

extra large *ek-sseu-ra-ji* 엑쓰라지

eye *nun* 눈

eyebrow pencil *nun-sseop yeon-p'il* 눈썹연필

eyedrops *an-yak* 안약

eyeliner *a-i ra-i-neo* 아이 라이너

eye shadow *a-i shae-do-u* 아이 새도우

F

face *eol-gul* 얼굴

face powder *pun* 분

facilities *shi-seol-mul* 시설물

fall (season) *ka-eul* 가을

fall colors *tan-p'ung* 단풍

to **fall down** *neom-eo-ji-da(neom-eo-jyeo-yo)* 넘어지다 (넘어져요)

to **fall off** *tteo-reo-ji-da(tteo-reo-jyeo-yo)* 떨어지다 (떨어져요)

family *ka-jok* 가족

to be **famous** *yu-myeong-ha-da(hae-yo)* 유명하다 (해요)

fan *pu-ch'ae* 부채

to be **far** *meol-da(meo-reo-yo)*
멀다(멀어요)

fare *yo-geum* 요금

farewell party *song-byeol-hoe*
송별회

farm *nong-ga* 농가

farmer's music (traditional
Korean) *nong-ak* 농악

to be **fast** *ppa-reu-da(ppal-la-yo)* 빠르다(빨라요)

father *a-beo-ji* 아버지

to **ask a favor** *pu-t'ak-k'a-da(k'ae-yo)* 부탁하다(해요)

favorite *che-il cho-a-ha-da(hae-yo)* 제일 좋아하다
(해요)

favorite place (where one is a
regular customer) *tan-gol*
단골

February *i-weol* 이월

fee *yo-geum* 요금

fencing *p'en-shing* 펜싱

ferry *p'e-ri* 페리

festival *ch'uk-jje* 축제

to **have a fever** *yeo-ri it-tta(i-sseo-yo)* 열이 있다(있어요)

to be **few** *keo-eui eop-tta(eop-sseo-yo)* 거의 없다(없어요)

field *teul-p'an* 들판

filling (tooth) *ppong* 뽕

filling station *chu-yu-so*
주유소

film (photography) *p'il-leum*
필름

finger *son-kka-rak* 손가락

to **finish** *kkeun-nae-da(kkeun-nae-yo)* 끝내다(끝내요)

first *ch'eot/meon-jeo* 첫/먼저

the **first time/at first** *ch'eot-ppeon/ch'eo-eum-e* 첫번/
처음에

first aid kit *eung-geup ch'eo-ch'i-ham* 응급 처치함

first class *il-tteung* 일등

first-class ticket *il-tteung
p'yo* 일등 표

fish *saeng-seon* 생선

fish (sliced, raw) *hoe* 회

fish (grilled) *saeng-seon-gu-i*
생선구이

fish market *su-san-mul shi-jang* 수산물 시장

to **fit** *mat-tta(ma-ja-yo)* 맞다
(맞아요)

fitness club *hel-seu-k'eul-leop*
헬스클럽

fixed price *cheong-ga* 정가

flashlight *p'eul-lae-shi* 플래시

flight number *hang-gong-beon-ho* 항공번호

flood *hong-su* 홍수

flower *kkot* 꽃

flower shop *kkot-jjip* 꽃집

flu *mom-sal* 몸살

flu (to get) *mom-sal na-da(na-yo)* 몸살 나다(나요)

folding chair *cheom-neun
eui-ja* 접는 의자

folk art *min-sok ye-sul*
민속예술

folk songs *tae-jung-ga-yo*
대중가요

food *eum-shik/shik-p'um*
음식/식품

    Korean-style food *han-shik* 한식

    Western-style food *yang-shik* 양식

food court *chi-ha-eum-shik-sang-ga* 지하음식상가

foot *pal* 발

football (American) *mi-shik-ch'uk-kku* 미식축구

foreigner *woe-guk sa-ram*
외국 사람

forest *sup* 숲

fork *p'o-k'eu* 포크

France *P'eu-rang-seu* 프랑스

French (lang.) *P'eu-rang-seu-eo/Pu-reo* 프랑스어/불어

French (person) *P'eu-rang-seu
sa-ram* 프랑스 사람

frequent customer *tan-gol
son-nim* 단골 손님

to be **fresh** *shing-shing-ha-da(hae-yo)* 싱싱하다(해요)

Friday *keum-yo-il* 금요일
friend *ch'in-gu* 친구
from *e-seo/pu-t'eo* 에서/부터
from_____to_____ (from 6:00
to 10:00) _____*put'eo*
_____*kkaji* _____부
터 _____까지
front *ap* 앞
fruit *kwa-il* 과일
fruit cocktail *p'eu-ru-t'eu
k'ak-t'e-il* 프루트 칵테일
to **fry** *t'wi-gi-da(t'wi-gyeo-yo)*
튀기다(튀겨요)
to be **full** *ka-deuk-ch'a-
da(ch'a-yo)* 가득차다(차요)
furniture *ka-gu* 가구

G

game (athletic event) *kyeong-
gi* 경기
garden *cheong-weon* 정원
gas *kka-sseu* 가스
gasoline *hwi-bal-lyu* 휘발유
premium *ko-geup-hwi-bal-
lyu* 고급휘발유
regular *po-t'ong-hwi-bal-
lyu* 보통휘발유
gas station *chu-yu-so* 주유소
gauze *ka-a-je* 가아제
German (lang.) *To-gi-reo*
독일어
German (person) *To-gil sa-
ram* 독일 사람
Germany *To-gil* 독일
to **get** (obtain) *ku-ha-da(hae-
yo)* 구하다(해요)
to **get off** *nae-ri-da(nae-ryeo-
yo)* 내리다(내려요)
to **get up** *i-reo-na-da(i-reo-na-
yo)* 일어나다(일어나요)
gift *seon-mul* 선물
gift shop *seon-mul ka-ge* 선물
가게
to **gift wrap** *seon-mul-p'o-
jang-ha-da(hae-yo)*
선물포장하다(해요)

gin *chin* 진
ginger *saeng-gang* 생강
ginseng *in-sam* 인삼
ginseng chicken *sam-gye-
t'ang* 삼계탕
ginseng shop *in-sam ka-ge*
인삼 가게
girl *yeo-ja a-i* 여자 아이
to **give** *chu-da(chweo-yo)*
주다(줘요)
to **give** (honorific) *teu-ri-
da(teu-ryeo-yo)* 드리다
(드려요)
to be **glad** *ki-ppeu-da(ki-ppeo-
yo)* 기쁘다(기뻐요)
glass (drinking) *chan* 잔
glass (window) *yu-ri* 유리
glasses *an-gyeong* 안경
gloves *chang-gap* 장갑
to **go** *ka-da(ka-yo)* 가다(가요)
to **go in** *teu-reo ka-da(teu-reo
ka-yo)* 들어 가다(들어 가요)
gold *keum* 금
golf *kol-p'eu* 골프
to be **good** *cho-t'a(cho-a-yo)*
좋다(좋아요)
Good-bye. *An-nyeong-hi ka-
se-yo.* 안녕히 가세요.
Good afternoon. **Good
evening.** **Good morning.**
An-nyeong-ha-se-yo?
안녕하세요?
Good night. (before
sleeping) *An-nyeong-hi
chu-mu-se-yo.* 안녕히
주무세요.
GPS (global positioning
system) *ne-bi-ge-i-shyeon/
chi-p'i-e-seu* 네비게이션/
지피에스
grandfather *ha-ra-beo-ji*
할아버지
grandmother *hal-meo-ni*
할머니
grapes *p'o-do* 포도
gray *hoe-saek* 회색
green *nok-saek/ch'o-rok* 녹색/
초록

grocery store *shik-p'um-jeom*
식품점
guide (person) *an-nae-weon*
안내원
gymnasium *ch'e-yuk-kkwan*
체육관
gymnastics *ch'e-jo* 체조

H

hair *meo-ri(k'a-rak)* 머리
(카락)
hair color *meo-ri saek-kkal*
머리 색깔
haircut *i-bal* 이발
  to get a haircut (man) *i-bal-ha-da(hae-yo)* 이발하다
(해요)
  to get a haircut (woman)
k'eo-t'eu-ha-da(hae-yo)
커트하다(해요)
hair dryer *he-eo teu-ra-i-eo*
헤어 드라이어
hair spray *he-eo seu-p'eu-re-i*
헤어 스프레이
half-fare *pan-aek* 반액
hamburger steak *haem-beo-geo seu-t'e-i-k'eu* 햄버거
스테이크
hammer *mang-ch'i* 망치
hand *son* 손
handbag *ka-bang* 가방
handball *haen-deu-bol*
핸드볼
handicrafts *su-gong-ye-p'um*
수공예품
handkerchief *son-ssu-geon*
손수건
hand lotion *haen-deu ro-shyeon* 핸드 로션
handmade *su-je-p'um* 수제품
harbor *hang-gu* 항구
hat *mo-ja* 모자
to have *it-tta(i-sseo-yo)* 있다
(있어요)
  not to have *eop-tta(eop-sseo-yo)* 없다(없어요)

to have to _____ _____ *ya
toeda(twaeyo)* _____ 야
되다(돼요)
hay fever *keon-ch'o-yeol*
건초열
he/she (honorific) *keu pun*
그 분
he/she *keu sa-ram* 그 사람
head *meo-ri* 머리
headache *tu-t'ong* 두통
headache (to have) *meo-ri-ga
a-p'eu-da(a-p'a-yo)* 머리가
아프다(아파요)
health club *hel-seu-k'eul-leop* 헬스클럽
hearing aid *po-ch'eong-gi*
보청기
heart *shim-jang* 심장
heart attack *shim-jang-ma-bi*
심장마비
heater *hi-t'eo* 히터
to be heavy *mu-geop-tta(mu-geo-weo-yo)* 무겁다
(무거워요)
heel *twi-ch'uk* 뒤축
height *k'i* 키
Hello. (telephone) *Yeo-bo-se-yo.* 여보세요.
to help *to-wa chu-da(to-wa
chweo-yo)* 도와 주다(도와
줘요)
hepatitis *kan-yeom* 간염
here *yeo-gi* 여기
to be high *nop-tta(no-p'a-yo)*
높다(높아요)
highway *ko-sok-tto-ro*
고속도로
to hike *ha-i-k'ing-ha-da(hae-yo)* 하이킹하다(해요)
hill *eon-deok* 언덕
history *yeok-sa* 역사
HIV test *e-i-ch'i-a-i-beu-i
keom-sa* 에이치아이브이
검사
hockey *ha-k'i* 하키
hof (pub/bar) *ho-p'eu-jip*
호프집
holiday *hyu-il* 휴일

hometown *ko-hyang* 고향
Hong Kong *Hong-k'ong* 홍콩
horn *k'eu-rak-shyeon* 크락션
hospital *pyeong-weon* 병원
hostess/helper *to-u-mi* 도우미
to be **hot** *teop-tta(teo-weo-yo)* 덥다(더워요)
to be **hot** (spicy) *maep-tta(mae-weo-yo)* 맵다 (매워요)
hot springs *on-ch'eon* 온천
hotel *ho-t'el* 호텔
motel *mo-t'el* 모텔
inn *yeo-gwan* 여관
hour *shi-gan* 시간
house *chip* 집
how *eo-tteo-k'e* 어떻게
How are you? *An-nyeong-ha-se-yo?* 안녕하세요?
How do you do? *Ch'eo-eum poep-kke-sseo-yo.* 처음 뵙겠어요.
how long *eol-ma tong-an* 얼마 동안
how much *eol-ma* 얼마
How much is it? *Eol-ma-ye-yo?* 얼마예요?
to be **humid** *seup-kki it-tta (i-sseo-yo)* 습기 있다 (있어요)
to be **hungry** *pae-ga ko-p'eu-da(ko-p'a-yo)* 배가 고프다 (고파요)
husband (someone else's) *pu-gun* 부군
husband (your own) *nam-p'yeon* 남편

I

I (modest form) *che-ga/cheo-neun* 제가/저는
I *nae-ga/na-neun* 내가/나는
I'm sorry. *Mi-an-ham-ni-da.* 미안합니다.
ice *eo-reum* 얼음

ice cream *a-i-seu k'eu-rim* 아이스 크림
immediately *tang-jang* 당장
in *an-e* 안에
to **include** *p'o-ham-ha-da(hae-yo)* 포함하다(해요)
indigestion *so-hwa-pul-lyang* 소화불량
Indonesia *In-do-ne-shi-a* 인도네시아
to be **inexpensive** *ssa-da(ssa-yo)* 싸다(싸요)
to be **infected** *kam-yeom-doe-da(dwae-yo)* 감염되다 (돼요)
infection *kam-yeom* 감염
to **inform** *al-lyeo chu-da(chweo-yo)* 알려 주다 (줘요)
information *an-nae* 안내
information desk *an-nae-so* 안내소
in front *a-p'e* 앞에
injection *chu-sa* 주사
to be **injured** *ta-ch'i-da(ta-ch'yeo-yo)* 다치다(다쳐요)
insect bite (to receive) *peol-le-e mul-li-da(mul-lyeo-yo)* 벌레에 물리다(물려요)
insect repellent *pang-ch'ung-je* 방충제
to **insert** *kki-u-da(kki-weo-yo)* 끼우다 (끼워요)
insomnia *pul-myeon-jeung* 불면증
insulin *in-syul-lin* 인슐린
insurance *po-heom* 보험
to be **intelligent** *meo-ri cho-t'a(cho-a-yo)* 머리 좋다 (좋아요)
to be **interested in** _____ _____*e kwan-shi-mi it-tta(isseoyo)* _____에 관심이 있다 (있어요)
to be **interesting** *chae-mi-it-tta(i-sseo-yo)* 재미있다 (있어요)

international *kuk-jje* 국제

Internet *In-t'eo-net* 인터넷

Internet cafe *In-t'eo-net kka-p'e* 인터넷 까페

interpreter *t'ong-yeok-kkwan* 통역관

intersection (four-way) *ne-geo-ri* 네거리

to **introduce oneself/to greet** *in-sa-ha-da(hae-yo)* 인사하다(해요)

to **invite** *ch'o-dae-ha-da(hae-yo)* 초대하다(해요)

iodine *ok-tto-jeong-gi* 옥도정기

iron *ta-ri-mi* 다리미

to **iron** *ta-ri-da(ta-ryeo-yo)* 다리다(다려요)

is (to be) *(i)-e-yo* (이)에요

island *seom* 섬

Italy *I-t'ae-ri* 이태리

itinerary *seu-k'e-jul* 스케줄

J

jacket *cha-k'et* 자켓

jade *pi-ch'wi* 비취

January *i-rweol* 일월

Japan *Il-bon* 일본

Japanese (lang.) *Il-bon-eo* 일본어

Japanese (person) *Il-bon sa-ram* 일본 사람

jazz *jjae-jeu* 째즈

jeans *ch'eong-ba-ji* 청바지

jewelry *po-seok* 보석

jewelry store *po-seok-sang* 보석상

to **jog** *cho-ging-ha-da(hae-yo)* 조깅하다(해요)

joint (body) *kwan-jeol* 관절

judo *yu-do* 유도

juice *chyu-seu* 쥬스

July *ch'i-rweol* 칠월

June *yu-weol* 유월

K

karat (for diamond) *k'ae-reot* 캐럿

karat (for gold) *k'e-i* 케이

ketchup *k'e-ch'eop* 케첩

key *yeol-soe* 열쇠

keyboard *k'i-bo-deu* 키보드

kilogram *k'il-lo-geu-raem* 킬로그램

kimchi (cabbage) *kim-ch'i* 김치

kimchi (cucumber) *o-i-so-bak-i* 오이소박이

kimchi (radish) *kkak-ttu-gi* 깍두기

kimchi stew *kim-ch'i-jji-gae* 김치찌개

to be **kind** *ch'in-jeol-ha-da(hae-yo)* 친절하다(해요)

king *wang* 왕

kisaeng (professional entertainer) *ki-saeng* 기생

knee *mu-reup* 무릎

knife (dinner) *na-i-p'eu* 나이프

knife (cutting) *k'al* 칼

to **know** *al-da(a-ra-yo)* 알다 (알아요)

not to know *mo-reu-da(mol-la-yo)* 모르다 (몰라요)

Korea *Han-guk* 한국

Korean (lang.) *Han-gung-mal/ Han-gu-geo* 한국말/한국어

Korean (person) *Han-guk sa-ram* 한국 사람

Korean language book *Han-gung-mal ch'aek* 한국말 책

Korean (writing system) *Han-geul* 한글

Korean-made *kuk-ssan-p'um* 국산품

L

lacquerware *na-jeon-ch'il-gi* 나전칠기

lake   *ho-su*   호수
language   *mal*   말
to be large/big   *k'eu-da(k'eo-yo)*   크다(커요)
large (size)   *ra-ji*   라지
last   *ma-ji-mak*   마지막
to be late   *neu-tta(neu-jeo-yo)*   늦다(늦어요)
later   *na-jung-e*   나중에
laundry (clothes)   *ppal-lae*   빨래
laundry (place)   *se-t'ak-so*   세탁소
lawyer   *pyeon-ho-sa*   변호사
laxative   *wan-ha-je/pyeon-bi-yak*   완하제/변비약
to learn   *pae-u-da(pae-weo-yo)*   배우다(배워요)
leather   *ka-juk*   가죽
left   *woen-jjok*   왼쪽
to be left over   *nam-a it-tta(i-sseo-yo)*   남아 있다(있어요)
leg   *ta-ri*   다리
lemon-lime soda   *sa-i-da*   사이다
lens   *ren-jeu*   렌즈
letter (mail)   *p'yeon-ji*   편지
lettuce   *yang-sang-ch'u*   양상추
library   *to-seo-gwan*   도서관
lifeguard   *in-myeong ku-jo-weon*   인명 구조원
light   *pul/pit*   불/빛
to be light   *ka-byeop-tta(ka-byeo-weo-yo)*   가볍다(가벼워요)
lightbulb   *cheon-gu*   전구
lighter   *ra-i-t'eo*   라이터
to like   *cho-a-ha-da(hae-yo)*   좋아하다(해요)
linen   *ma*   마
lip   *ip-ssul*   입술
lipstick   *rip-seu-t'ik*   립스틱
to listen   *teut-tta(teu-reo-yo)*   듣다(들어요)
a little   *cho-geum*   조금
to live   *sal-da(sa-ra-yo)*   살다(살아요)

liver   *kan*   간
lobster   *pa-dat-kka-jae*   바닷가재
to lock   *cham-geu-da(cham-ga-yo)*   잠그다(잠가요)
to be locked   *cham-gi-da(cham-gyeo-yo)*   잠기다(잠겨요)
lodging cost   *suk-ppak-ppi*   숙박비
to be long   *kil-da(ki-reo-yo)*   길다(길어요)
to look at/look around   *ku-gyeong-ha-da(hae-yo)*   구경하다(해요)
to look for   *ch'at-tta(ch'a-ja-yo)*   찾다(찾아요)
to be loose   *heol-leong-ha-da(hae-yo)*   헐렁하다(해요)
to lose   *i-reo-beo-ri-da(i-reo-beo-ryeo-yo)*   잃어버리다(잃어버려요)
to lose one's way   *ki-reul i-reo-beo-ri-da(i-reo-beo-ryeo-yo)*   길을 잃어버리다(잃어버려요)
lost and found office   *pun-shil-mul ch'wi-geup-so*   분실물 취급소
to love   *sa-rang-ha-da(hae-yo)*   사랑하다(해요)
to be low   *nat-tta(na-ja-yo)*   낮다(낮아요)
lunch   *cheom-shim shik-sa*   점심 식사

M

magazine   *chap-jji*   잡지
maid   *ch'eong-so-bu*   청소부
to mail   *pu-ch'i-da(pu-ch'yeo-yo)*   부치다(부쳐요)
mailbox   *u-ch'e-t'ong*   우체통
to make   *man-deul-da(man-deu-reo-yo)*   만들다(만들어요)

Malaysia *Mal-le-i-ji-a*
말레이지아

man *nam-ja* 남자

manager *chi-bae-in* 지배인

manicure *mae-ni-k'yu-eo*
매니큐어

to be many *man-t'a(man-na-yo)* 많다(많아요)

map *chi-do* 지도

   map (hand-drawn) *yak-tto*
약도

   city map *shi-nae chi-do*
시내 지도

   road map *to-ro chi-do* 도로
지도

March *sam-weol* 삼월

market (traditional) *shi-jang*
시장

to marry *kyeo-ron-ha-da(hae-yo)* 결혼하다(해요)

martial arts (Korean) *t'ae-kkweon-do* 태권도

mascara *ma-seu-k'a-ra*
마스카라

mask dance *t'al-ch'um* 탈춤

massage *mas-sa-ji* 맛사지

   facial massage *eol-gul
mas-sa-ji* 얼굴 맛사지

   massage therapist *mas-sa-ji-sa* 맛사지사

mat (straw) *tot-jja-ri* 돗자리

to match *eo-ul-li-da(eo-ul-lyeo-yo)* 어울리다(어울려요)

matches *seong-nyang* 성냥

matinee *nat kong-yeon*
낮 공연

mattress (Korean-style) *yo* 요

May *o-weol* 오월

to have a meal *shik-sa-ha-da(hae-yo)* 식사하다(해요)

meal cost *shik-ppi* 식비

to measure *chae-da(chae-yo)*
재다(재요)

mechanic *cheong-bi-gong*
정비공

medicine *yak* 약

medicine (herbal) *han-yak*
한약

medium (size) *mi-di-um*
미디움

to meet *man-na-da(man-na-yo)* 만나다(만나요)

melon (small, yellow) *ch'am-oe* 참외

member *hoe-weon* 회원

menu *me-nyu* 메뉴

message *me-sshi-ji* 메시지

Mexico *Mek-shi-k'o* 멕시코

middle *ka-un-de* 가운데

milk *u-yu* 우유

minister/minister (honorific)
mok-ssa/mok-ssa-nim 목사/
목사님

minute (time) *pun* 분

mirror *keo-ul* 거울

mistake (to make) *chal-mot-t'a-da(t'ae-yo)* 잘못하다
(해요)

monitor *mo-ni-t'eo* 모니터

monk/monk (honorific) *chung/
seu-nim* 중/스님

monk's dance *seung-mu* 승무

Monday *weo-ryo-il* 월요일

money *ton* 돈

month *tal* 달

morning *a-ch'im* 아침

mosque *hoe-gyo sa-weon* 회교
사원

mother *eo-meo-ni* 어머니

mountain *san* 산

to move *um-ji-gi-da(um-ji-gyeo-yo)* 움직이다
(움직여요)

movie *yeong-hwa* 영화

**Mr./Mrs./Ms./Miss_____
_____-sshi** _____ 씨

MSG (monosodium
glutamate) *hwa-hak cho-mi-ryo* 화학 조미료

mung bean pancakes *pin-dae-tteok* 빈대떡

muscle *keun-yuk* 근육

museum *pang-mul-gwan*
박물관

music *eum-ak* 음악

musical *myu-ji-k'al* 뮤지칼

mustache *k'o-mit su-yeom* 코밑 수염

my/my (modest form) *nae/che* 내/제

mystery *mi-seu-t'e-ri* 미스테리

N

nail (finger) *son-t'op* 손톱

nail clipper *son-t'op kka-kki* 손톱 깎기

nail file *son-t'op ta-deum-neun chul* 손톱 다듬는 줄

nail polish *mae-ni-k'yu-eo* 매니큐어

nail polish remover *mae-ni-k'yu-eo chi-u-gae* 매니큐어 지우개

name *i-reum* 이름

name (honorific) *seong-ham* 성함

napkin *naep-k'in* 냅킨

to be narrow *chop-tta(cho-ba-yo)* 좁다(좁아요)

nationality *kuk-jjeok* 국적

national park *kung-nip-kong-weon* 국립공원

to be nauseous *me-seu-kkeop-tta(me-seu-kkeo-weo-yo)* 메스껍다(메스꺼워요)

to be near *ka-kkap-tta(ka-kka-wa-yo)* 가깝다(가까워요)

neck *mok* 목

necklace *mok-kkeo-ri* 목걸이

to need *p'i-ryo-ha-da(hae-yo)* 필요하다(해요)

to be new *sae-rop-tta(sae-ro-wa-yo)* 새롭다(새로와요)

newspaper *shin-mun* 신문

newspaper (English language) *Yeong-jja shin-mun* 영자 신문

newsstand *shin-mun p'an-mae-dae* 신문 판매대

New Zealand *Nyu-jil-laen-deu* 뉴질랜드

next *ta-eum* 다음

night *pam* 밤

nightclub *na-i-t'eu k'eul-leop* 나이트 클럽

no *a-ni-yo* 아니요

to be noisy *shi-kkeu-reop-tta(shi-kkeu-reo-weo-yo)* 시끄럽다(시끄러워요)

noodles *kuk-ssu* 국수

noodles (cold, with beef and vegetables) *naeng-myeon* 냉면

noodles (with black bean sauce) *jja-jang-myeon* 짜장면

noodles (with meat and vegetables) *chap-ch'ae* 잡채

noon *cheong-o* 정오

north *puk-jjok* 북쪽

North Korea (Democratic People's Republic of Korea) *Puk-han (Cho-seon min-ju-ju-eui in-min-gong-hwa-guk)* 북한 (조선 민주주의 인민공화국)

nose *k'o* 코

November *ship-i-rweol* 십일월

now *chi-geum* 지금

nowadays *yo-jeu-eum* 요즈음

number *peon-ho* 번호

nurse *kan-ho-sa* 간호사

nylon *na-il-lon* 나일론

O

oatmeal *o-t'eu-mil* 오트밀

occupation *chi-geop* 직업

ocean *pa-da* 바다

October *shi-weol* 시월

octopus (small, fried) *nak-jji po-kkeum* 낙지 볶음

of course *mul-lon* 물론

office *sa-mu-shil* 사무실

office worker *sa-mu-weon* 사무원

oil (cooking) *ki-reum* 기름

oil (auto) *o-il* 오일
to be old (object) *nal-tta(nal-ga-sseo-yo)* 낡다(낡았어요)
to be old (person) *neul-tta(neul-geo-sseo-yo)* 늙다 (늙었어요)
on *wi-e* 위에
one-way (trip) *p'yeon-do* 편도
one-way ticket *p'yeon-do-p'yo* 편도표
onion *yang-p'a* 양파
to open *yeol-da(yeo-reo-yo)* 열다(열어요)
opening ceremony *kae-mak-shik* 개막식
opera *o-p'e-ra* 오페라
opponent/counterpart *sang-dae-bang* 상대방
optician *an-gyeong-jeom* 안경점
orange *o-ren-ji* 오렌지
orchestra *o-k'e-seu-t'eu-ra* 오케스트라
to place an order *chu-mun-ha-da(hae-yo)* 주문하다 (해요)
to be out of order *ko-jang-na-da(ko-jang-na-sseo-yo)* 고장나다(고장났어요)
outside *pa-kke* 밖에
overcoat *weo-t'u* 외투
overnight *ha-rut-ppam* 하룻밤
oysters *kul* 굴

P

Pacific Ocean *T'ae-p'yeong-yang* 태평양
package *chim* 짐
paduk (board game, go) *pa-duk* 바둑
to be painful *a-p'eu-da(a-p'a-yo)* 아프다(아파요)
painkiller *chin-t'ong-je* 진통제
pajamas *cham-ot* 잠옷

palace *kung-jeon/wang-gung* 궁전/왕궁
panty *p'aen-t'i* 팬티
pantyhose *p'aen-t'i seu-t'a-k'ing* 팬티 스타킹
paper *chong-i* 종이
parcel *so-p'o* 소포
park *kong-weon* 공원
to park *chu-ch'a-ha-da(hae-yo)* 주차하다 (해요)
parking lot *chu-ch'a-jang* 주차장
passenger *seung-gaek* 승객
passport *yeo-kkweon* 여권
to pay *nae-da(nae-yo)* 내다 (내요)
to pay the bill *kye-san-ha-da(hae-yo)* 계산하다(해요)
peach *pok-sung-a* 복숭아
peanuts *ttang-k'ong* 땅콩
pear *pae* 배
pen *p'en* 펜
pencil *yeon-p'il* 연필
pentathlon *keun-dae-o-jong-kyeong-gi* 근대오종경기
pepper (black) *hu-ch'u* 후추
pepper (hot) *ko-ch'u* 고추
performance (drama) *kong-yeon* 공연
perfume *hyang-su* 향수
permanent (hair) *p'a-ma* 파마
persimmon *kam* 감
persimmon punch *su-jeong-gwa* 수정과
person *sa-ram* 사람
person (honorific) *pun* 분
personal check *kae-in su-p'yo* 개인 수표
pharmacy *yak-kkuk* 약국
Philippines *P'il-li-p'in* 필리핀
photograph *sa-jin* 사진
photography studio *sa-jin-gwan* 사진관
pier *pu-du* 부두
pillow *pe-gae* 베개
pin *p'in* 핀
ping pong *t'ak-kku* 탁구
pink *pun-hong-saek* 분홍색

pipe *p'a-i-p'eu* 파이프
pipe tobacco *p'a-i-p'eu tam-bae* 파이프 담배
pizza *p'i-ja* 피자
place/location *kot/chang-so* 곳/장소
plaid *kyeok-jja mu-ni* 격자 무늬
plan *kye-hoek* 계획
plant *hwa-ch'o* 화초
plate *cheop-shi* 접시
platinum *paek-kkeum* 백금
to **play** (amusement) *nol-da(no-ra-yo)* 놀다(놀아요)
to **play** (board games) *tu-da(tu-eo-yo)* 두다(두어요)
to **play** (concert) *yeon-ju-ha-da(hae-yo)* 연주하다(해요)
play (drama) *yeon-geuk* 연극
please *chom/che-bal* 좀/제발
Pleased to meet you. *Pan-gap-sseum-ni-da.* 반갑습니다.
pliers *p'en-jji* 펜찌
to **plug in/stick in** *kki-u-da(kki-weo-yo)* 끼우다 (끼워요)
plum *cha-du* 자두
to **point out** *chi-jeok-k'a-da(k'ae-yo)* 지적하다 (해요)
police *kyeong-ch'al* 경찰
to **polish** *takk-tta(ta-kka-yo)* 닦다(닦아요)
politician *cheong-ch'i-ga* 정치가
polyester *p'ol-li-e-seu-t'el* 폴리에스텔
pond *yeon-mot* 연못
to be **popular** *in-kki-(ga) it-tta(i-sseo-yo)* 인기(가) 있다 (있어요)
popular music *p'ap-ssong* 팝송
population *in-gu* 인구
porcelain *to-ja-gi* 도자기
pork *twae-ji-go-gi* 돼지고기
port *hang-gu* 항구

Portugal *P'o-reu-t'u-gal* 포르투갈
Portuguese (lang.) *P'o-reu-t'u-gal-eo* 포르투갈어
postcard *yeop-sseo* 엽서
picture postcard *keu-rim yeop-sseo* 그림 엽서
post office *u-ch'e-guk* 우체국
potable water *shik-ssu* 식수
potato *kam-ja* 감자
pound *p'a-un-deu* 파운드
to **pray** *ki-do-ha-da(hae-yo)* 기도하다 (해요)
to be **pregnant** *im-shin-jung-i-da(i-e-yo)* 임신중이다 (이에요)
prescription *ch'eo-bang* 처방
to be **pretty** *ye-ppeu-da(ye-ppeo-yo)* 예쁘다 (예뻐요)
price *kap* 값
priest/priest (honorific) *shin-bu/shin-bu-nim* 신부/ 신부님
print (pattern) *yeon-sok mu-ni* 연속 무늬
to **print** *p'eu-rin-t'eu-ha-da(hae-yo)* 프린트하다 (해요)
private room *pyeol-shil* 별실
professor *kyo-su* 교수
program *p'eu-ro-geu-raem* 프로그램
province *to* 도
provincial capital *to-ch'eong so-jae-ji* 도청 소재지
to **pull** *kkeul-da(kkeu-reo-yo)* 끌다(끌어요)
purple *po-ra-saek* 보라색
to **push** *mil-da(mi-reo-yo)* 밀다(밀어요)
pushcart *son-su-re* 손수레
to **put in** *neo-t'a(neo-eo-yo)* 넣다(넣어요)
to **put on** (place) *no-t'a(no-a-yo)* 놓다(놓아요)

Q

queen *yeo-wang/wang-bi* 여왕/왕비

question *chil-mun* 질문

to be **quiet** *cho-yong-ha-da(hae-yo)* 조용하다(해요)

to **quit; sever; hang up** *kkeun-t'a(kkeu-neo-yo)* 끊다 (끊어요)

R

rabbi *rap-ppi* 랍비

racket *ra-k'et* 라켓

radiator *naeng-gak-kki* 냉각기

radio *ra-di-o* 라디오

radish *mu* 무

rain *pi* 비

raincoat *u-bi* 우비

rainy season *chang-ma-ch'eol* 장마철

raisins *keon-p'o-do* 건포도

rate *pi-yul* 비율

raw (uncooked) *nal-geot* 날것

razor *myeon-do-k'al* 면도칼

razor blades *myeon-do-nal* 면도날

to **read** *il-tta(il-geo-yo)* 읽다 (읽어요)

really *cheong-mal* 정말

receipt *yeong-su-jeung* 영수증

to **receive** *pat-tta(pa-da-yo)* 받다(받아요)

to **recharge** *ch'ung-jeon-ha-da(hae-yo)* 충전하다 (해요)

recommend/introduce *so-gae-ha-da(hae-yo)* 소개하다 (해요)

reconfirm *chae-hwa-gin-ha-da(hae-yo)* 재확인하다 (해요)

record *re-k'o-deu* 레코드

to **record** *no-geum-ha-da(hae-yo)* 녹음하다(해요)

red *ppal-gang/ppal-gan-saek* 빨강/빨간색

red pepper paste *ko-ch'u-jang* 고추장

red pepper powder *ko-ch'ut-ga-ru* 고춧가루

to **refund** *hwan-bul-ha-da(hae-yo)* 환불하다(해요)

regards (to give) *an-bu cheon-hae chu-da(chweo-yo)* 안부 전해 주다(줘요)

region *chi-bang* 지방

to be **religious** *chong-gyo-jeok-i-da(i-e-yo)* 종교적이다 (이에요)

religious service *ye-bae* 예배

to **remain** *nam-tta(nam-a-yo)* 남다(남아요)

to **remove** *ppae-da(ppae-yo)* 빼다(빼요)

to **rent** *pil-li-da(pil-lyeo-yo)* 빌리다(빌려요)

to **repair** *ko-ch'i-da(ko-ch'yeo-yo)* 고치다(고쳐요)

repair shop *cheong-bi-so* 정비소

to **replace** *kal-da(ka-ra-yo)* 갈다(갈아요)

reservation *ye-yak* 예약

reserved seat *chi-jeong-seok* 지정석

restaurant *eum-shik-jjeom/shik-ttang* 음식점/식당

  barbecue meat restaurant *pul-go-gi-jjip* 불고기집

  Chinese restaurant *chung-guk-jjip* 중국집

  dumpling restaurant *man-du-jjip* 만두집

  ginseng chicken restaurant *sam-gye-t'ang-jjip* 삼계탕집

  Japanese restaurant *il-shik-jjip* 일식집

  raw fish restaurant *hoe-jjip* 횟집

steamed rice and side dishes restaurant *paek-ppan-jjip* 백반집

drinking establishment *sul-jjip* 술집

restroom *hwa-jang-shil* 화장실

retail *so-mae* 소매

to **return** (v.i.) *to-ra-o-da(to-ra-wa-yo)* 돌아오다 (돌아와요)

rib *kal-bi-ppyeo* 갈비뼈

rice (cooked) *pap* 밥

rice (uncooked) *ssal* 쌀

    rice (with curry sauce) *k'a-re-ra-i-seu* 카레라이스

    rice (with side dishes) *paek-ppan* 백반

    rice (mixed with vegetables) *pi-bim-ppap* 비빔밥

rice cake *tteok* 떡

rice omelet *o-meu-ra-i-seu* 오므라이스

rice paddy *non* 논

rice punch *shik-k'ye* 식혜

rice wine *cheong-jong* 정종

rice/barley wine *mak-kkeol-li* 막걸리

to be **right** (correct) *mat-tta(ma-ja-yo)* 맞다 (맞아요)

right (direction) *o-reun-jjok* 오른쪽

ring *pan-ji* 반지

river *kang* 강

road *kil* 길

rock café *rak-k'a-p'e* 락카페

rock 'n' roll *ro-k'eun-rol* 로큰롤

romance *ae-jeong* 애정

room *pang* 방

    double room *i-in-yong pang* 이인용 방

    single room *tok-ppang* 독방

    Korean-style room *on-dol pang* 온돌 방

western-style room *ch'im-dae pang* 침대 방

room salon *rum-sal-long* 룸살롱

room service *rum sseo-bi-seu* 룸 서비스

rouge/blush *ru-jeu/ip-sul-yeon-ji* 루즈/입술연지

round-trip *wang-bok* 왕복

rowing *cho-jeong* 조정

rubber bands *ko-mu-jul* 고무줄

ruler (measure) *cha* 자

rum *reom* 럼

rush hour *reo-shi-a-weo* 러시아워

Russia *So-ryeon/Reo-shi-a* 소련/러시아

Russian (lang.) *So-ryeon-eo/Reo-shi-a-eo* 소련어/러시아어

Russian (person) *So-ryeon sa-ram/Reo-shi-a sa-ram* 소련 사람/러시아 사람

S

to be **safe** *an-jeon-ha-da(hae-yo)* 안전하다(해요)

safe (valuables) *keum-go* 금고

to leave for **safekeeping** *mat-kki-da(mat-kkyeo-yo)* 맡기다(맡겨요)

safety pin *an-jeon-p'in* 안전핀

salad *sael-leo-deu* 샐러드

sale *ha-rin p'an-mae* 할인 판매

salmon *yeon-eo* 연어

salt *so-geum* 소금

to be **salty** *jja-da(jja-yo)* 짜다(짜요)

to be **the same** *kat-tta(ka-t'a-yo)* 같다(같아요)

sandwich *saen-deu-wi-ch'i* 샌드위치

sanitary napkins *saeng-ni-dae* 생리대

to be **satisfied with** *ma-eum-e teul-da(teu-reo-yo)* 마음에 들다(들어요)

Saturday *t'o-yo-il* 토요일

sauna *sa-u-na* 사우나

to **scan** *seu-k'aen-ha-da(hae-yo)* 스캔하다(해요)

scarf *mok-tto-ri* 목도리

schedule *seu-k'e-jul* 스케줄

school *hak-kkyo* 학교

science fiction film *kong-sang kwa-hak yeong-hwa* 공상 과학영화

scissors *ka-wi* 가위

scissors (nail) *son-t'op ka-wi* 손톱 가위

scotch (whiskey) *seu-k'a-ch'i* 스카치

Scotch® tape *seu-k'a-ch'i t'e-i-p'eu* 스카치 테이프

screen (folding) *pyeong-p'ung* 병풍

screwdriver *teu-ra-i-beo* 드라이버

scroll (wall hanging) *chok-jja* 족자

sculptor *cho-gak-kka* 조각가

sea mail *seon-bak-p'yeon* 선박편

seashore *hae-byeon* 해변

to be **seasick** *pae-meol-mi na-da(na-yo)* 배멀미 나다(나요)

season *kye-jeol* 계절

seat *chwa-seok/eui-ja* 좌석/의자

seaweed (toasted) *kim* 김

second-class ticket *i-deung-p'yo* 이등표

secretary *pi-seo* 비서

to **see** *po-da(pwa-yo)* 보다(봐요)

to be worth **seeing** *pol man-ha-da(hae-yo)* 볼 만하다(해요)

to **see one off** *cheon-song-ha-da(hae-yo)* 전송하다(해요)

See you later. *Na-jung-e poep-kke-sseo-yo.* 나중에 뵙겠어요.

to **seem** _____ _____ *(-eun/neun keot) kat-tta(ka-t'a-yo)* _____ (은/는 것) 같다(같아요)

to **sell** *p'al-da(p'a-ra-yo)* 팔다(팔아요)

to **send** *po-nae-da(po-nae-yo)* 보내다(보내요)

senior citizen *no-in* 노인

Seoul Olympic Games *Seo-ul ol-lim-p'ik tae-hoe* 서울 올림픽 대회

September *ku-weol* 구월

service charge *pong-sa-ryo/t'ip* 봉사료/팁

sesame oil *ch'am-gi-reum* 참기름

Shall we _____? _____ *hal-kka-yo?* _____ 할까요?

shampoo *shyam-p'u* 샴푸

to **shampoo** *meo-ri-reul kam-tta(kam-a-yo)* 머리를 감다(감아요)

to **shave** *myeon-do-ha-da(hae-yo)* 면도하다(해요)

shaving cream *myeon-do k'eu-rim* 면도 크림

she/he (honorific) *keu pun* 그 분

she/he *keu sa-ram* 그 사람

ship *pae* 배

shirt *wa-i-shyeo-ch'eu* 와이셔츠

shoes *shin-bal/ku-du* 신발/구두

shoelaces *ku-du-kkeun* 구두끈

shoe store *yang-hwa-jeom* 양화점

shooting (sport) *sa-gyeok* 사격

to **shop** *shyo-p'ing-ha-da(hae-yo)* 쇼핑하다(해요)

shopping mall *shyo-p'ing-mol*
쇼핑몰

to be short *jjal-tta(jjal-ba-
yo)* 짧다(짧아요)

shoulder *eo-kkae* 어깨

to show *po-yeo chu-da(chweo-
yo)* 보여 주다(줘요)

shower (place) *sha-weo-jang*
샤워장

showing (movie) *sang-yeong*
상영

shrimp *sae-u* 새우

sick (to get) *pyeong-i na-
da(na-yo)* 병이 나다(나요)

side dishes *pan-ch'an* 반찬

to sightsee *kwan-gwang-ha-
da(hae-yo)* 관광하다
(해요)

to sign *ssa-in-ha-da(hae-yo)*
싸인하다(해요)

signature *seo-myeong* 서명

silk *shil-k'eu* 실크

silver *eun* 은

to be similar *pi-seut-t'a-
da(t'ae-yo)* 비슷하다(해요)

to sing *no-rae-ha-da(hae-yo)*
노래하다(해요)

singing room *no-rae-bang*
노래방

Singapore *Shing-ga-p'o-reu*
싱가포르

to be single *mi-hon-i-da(i-e-
yo)* 미혼이다(이에요)

sink *sshing-k'eu-dae* 씽크대

to sit *an-tta(an-ja-yo)* 앉다
(앉아요)

size *ssa-i-jeu* 싸이즈

to ski *seu-k'i-t'a-da(t'a-yo)*
스키타다(타요)

skin *p'i-bu* 피부

skirt *ch'i-ma/seu-k'eo-t'eu*
치마/스커트

slacks *pa-ji* 바지

to sleep *cha-da(cha-yo)* 자다
(자요)

to sleep (honorific) *chu-mu-
shi-da(chu-mu-shyeo-yo)* 주
무시다(주무셔요)

sleeping car (train) *ch'im-
dae-ch'a* 침대차

sleeping pills *su-myeon-je*
수면제

to be sleepy *chol-li-da(chol-
lyeo-yo)* 졸리다(졸려요)

sleeve (long) *kin so-mae* 긴
소매

sleeve (short) *jjal-beun so-
mae* 짧은 소매

slip *seul-lip/sok-ch'i-ma* 슬립/
속치마

slippers *seul-li-p'eo* 슬리퍼

to be slow *neu-ri-da(neu-
ryeo-yo)* 느리다(느려요)

slowly *ch'eon-ch'eon-hi*
천천히

to be small *chak-tta(cha-ga-
yo)* 작다(작아요)

small (size) *seu-mol* 스몰

to smile *mi-so-jit-tta(mi-so-ji-
eo-yo)* 미소짓다
(미소지어요)

to smoke (tobacco) *p'i-u-
da(p'i-weo-yo)* 피우다
(피워요)

no smoking *keum-yeon*
금연

non-smoking seat *keum-
yeon-seok* 금연석

snow *nun* 눈

soap *pi-nu* 비누

soccer *ch'uk-kku* 축구

socks *yang-mal* 양말

soju (sweet potato wine) *so-ju*
소주

somebody *nu-gu* 누구

soldier *kun-in* 군인

son *a-deul* 아들

song *no-rae* 노래

soon *kot* 곧

sore throat (to have) *mok
(-gu-meong)-i a-p'eu-da(a-
p'a-yo)* 목(구멍)이 아프다
(아파요)

soup *kuk* 국

    bean sprout soup *k'ong-
na-mul-kkuk* 콩나물국

fish soup (spicy) *mae-un-t'ang* 매운탕

meat dumpling soup *man-du-kkuk* 만두국

rib soup *kal-bi-t'ang* 갈비탕

seaweed soup *mi-yeok-kkuk* 미역국

spicy seafood noodle soup *jjam-ppong* 짬뽕

south *nam-jjok* 남쪽

South America *Nam-a-me-ri-k'a* 남아메리카

South American (person) *Nam-a-me-ri-k'a sa-ram* 남아메리카 사람

South Korea (Republic of Korea) *Tae-han-min-guk* 대한민국

souvenir *ki-nyeom-p'um* 기념품

souvenir shop *seon-mul ka-ge* 선물 가게

soy sauce *kan-jang* 간장

spa *jjim-jil-bang* 찜질방

Spain *Seu-p'e-in* 스페인

Spanish (lang.) *Seu-p'e-in-eo* 스페인어

spark plugs *cheom-hwa-jeon* 점화전

to speak *mal-ha-da(hae-yo)* 말하다 (해요)

to speak (honorific) *mal-sseum-ha-shi-da(ha-se-yo)* 말씀하시다 (하세요)

specialty *cheon-mun* 전문

to spend time *chi-nae-da(chi-nae-yo)* 지내다 (지내요)

spinach (seasoned, blanched) *shi-geum-ch'i-na-mul* 시금치나물

spine *ch'eok-ch'u* 척추

sponge *seu-p'on-ji* 스폰지

spoon *su-kka-rak* 숟가락

sports *un-dong* 운동

to sprain *ppi-da(ppi-eo-sseo-yo)* 삐다 (삐었어요)

spray *seu-p'eu-re-i* 스프레이

spring *pom* 봄

squid *o-jing-eo* 오징어

stadium *un-dong-jang* 운동장

baseball stadium *ya-gu-jang* 야구장

stain *eol-luk* 얼룩

stainless steel *seu-t'en-re-seu* 스텐레스

stamp *u-p'yo* 우표

to stand *seo-da(seo-yo)* 서다 (서요)

station *yeok* 역

stationery store *mun-pang-gu-jeom* 문방구점

to stay (as in hotel) *muk-tta (mu-geo-yo)* 묵다 (묵어요)

to steal *hum-ch'i-da(hum-ch'yeo-yo)* 훔치다 (훔쳐요)

stew (soy bean paste and vegetables) *toen-jang-jji-gae* 된장찌개

sting (to receive) *sso-i-da(sso-yeo-yo)* 쏘이다 (쏘여요)

stomach *pae* 배

stomachache (to have) *pae-ga a-p'eu-da(a-p'a-yo)* 배가 아프다 (아파요)

stone (jewelry) *po-seok* 보석

to stop (v.t.) *se-u-da(se-weo-yo)* 세우다 (세워요)

store *ka-ge* 가게

straight (direction) *ttok-ppa-ro* 똑바로

strawberry *ttal-gi* 딸기

stream *shi-nae-mul* 시냇물

street *to-ro* 도로

string *kkeun* 끈

stripes *chul-mu-ni* 줄무늬

to be strong *kang-ha-da(hae-yo)* 강하다 (해요)

student *hak-ssaeng* 학생

style *seu-t'a-il* 스타일

subtitles (movie) *cha-mak* 자막

English subtitles *Yeong-eo-ja-mak* 영어자막

subway *chi-ha-ch'eol* 지하철

sugar *seol-t'ang* 설탕

suit (men's) *nam-ja yang-bok*
남자양복

summer *yeo-reum* 얼음

to **summon** *pu-reu-da(pul-leo-yo)* 부르다(불러요)

Sunday *i-ryo-il* 일요일

sunglasses *seon-geul-lae-seu*
선글래스

sunscreen *seon-seu-k'eu-rin*
선스크린

suntan lotion *seon-t'aen ro-shyeon* 선탠 로션

supermarket *su-p'eo-ma-k'et*
수퍼마켓

suppositories *chwa-yak* 좌약

surgeon *oe-kkwa-eui-sa*
외과의사

  surgeon (cosmetic) *seong-hyeong-oe-kkwa eui-sa*
  성형외과 의사

sushi restaurant *hoe-jjip*
횟집

sweater *seu-we-t'eo* 스웨터

to **be sweet** *tal-da(ta-ra-yo)*
달다(달아요)

sweat suit *ttam-bok* 땀복

to **swell** *put-tta(pu-eo-yo)*
붓다(부어요)

to **swim** *su-yeong-ha-da(hae-yo)* 수영하다 (해요)

swimming pool *su-yeong-jang*
수영장

swimsuit *su-yeong-bok*
수영복

synagogue *yu-t'ae-gyo hoe-dang* 유태교 회당

synthetic *hap-seong* 합성

T

table *t'e-i-beul* 테이블
tablet *al-lyak* 알약
table tennis *t'ak-kku* 탁구
tailor *yang-bok-jjeom* 양복점
Taiwan *Tae-man* 대만
to **take** (transportation) *t'a-da(t'a-yo)* 타다(타요)

to **take lessons** *kang-seup-eul pat-tta(pa-da-yo)* 강습을
받다(받아요)

to **take off** (clothes) *peot-tta (peo-seo-yo)* 벗다(벗어요)

to **take a picture** *sa-jin jjik-tta(jji-geo-yo)* 사진 찍다
(찍어요)

to **take time** *keol-li-da(keol-lyeo-yo)* 걸리다(걸려요)

talcum powder *pun* 분

to **be tall** *k'i-ga k'eu-da(k'eo-yo)* 키가 크다(커요)

tampon *t'am-p'on* 탐폰
tangerine *kyul* 귤
tax *se-geum* 세금
taxi *t'aek-shi* 택시
tea *hong-ch'a* 홍차

  ginger tea *saeng-gang-ch'a*
  생강차

  ginseng tea *in-sam-ch'a*
  인삼차

  green tea *nok-ch'a* 녹차

  jujube tea *tae-ch'u-ch'a*
  대추차

to **teach** *ka-reu-ch'i-da(ka-reu-ch'yeo-yo)* 가르치다
(가르쳐요)

teacher/teacher (honorific)
seon-saeng/seon-saeng-nim 선생/선생님

teahouse *ch'a-jjip* 찻집
team *t'im* 팀
tee shirt *t'i-shyeo-ch'eu*
티셔츠
telegram *cheon-bo* 전보
telephone/telephone

  call *cheon-hwa* 전화
  collect call *su-shin-in chi-bul cheon-hwa* 수신인 지불
  전화
  international call
  kuk-jje cheon-hwa 국제
  전화
  local call *shi-nae cheon-hwa* 시내 전화
  long-distance call *shi-woe cheon-hwa* 시외 전화

public telephone *kong-jung cheon-hwa* 공중 전화

to telephone *cheon-hwa-ha-da(hae-yo)* 전화하다(해요)

telephone directory *cheon-hwa peon-ho-bu* 전화 번호부

telephone number *cheon-hwa peon-ho* 전화 번호

telephone operator *kyo-hwan* 교환

television *t'el-le-bi-jeon* 텔레비전

temple (Buddhist) *cheol* 절

temple stay program *t'em-p'eul seu-t'e-i p'eu-ro-geu-raem* 템플 스테이 프로그램

temporarily *im-shi-ro* 임시로

tennis *t'e-ni-seu* 테니스

tennis shoes *t'e-ni-seu-hwa* 테니스화

Thai (lang.) *T'ae-gu-geo* 태국어

Thailand *T'ae-guk* 태국

Thank you. *Kam-sa-ham-ni-da.* 감사합니다. *Ko-map-sseum-ni-da.* 고맙습니다. *Su-go-ha-shyeo-sseo-yo.* 수고하셨어요.

that *keu-geot/cheo-geot* 그것/저것

theater *keuk-jjang* 극장

there *keo-gi/cheo-gi* 거기/저기

thermometer *ch'e-on-gye* 체온계

they (honorific) *keu pun-deul* 그 분들

they *keu-deul* 그들

thigh *neolp-jjeok-tta-ri* 넓적다리

to be thirsty *mok-i ma-reu-da(mal-la-yo)* 목이 마르다 (말라요)

this *i-geot* 이것

thriller movie *kong-p'o yeong-hwa* 공포영화

throat *mok-kku-meong* 목구멍

to throw away *peo-ri-da(peo-ryeo-yo)* 버리다(버려요)

thumb *eom-ji-son-kka-rak* 엄지손가락

Thursday *mok-yo-il* 목요일

ticket *p'yo* 표

　　ticket (regular) *il-ban-shil p'yo* 일반실 표

　　ticket (standing) *cha-yu-seok p'yo* 자유석 표

ticket machine *ch'a-p'yo cha-dong p'an-mae-gi* 차표 자동 판매기

ticket office *mae-p'yo-so* 매표소

ticket window *mae-p'yo-gu* 매표구

tie *nek-t'a-i* 넥타이

to be tight *kkok kki-da(kkok kkyeo-yo)* 꼭 끼다(꼭 껴요)

time *shi-gan* 시간

timetable *shi-gan-p'yo* 시간표

tip/service charge *t'ip/pong-sa-ryo* 팁/봉사료

tire *t'a-i-eo* 타이어

to be tired *p'i-gon-ha-da(hae-yo)* 피곤하다(해요)

tissue *t'i-shyu* 티슈

title *che-mok* 제목

T-money card *Kyo-t'ong-k'a-deu* 교통카드

to *e* 에

toast *t'o-seu-t'eu* 토스트

tobacco shop *tam-bae ka-ge* 담배 가게

today *o-neul* 오늘

toe *pal-kka-rak* 발가락

toilet *pyeon-gi* 변기

toilet paper *hyu-ji/hwa-jang-ji* 휴지/화장지

toiletries *hwa-jang-p'um* 화장품

tomato *t'o-ma-t'o* 토마토

tomato juice *t'o-ma-t'o chyu-seu* 토마토 쥬스

tomorrow *nae-il* 내일

tongue *hyeo* 혀

tonight *o-neul-ppam* 오늘밤
tool *to-gu* 도구
too much *neo-mu* 너무
tooth/teeth *i* 이
toothache *ch'i-t'ong* 치통
toothbrush *ch'i-ssol* 칫솔
toothpaste *ch'i-yak* 치약
toothpick *i-ssu-shi-gae* 이쑤시개
topaz *hwang-ok* 황옥
to **tour** *kwan-gwang-ha-da(hae-yo)* 관광하다(해요)
tour guide book *kwan-gwang an-nae-seo* 관광 안내서
tourist *kwan-gwang-gaek* 관광객
tourist information center *kwan-gwang an-nae-so* 관광 안내소
towel *t'a-ol/su-geon* 타올/수건
 scrub towel *i-t'ae-ri t'a-ol* 이태리 타올
toy *chang-nan-kkam* 장난감
track and field *yuk-ssang* 육상
to be **traditional** *cheon-t'ong-jeok-i-da(i-e-yo)* 전통적이다(이에요)
tragedy *pi-geuk* 비극
train *yeol-ch'a/ki-ch'a* 열차/기차
tranquilizers *chin-jeong-je* 진정제
to **transfer** (transportation) *ka-ra-t'a-da(t'a-yo)* 갈아타다(타요)
to **translate** *peon-yeok-k'a-da(k'ae-yo)* 번역하다(해요)
to **travel** *yeo-haeng-ha-da(hae-yo)* 여행하다(해요)
travel agency *yeo-haeng-sa* 여행사
travelers checks *yeo-haeng-ja su-p'yo* 여행자 수표
treatment (medical) *ch'i-ryo* 치료
trees *na-mu* 나무

to **trim** *ta-deum-tta(ta-deu-meo-yo)* 다듬다(다듬어요)
trip *yeo-haeng* 여행
trousers *pa-ji* 바지
to **try on** *i-beo po-da(i-beo pwa-yo)* 입어 보다(입어 봐요)
Tuesday *hwa-yo-il* 화요일
tweezers *jjok-jjip-kke* 쪽집게
type/style *t'a-ip/seu-t'a-il* 타입/스타일
typhoon *t'ae-p'ung* 태풍

U

to be **ugly** *mip-tta(mi-weo-yo)* 밉다(미워요)
ulcer (stomach) *wi-gwe-yang* 위궤양
umbrella *u-san* 우산
undershirt *reon-ning-shyeo-ch'eu* 런닝셔츠
undershorts (men's) *p'aen-t'i* 팬티
to **understand** *al-da(a-ra-yo)* 알다(알아요)
 I understand. *Al-ge-sseo-yo.* 알겠어요.
 I don't understand. *Mo-reu-ge-sseo-yo.* 모르겠어요.
underwear *so-got* 속옷
 underwear (long) *nae-bok* 내복
United States *Mi-guk* 미국
university *tae-hak-kkyo* 대학교
up *wi(-ro)* 위(로)
to **use** *sseu-da(sseo-yo)* 쓰다(써요)
usually *po-t'ong* 보통

V

vacation *hyu-ga* 휴가
valley *kol-jja-ki* 골짜기

valuables *kwi-jung-p'um* 귀중품

vegetables *ya-ch'ae/ch'ae-so* 야채/채소

vegetarian restaurant *ch'ae-shik shik-dang* 채식 식당

vehicle *ch'a* 차

vending machine *cha-dong-p'an-mae-gi* 자동판매기

venue *kyeong-gi-jang* 경기장

very much *tae-dan-hi/a-ju* 대단히/아주

Vietnam *Pe-t'eu-nam* 베트남

Vietnamese (lang.) *Pe-t'eu-nam-eo* 베트남어

view *kyeong-ch'i* 경치

village *ma-eul* 마을

vinegar *shik-ch'o* 식초

vinyl *pi-nil* 비닐

to visit *pang-mun-ha-da(hae-yo)* 방문하다(해요)

vitamins *pi-t'a-min* 비타민

vodka *po-deu-k'a* 보드카

volcano *hwa-san* 화산

volleyball *pae-gu* 배구

voltage *cheon-ap* 전압

W

to wait *ki-da-ri-da(ki-da-ryeo-yo)* 기다리다(기다려요)

to wake up *kkae-u-da(kkae-weo-yo)* 깨우다(깨워요)

to walk *keot-tta(keo-reo-yo)* 걷다(걸어요)

wallet *chi-gap* 지갑

to want *weon-ha-da(hae-yo)* 원하다(해요)

to want to _____ _____-go ship-tta(shi-p'eo-yo) _____ 고 싶다(싶어요)

war movie *cheon-jaeng yeong-hwa* 전쟁영화

to be warm *tta-tteut-t'a-da(t'ae-yo)* 따뜻하다(해요)

to wash (laundry) *ppal-da(ppa-ra-yo)* 빨다(빨아요)

watch/wristwatch *son-mok shi-gye* 손목 시계

to watch *ku-gyeong-ha-da(hae-yo)* 구경하다(해요)

watch and clock store *shi-gye-ppang* 시계방

water *mul* 물

water (boiled) *kkeu-rin mul* 끓인 물

water (bottled) *saeng-su* 생수

waterfall *p'ok-p'o* 폭포

watermelon *su-bak* 수박

water polo *su-gu* 수구

waves (water) *p'a-do* 파도

to be wavy (hair) *we-i-beu-ji-da(jyeo-yo)* 웨이브지다(져요)

we *u-ri* 우리

to be weak *yak-k'a-da(k'ae-yo)* 약하다(해요)

to wear *ip-tta(i-beo-yo)* 입다(입어요)

weather *nal-sshi* 날씨

weather forecast *il-gi-ye-bo* 일기예보

Wednesday *su-yo-il* 수요일

week *chu* 주

weekday *p'yeong-il* 평일

weekend *chu-mal* 주말

weight (body) *mom-mu-ge* 몸무게

weightlifting *yeok-tto* 역도

Welcome. *Eo-seo o-se-yo.* 어서 오세요.

well *chal* 잘

west *seo-jjok* 서쪽

western (film) *seo-bu yeong-hwa* 서부영화

what *mu-eot* 무엇

what kind *mu-seun/eo-tteon* 무슨/어떤

when *eon-je* 언제

where *eo-di* 어디

which *eo-neu* 어느

whiskey *wi-seu-k'i* 위스키

white *ha-yang/ha-yan-saek* 하양/하얀색

who *nu-gu* 누구

wholesale *to-mae* 도매

why *wae* 왜
to be **wide** *neol-tta(neol-beo-yo)* 넓다(넓어요)
wife (one's own) *a-nae* 아내
wife (someone else's) *pu-in* 부인
to **win** *i-gi-da(i-gyeo-yo)* 이기다(이겨요)
wind *pa-ram* 바람
window *ch'ang-mun* 창문
wine (red) *cheok-p'o-do-ju/wa-in* 적포도주/와인
wine (white) *paek-p'o-do-ju/wa-in* 백포도주/와인
winter *kyeo-ul* 겨울
wireless Internet *mu-seon In-t'eo-net* 무선 인터넷
with _____*-gwa/wa ham-kke* _____ 과/와 함께
woman *yeo-ja* 여자
won (Korean currency) *weon* 원
wood *mok-jjae* 목재
wool *mo* 모
to **work** *il-ha-da(hae-yo)* 일하다(해요)
to **work hard** *su-go-ha-da(hae-yo)* 수고하다(해요)
to **wrap** *p'o-jang-ha-da(hae-yo)* 포장하다(해요)
wrench *seu-p'ae-neo/ren-ch'i* 스패너/렌치

wrestling *re-seul-ling* 레슬링
wrestling (traditional Korean) *sshi-reum* 씨름
wrist *son-mok* 손목
to **write** *sseu-da(sseo-yo)* 쓰다(써요)
to be **wrong** *t'eul-li-da(t'eul-lyeo-yo)* 틀리다(틀려요)

XYZ

X-ray *ek-sseu-re-i* 엑스레이
yachting *yo-t'eu-t'a-gi* 요트타기
year *nyeon* 년
yellow *no-rang/no-ran-saek* 노랑/노란색
yes *ne/ye* 네/예
yesterday *eo-je* 어제
you (sing., honorific) *seon-saeng-nim* 선생님
you (sing.) *ne-ga/neo-neun* 네가/너는
you (plural, honorific) *yeo-reo-bun* 여러분
you (plural) *neo-heui-deul* 너희들
zipper *chi-p'eo* 지퍼
zoo *tong-mul-weon* 동물원

KOREAN-ENGLISH DICTIONARY

A

a-beo-ji father 아버지
a-ch'im morning 아침
a-ch'im shik-sa breakfast 아침 식사
a-deul son 아들
a-dong-bok clothing (children's) 아동복
ae-gi baby 애기
ae-jeong romance 애정
aeng-du cherries 앵두
a-i/eo-rin-i child 아이/어린이
a-i-deul/eo-rin-i-deul children 아이들/어린이들
a-i ra-i-neo eyeliner 아이 라이너
a-i-seu k'eu-rim ice cream 아이스 크림
a-i shyae-do-u eye-shadow 아이 섀도우
al-lyak tablet 알약
al-da(a-ra-yo) to know/understand 알다(알아요)
Al-ge-sseo-yo. I understand. 알겠어요.
al-k'ol alcohol 알콜
al-lam-shi-gye alarm clock 알람시계
al-le-reu-gi allergy 알레르기
al-lyeo chu-da(chweo-yo) to inform 알려 주다(줘요)
a-nae wife (one's own) 아내
an-bu cheon-hae chu-da(chweo-yo) to give regards 안부 전해 주다 (줘요)
an-e in안에
an-gyeong glasses 안경
an-gyeong-jeom optician 안경점

a-ni-yo no 아니요
an-jeon-ha-da(hae-yo) to be safe 안전하다(해요)
an-jeon-p'in safety pin 안전핀
an-ju appetizers (for alcoholic drinks) 안주
an-nae information 안내
an-nae-so information desk 안내소
an-nae-weon guide (person) 안내원
An-nyeong-ha-se-yo? Good afternoon. Good evening. Good morning. How are you? 안녕하세요 ?
An-nyeong-hi chu-mu-se-yo. Good-night. (before sleeping) 안녕히 주무세요.
An-nyeong-hi ka-se-yo. Good-bye. 안녕히 가세요.
an-tta(an-ja-yo) to sit 앉다 (앉아요)
an-yak eyedrops 안약
ap front 앞
a-p'e in front 앞에
a-p'eu-da(a-p'a-yo) to be painful 아프다(아파요)
A-p'eu-ri-k'a Africa 아프리카
a-rae down 아래
a-reum-dap-tta(a-reum-da-weo-yo) to be beautiful 아름답다(아름다워요)
a-seu-p'i-rin aspirin 아스피린

Ch

cha ruler (measure) 자
cha-da(cha-yo) to sleep 자다(자요)

cha-dong-p'an-mae-gi vending machine 자동판매기

cha-du plum 자두

chae-da(chae-eo-yo) to measure 재다(재어요)

chae-hwa-gin-ha-da(hae-yo) reconfirm 재확인하다(해요)

chae-mi-it-tta(i-sseo-yo) to be interesting 재미있다 (있어요)

chae-tteo-ri ashtray 재떨이

cha-jeon-geo bicycle 자전거

cha-jeon-geo t'a-da(t'a-yo) to ride a bike 자전거 타다 (타요)

cha-ju saek burgundy (color) 자주 색

chak-kka writer 작가

chak-tta(cha-ga-yo) to be small 작다(작아요)

cha-k'et jacket 자켓

cha-mak subtitles (movie) 자막

cha-yu-seok p'yo ticket (standing) 자유석 표

chal well 잘

chal-mot-t'a-da(t'ae-yo) make a mistake 잘못하다 (해요)

cham-geu-da(cham-ga-yo) to lock 잠그다(잠가요)

cham-gi-da(cham-gyeo-yo) to be locked 잠기다 (잠겨요)

cham-ot pajamas 잠옷

chan glass (drinking) 잔

chan-don change (coins) 잔돈

chang-gap gloves 장갑

chang-gi chess (Korean-style) 장기

chang-go-ch'um drum dance (traditional Korean) 장고춤

chang-ma-ch'eol rainy season 장마철

chang-nan-kkam toy 장난감

chap-ch'ae noodles (with meat and vegetables) 잡채

chap-jji magazine 잡지

chap-su-shi-da(chap-su-shyeo-yo) to eat (honorific) 잡수시다 (잡수셔요)

cha-su-jeong amethyst 자수정

che-ga/che-neun I (modest form) 제가/저는

che-il cho-a-ha-da(hae-yo) favorite 제일 좋아하다 (해요)

che-mok title 제목

cheo-geot that 저것

cheo-ja author 저자

cheok-p'o-do-ju/wa-in wine (red) 적포도주/와인

cheok-ttang-ha-da(hae-yo) to be appropriate 적당하다 (해요)

cheo-kka-rak chopsticks 젓가락

cheol temple (Buddhist) 절

cheom-hwa-jeon spark plugs 점화전

cheom-neun eui-ja folding chair 접는 의자

cheom-shim(shik-sa) lunch 점심 (식사)

cheom-tta(cheol-meo-yo) young(adult) 젊다(젊어요)

cheon-ap voltage 전압

cheon-bo telegram 전보

cheon-bok abalone 전복

cheon-e before 전에

cheong-bi-gong mechanic 정비공

cheong-bi-so repair shop 정비소

cheong-ga fixed price 정가

cheon-gi electricity 전기

cheong-jong rice wine 정종

cheong-mal really 정말

cheong-o noon 정오

cheon-gu lightbulb 전구

cheong-weon garden 정원

cheon-hwa telephone/
telephone call 전화

cheon-hwa-ha-da(hae-yo)
to telephone 전화하다(해요)

cheon-hwa peon-ho
telephone number 전화 번호

cheon-hwa peon-ho-bu
telephone directory 전화
번호부

cheon-jaeng yeong-hwa war
movie 전쟁영화

cheon-ja-je-p'um-jeom
electrical appliance store
전자제품점

cheon-mun specialty 전문

cheon-song-ha-da(hae-yo)
to see one off 전송하다
(해요)

cheon-shi-ha-da(hae-yo) to
exhibit 전시하다(해요)

cheon-t'ong-jeok-i-da to be
traditional 전통적이다

cheo-nyeok evening 저녁

cheo-nyeok(shik-sa)
dinner 저녁(식사)

cheop-ch'ak t'e-i-p'eu
adhesive tape 접착 테이프

cheop-shi plate 접시

che-san-je antacid 제산제

***cheul-geop-tta(cheul-geo-
weo-yo)*** to enjoy 즐겁다
(즐거워요)

chi-ap acupressure 지압

chi-ap-sa acupressurist
지압사

chi-bae-in manager 지배인

chi-bang region 지방

chi-do map 지도

chi-gap wallet 지갑

chi-geop occupation 직업

chi-geum now 지금

chi-ha-ch'eol subway 지하철

chi-ha-eum-shik-sang-ga
food court 지하음식상가

chi-jeok-k'a-da(k'ae-yo) to
point out 지적하다(해요)

chi-jeong-seok reserved seat
지정석

chi-jin earthquake 지진

chik-k'aeng direct (route)
직행

chil-mun question 질문

chim package/baggage 짐

chin gin 진

chi-nae-da(chi-nae-yo) to
spend time 지내다(지내요)

chin-jeong-je tranquilizers
진정제

chin-t'ong-je painkiller
진통제

chip house 집

chi-p'eo zipper 지퍼

chi-p'i-e-seu/ne-bi-ge-i-shyeon
GPS (global positioning
system) 지피에스/
네비게이션

chi-p'ye bills (currency) 지폐

chit-tta(chi-eo-yo) to build
짓다(지어요)

chi-u-gae eraser 지우개

cho-a-ha-da(hae-yo) to like
좋아하다(해요)

cho-gak-kka sculptor 조각가

cho-geum a little 조금

cho-ging-ha-da(hae-yo) to
jog 조깅하다(해요)

cho-jeong rowing 조정

chok-jja scroll (wall
hanging) 족자

chol-li-da(chol-lyeo-yo) to be
sleepy 졸리다(졸려요)

chom/che-bal please 좀/
제발

chong-gi-ga na-da(na-yo)
to have an abscess
종기가 나다(나요)

chong-gyo-jeok-i-da(i-e-yo)
to be religious 종교적이다
(이에요)

chong-i paper 종이

chong-i ki-jeo-gwi diapers
(disposable) 종이 기저귀

chop-tta(cho-ba-yo) to be
narrow 좁다(좁아요)

cho-shim-ha-da(hae-yo) to
be careful 조심하다(해요)

cho-t'a(*cho-a-yo*) to be good 좋다(좋아요)

cho-yong-ha-da(*hae-yo*) to be quiet 조용하다(해요)

chu week 주

chu-ch'a-ha-da(*hae-yo*) to park 주차하다(해요)

chu-ch'a-jang parking lot 주차장

chu-da(*chweo-yo*) to give 주다(줘요)

chuk-tta(*chu-geo-yo*) to die 죽다(죽어요)

chul-mu-ni stripes 줄무늬

chu-mal weekend 주말

chu-mun-ha-da(*hae-yo*) to place an order 주문하다 (해요)

chu-mu-shi-da(*chu-mu-shyeo-yo*) to sleep (honorific) 주무시다(주무셔요)

chung/seu-nim monk/monk (honorific) 중/스님

Chung-guk China 중국

Chung-guk-jjip Chinese restaurant 중국집

Chung-guk sa-ram Chinese (person) 중국 사람

Chung-gu-keo Chinese (lang.) 중국어

chu-sa injection 주사

chu-so address 주소

chu-yu-so filling station/gas station 주유소

chwa-seok seat 좌석

chwa-yak suppositories 좌약

chyu-seu juice 쥬스

Ch'

ch'a car/vehicle 차

ch'ae-shik shik-dang vegetarian restaurant 채식 식당

ch'aek book 책

ch'a-jjip teahouse 찻집

ch'am-gi-reum sesame oil 참기름

ch'am-oe melon (small, yellow) 참외

ch'ang-mun window 창문

ch'a-p'yo cha-dong p'an-mae-gi ticket machine 차표 자동 판매기

ch'at-tta(*ch'a-ja-yo*) to look for 찾다(찾아요)

ch'e-in chain 체인

ch'e-jo gymnastics 체조

ch'e-k'eu mu-ni check (pattern) 체크 무늬

ch'eo-bang prescription 처방

ch'eok-ch'u spine 척추

Ch'eo-eum poep-kke-sseo-yo. How do you do? 처음 뵙겠어요.

ch'eon-ch'eon-hi slowly 천천히

ch'eong-ba-ji jeans 청바지

ch'eong-so-bu maid 청소부

ch'eong-so-ha-da(*hae-yo*) to clean (room) 청소하다 (해요)

ch'e-on-gye thermometer 체온계

Ch'eon-man-e-yo. You're welcome. 천만에요.

ch'eot/meon-jeo first 첫/ 먼저

ch'eot-ppeon/ch'eo-eum-e the first time/at first 첫번/처음에

ch'e-yuk-kkwan gymnasium 체육관

ch'i-kkwa eui-sa dentist 치과 의사

ch'il-bo cloisonne 칠보

ch'i-ma/seu-k'eo-t'eu skirt 치마/스커트

ch'im-ch'i-ryo acupuncture 침치료

ch'im-dae bed 침대

ch'im-dae-ch'a sleeping car (train) 침대차

ch'im-dae pang western-style room 침대 방

ch'im-sul-sa acupuncturist
침술사
ch'in-gu friend 친구
ch'in-jeol-ha-da(hae-yo)
to be kind 친절하다(해요)
Ch'i-rweol July 칠월
ch'i-ryo treatment (medical)
치료
ch'i-ssol toothbrush 칫솔
ch'i-t'ong toothache 치통
ch'i-u-da(ch'i-weo-yo) to
clean 치우다(치워요)
ch'i-yak toothpaste 치약
ch'o-dae-ha-da(hae-yo) to
invite 초대하다(해요)
ch'o-k'ol-let chocolate 초콜렛
ch'uk-jje festival 축제
ch'uk-kku soccer 축구
ch'ul-bal-gu departure gate
출발구
ch'ul-bal-ha-da(hae-yo) to
depart 출발하다(해요)
ch'ul-gu exit 출구
*ch'um-ch'u-da(ch'um-ch'weo-
yo)* to dance 춤추다
(춤춰요)
ch'ung-bun-ha-da(hae-yo)
to be enough 충분하다(해요)
ch'ung-ch'i cavity 충치
ch'ung-jeon-ha-da(hae-yo)
to recharge 충전하다(해요)
ch'up-tta(ch'u-weo-yo) to be
cold 춥다(추워요)

E

e to 에
e-eo-k'on air conditioner
에어콘
e-i-ch'i-a-i-beu-i keom-sa
HIV test 에이치아이브이검사
ek-sseu-ra-ji extra large
엑쓰라지
ek-sseu-re-i X-ray 엑스레이
el-li-be-i't'eo elevator
엘리베이터
en-jin engine 엔진

eo-di where 어디
eo-dup-tta(eo-du-weo-yo) to
be dark 어둡다(어두워요)
eo-je yesterday 어제
eo-kkae shoulder 어깨
eol-gul face 얼굴
eol-gul mas-sa-ji facial
massage 얼굴 맛사지
eol-luk stain 얼룩
eol-ma how much 얼마
eol-ma tong-an how long
얼마 동안
Eol-ma-ye-yo? How much is
it? 얼마예요 ?
eo-meo-ni mother 어머니
eom-ji-son-kka-rak
thumb 엄지손가락
eon-deok hill 언덕
eo-neu which 어느
eon-je when 언제
eop-tta(eop-sseo-yo) not to
have 없다(없어요)
eo-reum ice 얼음
eo-ri-da(eo-ryeo-yo) to be
young (child) 어리다
(어려요)
eo-ryeop-tta(eo-ryeo-weo-yo)
to be difficult 어렵다
(어려워요)
Eo-seo o-se-yo. Welcome.
어서 오세요.
eo-tteo-k'e how 어떻게
eo-ul-li-da(eo-ul-lyeo-yo) to
match 어울리다(어울려요)
e-seo at 에서
e-seo/pu-t'eo from 에서/부터
e-seu-k'eol-le-i-t'eo
escalator 에스컬레이터
eui-sa doctor 의사
eum-ak music 음악
eum-nyo-su beverage
음료수
eum-shik-jjeom/shik-ttang
restaurant 음식점/식당
eum-shik/shik-p'um food
음식/식품
eun silver 은
eung-geup emergency 응급

eung-geup ch'eo-ch'i-ham
first-aid kit 응급 처치함
eun-haeng bank 은행

H

ha-da(hae-yo) to do 하다
(해요)
hae-an coast 해안
hae-byeon seashore 해변
haem-beo-geo seu-t'e-i-k'eu
hamburger steak 햄버거
스테이크
haen-deu-bol handball
핸드볼
haen-deu-p'on cell phone
핸드폰
haen-deu ro-shyeon hand
lotion 핸드 로션
haeng-sa activity 행사
hae-su-yok-jjang beach
해수욕장
ha-i-k'ing-ha-da(hae-yo) to
hike 하이킹하다(해요)
hak-ch'um crane dance 학춤
hak-kkyo school 학교
hak-ssaeng student 학생
ha-k'i hockey 하키
hal-meo-ni grandmother
할머니
_____ -***gwa/wa ham-kke***
with _____ 과/와 함께
han-bok dress (traditional
Korean) 한복
Han-geul Korean (writing
system) 한글
hang-gong-beon-ho flight
number 항공번호
hang-gong-p'yeon air
mail 항공편
hang-gong yeop-seo
aerogram 항공 엽서
hang-gu harbor/port 항구
hang-sang always 항상
hang-saeng-je antibiotics
항생제
Han-guk Korea 한국

Han-guk sa-ram Korean
(person) 한국 사람
Han-gung-mal/Han-gu-geo
Korean (lang.) 한국말/
한국어
Han-gung-mal ch'aek
Korean language book
한국말 책
han-shik Korean-style food
한식
han-yak herbal medicine
한약
hap-seong synthetic 합성
ha-ra-beo-ji grandfather
할아버지
ha-yang/ha-yan-saek
white 하양/하얀색
ha-rin-ha-da(hae-yo) to
discount 할인하다(해요)
ha-rin p'an-mae sale 할인
판매
ha-ru one day 하루
ha-ru-ppam overnight 하룻밤
he-eo seu-p'eu-re-i hair spray
헤어 스프레이
he-eo teu-ra-i-eo hair dryer
헤어 드라이어
hel-seu-k'eul-leop health/
fitness club 헬스클럽
heol-leong-ha-da(hae-yo) to
be loose 헐렁하다(해요)
hi-t'eo heater 히터
ho-bak zucchini 호박
hoe raw, sliced fish 회
hoe-jjip sushi restaurant 횟집
hoe-gyo sa-weon mosque
회교 사원
hoe-saek gray 회색
hoe-sa kan-bu executive
회사 간부
hoe-weon member 회원
Ho-ju Australia 호주
Ho-ju sa-ram Australian
(person) 호주 사람
hon-ja alone 혼자
hong-ch'a tea 홍차
Hong-K'ong Hong Kong 홍콩
hong-su flood 홍수

ho-p'eu-jip hof (pub/bar) 호프집

ho-su lake 호수

ho-t'el hotel 호텔

hu-ch'u pepper (black) 후추

hu-e after 후에

hum-ch'i-da*(hum-ch'yeo-yo)* to steal 훔치다(훔쳐요)

hwa-ch'o plant 화초

hwa-gin-ha-da*(hae-yo)* to confirm 확인하다(해요)

hwa-gin-seo confirmation 확인서

hwa-hak cho-mi-ryo MSG (monosodium glutamate) 화학 조미료

hwa-jang-p'um toiletries 화장품

hwa-jang-shil restroom/ bathroom 화장실

hwang-ok topaz 황옥

hwan-bul-ha-da*(hae-yo)* to refund 환불하다(해요)

hwan-yul exchange rate 환율

hwa-rang art gallery 화랑

hwa-san volcano 화산

hwa-sang burn (n.) 화상

hwa-t'u card game (Korean) 화투

hwa-yo-il Tuesday 화요일

hwi-bal-lyu gasoline 휘발유
  hwi-bal-lyu *(keo-geup)* gasoline (premium) 휘발유
  hwi-bal-lyu *(po-t'ong)* gasoline (regular) 휘발유

hyang-su perfume 향수

hyeo tongue 혀

hyeok-ttae belt 혁대

hyeon-geum-ja-dong-ch'ul-nap-kki ATM 현금자동출납기

hyeon-sang-ha-da*(hae-yo)* to develop (film) 현상하다 (해요)

hyeop-jju-gok concerto 협주곡

hyeo-rap blood pressure 혈압

hyu-ga vacation 휴가

hyu-il holiday 휴일

hyu-ji/hwa-jang-ji toilet paper 휴지/화장지

I

i tooth/teeth 이

i-bal haircut 이발

i-bal-ha-da*(hae-yo)* to get a haircut (men) 이발하다 (해요)

i-bal-so barber shop 이발소

i-beo po-da*(i-beo pwa-yo)* to try on 입어 보다(입어 봐요)

i-bul blanket/quilt (Korean-style) 이불

i-deung p'yo second-class ticket 이등 표

(i)-e-yo is (to be) (이)에요

i-geot this 이것

i-gi-da*(i-gyeo-yo)* to win 이기다(이겨요)

i-in-yong pang double room 이인용 방

ik-tta*(i-geo-yo)* to cook (v.i.) 익다(익어요)

il/nal day 일/날

il-ban-shil p'yo ticket (regular) 일반실 표

Il-bon Japan 일본

Il-bon-eo Japanese (lang.) 일본어

Il-bon sa-ram Japanese (person) 일본 사람

il-gi-ye-bo weather forecast 일기예보

il-ha-da*(hae-yo)* to work 일하다(해요)

il-hoe-yong pan-ch'ang-go Band-aid® 일회용 반창고

il-jjik early 일찍

ilk-tta*(il-geo-yo)* to read 읽다(읽어요)

il-shik-jjip Japanese restaurant 일식집

il-tteung first class 일등

il-tteung p'yo first-class ticket
일등 표

im-shi-ro temporarily
임시로

im-shin-jung-i-da(i-e-yo) to
be pregnant 임신중이다
(이에요)

In-do-ne-shi-a Indonesia
인도네시아

in-gu population 인구

in-hyeong doll 인형

in-kki(-ga) it-tta(i-sseo-yo)
to be popular 인기(가) 있다
(있어요)

in-myeong ku-jo-weon
lifeguard 인명 구조원

in-sa-ha-da(hae-yo) to
introduce oneself/to greet
인사하다(해요)

in-sam ginseng 인삼

in-sam-ch'a ginseng tea
인삼차

in-sam ka-ge ginseng shop
인삼 가게

in-syul-lin insulin 인슐린

In-t'eo-net Internet 인터넷

In-t'eo-net kka-p'e Internet
cafe 인터넷 까페

ip-jjang-nyo admission fee/
cover charge 입장료

ip-kku entrance 입구

ip-ssul lip 입술

ip-tta(i-beo-yo) to wear 입다
(입어요)

*i-reo-beo-ri-da(i-reo-beo-ryeo-
yo)* to lose 잃어버리다
(잃어버려요)

i-reo-na-da(i-reo-na-yo) to
get up 일어나다(일어나요)

i-reum name 이름

i-rweol January 일월

i-ryo-il Sunday 일요일

i-ssu-shi-gae toothpick
이쑤시개

it-tta(i-sseo-yo) to have/be
available 있다(있어요)

i-t'ae-ri t'a-ol scrub towel
이태리 타올

I-t'ae-ri Italy 이태리

i-weol February 이월

JJ

jja-da(jja-yo) to be salty
짜다(짜요)

jjae-jeu jazz 째즈

jja-jang-myeon noodles
(with black bean sauce)
짜장면

jjal-beun so-mae sleeve
(short) 짧은 소매

jjal-tta(jjal-ba-yo) to be
short 짧다(짧아요)

jjam-ppong spicy seafood
noodle soup 짬뽕

jjim-jil-bang spa 찜질방

jjok-jjip-kke tweezers
쪽집게

K

ka-a-je gauze 가아제

ka-bang bag/handbag/
briefcase 가방

*ka-byeop-tta(ka-byeo-weo-
yo)* to be light 가볍다
(가벼워요)

ka-da(ka-yo) to go 가다
(가요)

ka-deuk ch'a-da(ch'a-yo) to
be full 가득차다(차요)

kae-in su-p'yo personal check
개인 수표

kae-mak-shik opening
ceremony 개막식

ka-eul fall (season) 가을

ka-ge store 가게

ka-gu furniture 가구

ka-jeon che-p'um electrical
appliances 가전 제품

ka-jok family 가족

ka-juk leather 가죽

ka-kkap-tta(ka-kka-weo-yo)
to be near 가깝다(가까워요)

kal-bi-ppyeo rib 갈비뼈
kal-bi-t'ang rib soup 갈비탕
kal-da(*ka-ra-yo*) to replace
갈다(갈아요)
kal-saek brown 갈색
kam persimmon 감
kam-gi-e keol-li-da(*keol-lyeo-yo*) to catch cold
감기에 걸리다(걸려요)
kam-ja potato 감자
Kam-sa-ham-ni-da. Thank
you. 감사합니다.
kam-yeom infection 감염
kam-yeom-doe-da(*twae-yo*)
to be infected 감염되다
(돼요)
kan liver 간
ka-neung-han-han ppal-li
as soon as possible
가능한한 빨리
kang river 강
kang-ha-da(*hae-yo*) to be
strong 강하다(해요)
kang-seup-eul pat-tta(*pa-da-yo*) to take lessons 강습을
받다(받아요)
kan-ho-sa nurse 간호사
kan-jang soy sauce 간장
kan-yeom hepatitis 간염
kap price 값
kap-seul kka-kka chu-da
(*kka-kka chweo-yo*) to
cut the price for someone
값을 깎아 주다(깎아 줘요)
ka-ra-t'a-da(*t'a-yo*) to
transfer (transportation)
갈아타다(타요)
ka-reu-ch'i-da(*ka-reu-ch'yeo-yo*) to teach 가르치다
(가르쳐요)
ka-seu gas 가스
ka-seum chest (body) 가슴
kat-tta(*ka-t'a-yo*) to be the
same 같다(같아요)
_____(*-eun/ neun keot*) **kat-tta**(*ka-t'a-yo*) to seem
_____(은/ 는 것) 같다
(같아요)

ka-jyeo-o-da/ka-jyeo-ka-da to bring/take 가져오다/
가져가다
ka-un-de/ssen-t'eo middle/
center 가운데/쎈터
ka-wi scissors 가위
ka-ya-geum zither (12-string)
가야금
ke crab 게
keo-eui eop-tta(*eop-sseo-yo*)
to be few 거의 없다(없어요)
keo-gi/cheo-gi there 거기/
저기
keol-li-da(*keol-lyeo-yo*) to
take time 걸리다(걸려요)
keom-jeong/keom-eun-saek
black 검정/검은색
keom-t'o-ha-da(*hae-yo*) to
check/examine 검토하다
(해요)
keon-ch'o-yeol hay fever
건초열
keon-ch'uk architecture 건축
keon-ch'uk ki-sa architect
건축 기사
keon-jeon-ji battery 건전지
keon-neo-da(*keon-neo-yo*) to
cross 건너다(건너요)
keon-p'o-do raisins 건포도
keo-ri distance 거리
keot-tta(*keo-reo-yo*) to walk
걷다(걸어요)
keo-ul mirror 거울
keu pun he/she (honorific)
그 분
keu pun-deul they (honorific)
그 분들
keu-deul they 그들
keu-geot/cheo-geot that
그것/저것
keuk-jjang theater 극장
keum gold 금
keum-go safe (valuables)
금고
keum-yeon no smoking 금연
keum-yeon-seok non-smoking
seat 금연석
keum-yo-il Friday 금요일

keun-dae-o-jong-kyeong-gi
pentathlon 근대오종경기

keun-yuk muscle 근육

keu-reon-de but 그런데

keu-ri-da(*keu-ryeo-yo*) to
draw 그리다(그려요)

keu-rim yeop-sseo postcard
(picture) 그림 엽서

keu sa-ram he/she 그 사람

ki-bun feeling/mood/frame of
mind 기분

ki-ch'a/yeol-ch'a train 기차/
열차

ki-ch'im-ha-da(*hae-yo*) to
cough 기침하다(해요)

ki-ch'im kam-gi chest cold
기침 감기

ki-da-ri-da(*ki-da-ryeo-yo*)
to wait 기다리다(기다려요)

ki-do-ha-da(*hae-yo*) to pray
기도하다(해요)

ki-hu climate 기후

kil road 길

kil-da(*ki-reo-yo*) to be long
길다(길어요)

kim seaweed (toasted) 김

kim-ch'i kimchi (cabbage)
김치

kim-ch'i-jji-gae kimchi stew
김치찌개

kin so-mae sleeve (long) 긴
소매

ki-nyeom-p'um souvenir
기념품

ki-ppeu-da(*ki-ppeo-yo*) to be
glad 기쁘다(기뻐요)

ki-reul i-reo-beo-ri-da(*i-reo-
beo-ryeo-yo*) to lose one's
way 길을 잃어버리다
(잃어버려요)

ki-reum oil (cooking) 기름

ki-saeng kisaeng (professional
entertainer) 기생

ki-seong-bok clothing (ready-
to-wear) 기성복

ki-sul-jja engineer 기술자

ko-ch'i-da(*ko-ch'yeo-yo*) to
repair/alter 고치다(고쳐요)

ko-ch'u pepper (hot) 고추

ko-ch'ut-ga-ru red pepper
powder 고춧가루

ko-ch'u-jang red pepper
paste 고추장

ko-ga-gu antique furniture
고가구

ko-hyang hometown 고향

ko-jang-na-da(*ko-jang-
na-sseo-yo*) to be out
of order 고장나다
(고장났어요)

ko-jeon eum-ak classical
music 고전 음악

kol-jja-ki valley 골짜기

kol-mok alley 골목

kol-p'eu golf 골프

kol-ttong-p'um antique
골동품

Ko-map-sseum-ni-da. Thank
you. 고맙습니다.

ko-mu-ch'im-dae air
mattress 고무침대

ko-mu-jjul rubber bands
고무줄

kong-hang airport 공항

kong-jung cheon-hwa public
telephone 공중 전화

kong-p'o yeong-hwa thriller
movie 공포영화

***kong-sang gwa-hak yeong-
hwa*** science fiction
movie 공상 과학 영화

kong-weon park 공원

kong-yeon performance
(drama) 공연

kong-yeon an-nae-seo
entertainment guide 공연
안내서

kop-seul-ha-da(*hae-yo*) to
be curly 곱슬하다(해요)

ko-reu-da(*kol-la-yo*) to
choose 고르다(골라요)

ko-sok-ppeo-seu express bus
고속버스

ko-sok-tto-ro highway
고속도로

kot soon 곧

kot/chang-so place/location 곳/장소

ku-du-kkeun shoelaces 구두끈

ku-geup-ch'a ambulance 구급차

ku-gyeong-ha-da(*hae-yo*) to look at/look around/watch 구경하다(해요)

ku-ha-da(*hae-yo*) to get (obtain) 구하다(해요)

kuk soup 국

kuk-jje international 국제

kuk-jje cheon-hwa international call 국제 전화

kuk-jjeok nationality 국적

kuk-ssan-p'um Korean-made 국산품

kuk-ssu noodles 국수

kul oysters 굴

kung-jeon/wang-gung palace 궁전/왕궁

kung-nip kong-weon national park 국립 공원

kun-in soldier 군인

kup-tta(*ku-weo-yo*) grilled 굽다(구워요)

ku-reum cloud 구름

ku-weol September 구월

kwa-il fruit 과일

kwa-ja cookie 과자

kwan-gwang an-nae-seo tour guidebook 관광 안내서

kwan-gwang an-nae-so touist information center 관광 안내소

kwan-gwang-gaek tourist 관광객

kwan-gwang-ha-da(*hae-yo*) to tour/sightsee 관광하다 (해요)

kwan-jeol joint (body) 관절 _____-***e kwan-shim-i it-tta***(*i-sseo-yo*) to be interested in _____ 에 관심이 있다 (있어요)

kweon-t'u boxing 권투

kwi ear 귀

kwi-e neo-neun yak ear drops 귀에 넣는약

kwi-geo-ri earrings 귀걸이

kwi-jung-p'um valuables 귀중품

kye-hoek plan 계획

kye-jeol season 계절

kyeok-jja mu-ni plaid 격자 무늬

kyeol-jjeong-ha-da(*hae-yo*) decide 결정하다(해요)

kyeong-ch'al police 경찰

kyeong-ch'i view 경치

kyeong-gi game (athletic event) 경기

kyeong-gi-jang venue 경기장

kyeong-yu diesel 경유

kyeo-ron-ha-da(*hae-yo*) to marry 결혼하다(해요)

kyeo-ul winter 겨울

kye-ran egg 계란

kye-san-gi calculator 계산기

kye-san-ha-da(*hae-yo*) to settle the bill 계산하다(해요)

kye-san-seo check/bill 계산서

kye-sok-k'a-da(*k'ae-yo*) to continue 계속하다(해요)

kyo-hoe church 교회

kyo-hwan telephone operator 교환

kyo-su professor 교수

Kyo-t'ong-k'a-deu T-money card 교통카드

kyul tangerine 귤

K'

k'a-byu-re-t'eo carburetor 카뷰레터

k'aem-k'o-deo camcorder 캠코더

k'aem-ping-ha-da(*hae-yo*) to camp 캠핑하다(해요)

K'ae-na-da Canada 캐나다

K'ae-na-da sa-ram Canadian (person) 캐나다 사람

k'ae-reot karat (for diamond) 캐럿

k'ak-t'e-il cocktail 칵테일

k'al knife (cutting) 칼

k'a-me-ra camera 카메라

k'a-me-ra-jeom camera shop 카메라점

k'an-ch'yu-ri myu-jik country music 칸츄리 뮤직

k'a-nu canoeing 카누

k'a-re-ra-i-seu rice (with curry sauce) 카레라이스

k'e-ch'eop ketchup 케첩

k'e-i karat (for gold) 케이

k'e-i-k'eu cake 케이크

k'eom-p'aek-t'eu ti-seu-k'eu compact discs 컴팩트 디스크

k'eom-p'yu-t'eo computer 컴퓨터

k'eop cup 컵

k'eo-p'eu-seu-dan-ch'u cufflinks 커프스단추

k'eo-p'i coffee 커피

k'eo-p'i shyop coffee shop 커피 숍

k'e-o-t'eu-ha-da(hae-yo) to get a haircut (women) 커트하다(해요)

k'eu-da(k'eo-yo) to be large/big 크다(커요)

k'eul-len-jing k'eu-rim cleansing cream 클렌징 크림

k'eul-lip curlers 클립

k'eu-rak-shyeon horn 크락션

k'eu-re-dit k'a-deu credit card 크레딧 카드

k'i height 키

k'i-bo-deu keyboard 키보드

k'i-ga k'eu-da(k'eo-yo) to be tall 키가 크다(커요)

k'il-lo-geu-raem kilogram 킬로그램

k'o nose 코

k'ol-la cola 콜라

k'ol-lon-su cologne 콜론수

k'o-mi-di comedy 코미디

k'o-mit su-yeom mustache 코밑 수염

k'on-dom condom 콘돔

k'on-t'aek-t'eu ren-jeu contact lens 콘택트 렌즈

k'ong-na-mul bean sprouts 콩나물

k'ong-na-mul-kkuk bean sprout soup 콩나물국

k'ya-ba-re cabaret 캬바레

KK

kkae-ji-da(kkae-jyeo-yo) to break (glass) 깨지다(깨져요)

kkae-u-da(kkae-weo-yo) to wake up 깨우다(깨워요)

kkak-tta(kkak-kka-yo) to cut 깎다(깎아요)

kka-p'e cafe 까페

kkak-ttu-gi kimch'i (radish) 깍두기

kkeul-da(kkeu-reo-yo) to pull 끌다(끌어요)

kkeun string 끈

kkeun-na-da(kkeun-na-yo) to end/finish 끝나다 (끝나요)

kkeun-t'a (kkeu-neo-yo) to quit; sever; hang up 끊다 (끊어요)

kken-rin mul water (boiled) 끓인 물

kki-u-da (kki-weo-yo) to plug in/stick in/insert 끼우다 (끼워요)

kkok kki-da (kkok kkyeo-yo) to be tight 꼭 끼다 (꼭 껴요)

kkot flower 꽃

kkot-jjip flower shop 꽃집

M

ma linen 마

ma-ch'um-bok clothing (made-to-order) 마춤복

mae-il every day 매일

maek-jju beer 맥주

maeng-jang-yeom appendicitis 맹장염

mae-ni-k'yu-eo manicure/nail polish 매니큐어

mae-ni-k'yu-eo chi-u-gae nail polish remover 매니큐어 지우개

maep-tta*(mae-weo-yo)* to be hot(spicy) 맵다 (매워요)

mae-p'yo-gu ticket window 매표구

mae-p'yo-so ticket office 매표소

ma-eul village 마을

ma-eum-e teul-da*(teu-reo-yo)* to be satisfied with 마음에 들다 (들어요)

mae-un-t'ang fish soup (spicy) 매운탕

ma-ji-mak last 마지막

mak-kkeol-li rice/barley wine 막걸리

mal language 말

mal-ha-da*(hae-yo)* to speak 말하다 (해요)

mal-tta*(mal-ga-yo)* to be clear 맑다 (맑아요)

Mal-le-i-ji-a Malaysia 말레이지아

mal-sseum-ha-shi-da*(ha-se-yo)* to speak (honorific) 말씀하시다 (하세요)

man-deul-da*(man-deu-reo-yo)* to make 만들다 (만들어요)

man-du-jjip dumpling restaurant 만두집

man-du-kkuk meat dumpling soup 만두국

mang-ch'i hammer 망치

man-na-da*(man-na-yo)* to meet 만나다 (만나요)

man-t'a*(ma-na-yo)* to be many 많다 (많아요)

ma-reu-da*(mal-la-yo)* to be dry 마르다 (말라요)

ma-seu-k'a-ra mascara 마스카라

ma-shi-da*(ma-shyeo-yo)* to drink 마시다 (마셔요)

ma-shi eop-tta*(eop-sseo-yo)* not delicious 맛이 없다 (없어요)

ma-shi it-tta*(i-sseo-yo)* to be delicious 맛이 있다 (있어요)

mas-sa-ji massage 맛사지

mas-sa-ji-sa massage therapist 맛사지사

mat-kki-da*(mat-kkyeo-yo)* to leave for safekeeping 맡기다 (맡겨요)

mat-tta*(ma-ja-yo)* to be right/ to fit 맞다 (맞아요)

Mek-shi-k'o Mexico 멕시코

me-nyu menu 메뉴

meok-tta*(meo-geo-yo)* to eat 먹다 (먹어요)

meol-da*(meo-reo-yo)* to be far 멀다 (멀어요)

meo-ri head 머리

meo-ri-bit comb (n.) 머리빗

meo-ri cho-t'a*(cho-a-yo)* to be intelligent 머리 좋다 (좋아요)

meo-ri-ga a-p'eu-da*(a-p'a-yo)* to have a headache 머리가 아프다 (아파요)

meo-ri*(k'a-rak)* hair 머리 (카락)

meo-ri-reul kam-tta*(ka-ma-yo)* to shampoo 머리를 감다 (감아요)

meo-ri saek-kkal hair color 머리 색깔

me-seu-kkeop-tta*(me-seu-kkeo-weo-yo)* to be nauseous 메스껍다 (메스꺼워요)

me-sshi-ji message 메시지

Mi-an-ham-ni-da. I'm sorry. 미안합니다.

mi-di-um medium (size) 미디움

Mi-guk   United States 미국

Mi-guk sa-ram   American (person) 미국 사람

Mi-guk tae-sa-gwan   American Embassy 미국 대사관

mi-jang-weon   beauty salon 미장원

mil-da(*mi-reo-yo*)   to push 밀다 (밀어요)

min-sok ye-sul   folk art 민속예술

mip-tta(*mi-weo-yo*)   to be ugly 밉다 (미워요)

mi-ri   in advance 미리

mi-seu-t'e-ri   mystery 미스테리

mi-shik-ch'uk-kku   football (American) 미식축구

mi-so-jit-tta(*mi-so-ji-eo-yo*)   to smile 미소짓다 (미소지어요)

mi-sul   art (painting) 미술

mo   wool 모

mo-ja   hat 모자

mok   neck 목

mok-i ma-reu-da(*mal-la-yo*)   to be thirsty 목이 마르다 (말라요)

mok-jjae   wood 목재

mok-kkeo-ri   necklace 목걸이

mok-kku-meong   throat 목구멍

mok(-kku-meong)-i a-p'eu-da(*a-p'a-yo*)   to have a sore throat 목 (구멍)이 아프다 (아파요)

mok-sa/mok-sa-nim   minister/ minister (honorific) 목사/ 목사님

mok-tto-ri   scarf 목도리

mok-yo-il   Thursday 목요일

mok-yok-k'a-da(*k'ae-yo*)   to take a bath 목욕하다 (해요)

mok-yok-t'ang   bathhouse (public) 목욕탕

mok-yok-t'ong   bathtub 목욕통

mom-mu-ge   weight (body) 몸무게

mom-sal   flu 몸살

mo-ni-t'eo   monitor 모니터

mo-re   day after tomorrow 모레

mo-reu-da(*mol-la-yo*)   not to know/understand 모르다 (몰라요)

Mo-reu-ge-sseo-yo.   I don't understand. 모르겠어요.

mo-t'el   motel 모텔

mu   radish 무

mu-geop-tta(*mu-geo-weo-yo*)   to be heavy 무겁다 (무거워요)

muk-tta(*mu-geo-yo*)   to stay (as in a hotel) 묵다 (묵어요)

mul   water 물

mul-lon   of course 물론

mun   door 문

mun-pang-gu-jeom   stationery store 문방구점

mu-reup   knee 무릎

mu-seon In-t'eo-net   wireless Internet 무선 인터넷

mu-seun/eo-tteon   what kind 무슨/어떤

mu-yong-ha-da(*hae-yo*)   to dance (performance) 무용하다 (해요)

mu-eot   what 무엇

myeo-ch'il   a few days 며칠

myeon   cotton (fabric) 면

myeon-do-gi   electric razor 면도기

myeon-do-ha-da(*hae-yo*)   to shave 면도하다 (해요)

myeon-do-k'al   razor 면도칼

myeon-do k'eu-rim   shaving cream 면도 크림

myeon-do-nal   razor blades 면도날

myeong-ham   card (business, personal) 명함

myu-ji-k'al   musical 뮤지칼

N

nae/che my/my (modest form) 내/제

nae-bok underwear (long) 내복

nae-da(*nae-yo*) to pay 내다 (내요)

nae-ga/na-neun I 내가/나는

nae-il tomorrow 내일

naeng-gak-kki radiator 냉각기

naeng-myeon noodles (cold, with beef and vegetables) 냉면

naep-k'in napkin 냅킨

nae-ri-da(*nae-ryeo-yo*) to get off 내리다(내려요)

na-i age 나이

na-il-lon nylon 나일론

na-i-p'eu knife (dinner) 나이프

na-i-t'eu k'eul-leop nightclub 나이트 클럽

na-jeon-ch'il-gi lacquerware 나전칠기

na-jung-e later 나중에

Na-jung-e poep-kke-sseo-yo. See you later. 나중에 뵙겠어요.

nak-jji po-kkeum octopus (small, fried) 낙지 볶음

nal-jja date 날짜

nal-tta(*nal-ga-sseo-yo*) to be old (object) 낡다(낡았어요)

nal-sshi weather 날씨

na-ma it-tta(*i-sseo-yo*) to be left over 남아 있다 (있어요)

Nam-a-me-ri-k'a South America 남아메리카

Nam-a-me-ri-k'a sa-ram South American (person) 남아메리카 사람

nam-ja man 남자

nam-ja a-i boy 남자 아이

nam-ja-yang-bok suit (men's) 남자양복

nam-jjok south 남쪽

nam-p'yeon husband (your own) 남편

nam-tta(*nam-a-yo*) to remain 남다(남아요)

na-mu trees 나무

na-o-da(*na-wa-yo*) to come out 나오다(나와요)

na-ppeu-da(*na-ppa-yo*) to be bad 나쁘다(나빠요)

na-ra country 나라

nat kong-yeon matinee 낮 공연

nat-tta(*na-ja-yo*) to be low 낮다(낮아요)

ne/ye yes 네/예

ne-bi-ge-i-shyeon/chi-p'i-e-seu GPS (global positioning system) 네비게이션/지피에스

ne-ga/neo-neun you (sing.) 네가/너는

ne-geo-ri intersection (four-way) 네거리

nek-t'a-i tie 넥타이

neo-heui-deul you (plural) 너희들

neolp-jjeok-tta-ri thigh 넓적다리

neolp-tta(*neol-beo-yo*) to be wide 넓다(넓어요)

neom-eo-ji-da(*neom-eo-jyeo-yo*) to fall down 넘어지다 (넘어져요)

neo-mu too much 너무

neo-t'a(*neo-eo-yo*) to put in 넣다(넣어요)

neul-tta(*neul-geo-sseo-yo*) to be old (person) 늙다(늙었어요)

neu-ri-da(*neu-ryeo-yo*) to be slow 느리다(느려요)

neut-tta(*neu-jeo-yo*) to be late 늦다(늦어요)

no-geum-ha-da(*hae-yo*) to record 녹음하다(해요)

no-in senior citizen 노인

nok-ch'a green tea 녹차

nok-saek/ch'o-rok green
녹색/초록

nol-da(no-ra-yo) to play
(amusement) 놀다(놀아요)

non rice paddy 논

nong-ak farmer's music
(traditional Korean) 농악

nong-ga farm 농가

nong-gu basketball 농구

nop-tta(no-p'a-yo) to be high
높다(높아요)

no-rae song 노래

no-rae-bang singing room
노래방

no-rae-ha-da(hae-yo) to sing
노래하다(해요)

no-rang/no-ran-saek
yellow 노랑/노란색

not-ssoe brass 놋쇠

no-t'a(no-a-yo) to put on/
place 놓다(놓아요)

no-t'eu-buk k'eom-p'yu-t'eo
notebook computer 노트북
컴퓨터

nu-gu somebody, who 누구

nun eye 눈

nun snow 눈

nyeon year 년

Nyu-jil-laen-deu New
Zealand 뉴질랜드

O

o-da(wa-yo) to come 오다
(와요)

oe-kkwa-eui-sa surgeon
외과의사

o-han-i na-da(na-yo) to
chill (shiver) 오한이 나다
(나요)

o-hu afternoon 오후

o-i cucumber 오이

o-il oil 오일

o-i-so-ba-ki kimchi
(cucumber) 오이소박이

o-jing-eo squid 오징어

ok-ssu-su corn 옥수수

ok-tto-jeong-gi iodine
옥도정기

o-k'e-seu-t'eu-ra orchestra
오케스트라

o-meu-ra-i-seu rice omelet
오므라이스

on-ch'eon hot springs 온천

on-dol ppang Korean-style
room 온돌 방

o-neul today 오늘

o-neul-ppam tonight 오늘밤

o-p'e-ra opera 오페라

o-ren-ji orange 오렌지

o-reun-jjok right (direction)
오른쪽

o-ri duck 오리

ot clothes 옷

ot ka-ra-ip-tta(ka-ra-i-beo-yo) to change clothes
옷 갈아입다(갈아입어요)

o-t'eu-mil oatmeal 오트밀

o-t'o-mae-t'ik automatic
transmission 오토매틱

o-weol May 오월

P

pa-da ocean 바다

pa-dat-kka-je lobster
바닷가재

pa-di ro-shyeon body lotion
바디 로션

pa-duk paduk (board game;
go) 바둑

pae pear 배

pae ship/boat 배

pae stomach 배

pae-ga a-p'eu-da(a-p'a-yo)
to have a stomachache 배가
아프다(아파요)

pae-ch'u cabbage 배추

pae-dal-ha-da(hae-yo) to
deliver 배달하다(해요)

pae-ga ko-p'eu-da(ko-p'a-yo)
to be hungry 배가 고프다
(고파요)

pae-gu volleyball 배구

paek-ppan rice (with side dishes) 백반

paek-ppan-jjip steamed rice and side dishes restaurant 백반집

paek-k'wa-jeom department store 백화점

paek-kkeum platinum 백금

paek-p'o-do-ju/wa-in wine (white) 백포도주/와인

pae-meol-mi na-da(*na-yo*) to be seasick 배멀미 나다 (나요)

pae-t'eo-ri battery (car) 배터리

pae-u actor 배우

pae-u-da(*pae-weo-yo*) to learn 배우다(배워요)

pa-ji slacks/trousers 바지

pa-gu-ni baskets (straw) 바구니

pa-kke outside 밖에

pa-kku-da(*pa-kkweo-yo*) to change/exchange 바꾸다 (바꿔요)

pal foot 발

palk-tta(*pal-ga-yo*) to be bright 밝다(밝아요)

pal-kka-rak toe 발가락

pal-le ballet 발레

pal-mok ankle 발목

pam chestnuts 밤

pam night 밤

pan-aek half-fare 반액

pan-ch'an side dishes 반찬

pang room 방

Pan-gap-sseum-ni-da. Pleased to meet you. 반갑습니다.

pang-bu-je antiseptic 방부제

pang-ch'ung-je insect repellent 방충제

pang-ch'wi-je deodorant 방취제

pang-mul-gwan museum 박물관

pang-mun-ha-da(*hae-yo*) to visit 방문하다(해요)

pan-ji ring 반지

pap rice (cooked) 밥

pa-ppeu-da(*pa-ppa-yo*) to be busy 바쁘다(바빠요)

pa-ram wind 바람

pa-reu-da(*pal-la-yo*) to apply (lotion, medicine) 바르다 (발라요)

pat-tta(*pa-da-yo*) to receive 받다(받아요)

pe-da(*pe-eo-yo*) to cut (with a sharp object) 베다(베어요)

pe-gae pillow 베개

pel-bo-i bellhop 벨보이

peol-le-e mul-li-da(*mul-lyeo-yo*) to get an insect bite 벌레에 물리다(물려요)

peon-ho number 번호

peon-yeok-k'a-da(*k'ae-yo*) to translate 번역하다(해요)

peo-ri-da(*peo-ryeo-yo*) to throw away 버리다(버려요)

peo-seu t'eo-mi-neol bus terminal 버스 터미널

peot-tta(*peo-seo-yo*) to take off (clothes) 벗다(벗어요)

peo-t'eo butter 버터

Pe'eu-nam Vietnam 베트남

Pe-te'u-nam-eo Vietnamese (lang.) 베트남어

peul-la-u-seu blouse 블라우스

Peu-ra-jil Brazil 브라질

peu-rae-ji-eo bra 브래지어

peu-re-i-k'eu brakes 브레이크

peu-reo-shi brush 브러시

pi rain 비

pi-bim-ppap rice (mixed with vegetables) 비빔밥

pi-ch'wi jade 비취

pi-eo-hol beer hall 비어홀

pi-geuk tragedy 비극

pi-haeng-gi airplane 비행기

pi-ji-ni-seu sen-t'eo business center 비지니스 센터

pil-li-da(*pil-lyeo-yo*) to borrow/rent 빌리다(빌려요)

pin-dae-tteok mung bean pancakes 빈대떡

pi-nil vinyl 비닐

pi-nu soap 비누

pi-seo secretary 비서

pi-seut-t'a-da(*t'ae-yo*) to be similar 비슷하다(해요)

pi-ssa-da(*pi-ssa-yo*) to be expensive 비싸다(비싸요)

pit-tta(*pi-seo-yo*) to comb 빗다(빗어요)

pi-t'a-min vitamins 비타민

pi-yul rate 비율

po-ch'eong-gi hearing aid 보청기

po-da(*pwa-yo*) to see 보다 (봐요)

po-deu-k'a vodka 보드카

po-heom insurance 보험

pok-jjap-ha-da(*hae-yo*) to be crowded 복잡하다(해요)

pok-ssung-a peach 복숭아

pok-t'ong-i na-da(*na-yo*) to cramp 복통이 나다(나요)

pol man-ha-da(*hae-yo*) to be worth seeing 볼 만하다(해요)

pom spring 봄

po-nae-da(*po-nae-yo*) to send 보내다(보내요)

pong-sa-ryo/t'ip service charge/tip 봉사료/팁

pong-t'u envelope 봉투

po-ra-saek purple 보라색

po-ri-ch'a barley tea 보리차

po-seok stone/jewelry 보석

po-seok-ssang jewelry store 보석상

po-t'ong usually 보통

po-yeo chu-da(*chweo-yo*) to show 보여 주다(줘요)

pu-ch'ae fan 부채

pu-ch'i-da(*pu-ch'yeo-yo*) to mail 부치다(부쳐요)

pu-du pier 부두

pu-gun husband (someone else's) 부군

pu-in wife (someone else's) 부인

Puk-han (*Cho-seon min-ju-ju-eui in-min-gong-hwa-guk*) North Korea (Democratic People's Republic of Korea) 북한 (조선 민주주의 인민공화국)

puk-jjok north 북쪽

pul(*cheon-gi-*) electric light (전기)불

pul/pit light (n.) 불/빛

pul-gal-bi beef ribs (grilled) 불갈비

pul-go-gi beef (grilled) 불고기

pul-go-gi-jjip barbecue meat restaurant 불고기집

pul-myeon-jjeung insomnia 불면증

pun face powder/talcum powder 분

pun minute (time) 분

pun person (honorific) 분

pung-dae bandage 붕대

pung-hong-saek pink 분홍색

pun-shil-mul ch'wi-geup-so lost and found office 분실물 취급소

pun-wi-gi atmosphere 분위기

pu-reo-ji-da(*pu-reo-jyeo-yo*) to break (bone) 부러지다 (부러져요)

pu-reu-da(*pul-leo-yo*) to summon 부르다(불러요)

put-tta(*pu-eo-yo*) to swell 붓다(부어요)

pu-t'ak-k'a-da(*k'ae-yo*) to ask a favor 부탁하다(해요)

_____**pu-t'eo**_____**kka-ji** from_____ to _____ (from 6:00 to 10:00) _____ 부터 _____까지

pyeol-shil private room 별실

pyeon-bi-e keol-li-da(*keol-lyeo-yo*) to be constipated 변비에 걸리다(걸려요)

pyeong bottle 병

pyeon-gi toilet 변기

pyeong-i na-da(*na-yo*) to get sick 병이 나다(나요)

pyeong-p'ung screen (folding) 병풍
pyeong-weon hospital 병원
pyeon-ho-sa lawyer 변호사

P'

p'a-do waves (water) 파도
p'aen-t'i undershorts (men's) 팬티
p'aen-t'i panties (women's) 팬티
p'aen-t'i seu-t'a-k'ing pantyhose 팬티 스타킹
p'a-i-p'eu pipe 파이프
p'a-i-p'eu tam-bae pipe tobacco 파이프 담배
p'al arm 팔
p'al-da(*p'a-ra-yo*) to sell 팔다(팔아요)
p'al-jji bracelet 팔찌
p'al-kkum-ch'i elbow 팔꿈치
p'a-ma permanent (hair) 파마
p'an-sso-ri dramatic song (traditional Korean) 판소리
p'ap-ssong popular music 팝송
p'a-rang/p'a-ran-saek blue 파랑/파란색
p'a-rweol August 팔월
p'a-un-deu pound 파운드
p'en pen 펜
p'en-shing fencing 펜싱
p'e-ni-shil-lin penicillin 페니실린
p'en-jji pliers 펜찌
p'e-ri ferry 페리
p'eul-lae-shi flashlight 플래시
P'eu-rang-seu/Pul-lan-seo France 프랑스/불란서
P'eu-rang-seu-eo/Pu-reo French (lang.) 프랑스어/불어
P'eu-rang-seu sa-ram/Pul-lan-seo sa-ram French (person) 프랑스 사람/불란서 사람
p'eu-rin-t'eu-ha-da(*hae-yo*) to print 프린트하다(해요)

p'eu-ro-geu-raem program 프로그램
p'eu-ru-t'eu k'ak-t'e-il fruit cocktail 프루트 칵테일
p'i/hyeo-raek blood 피/혈액
p'i-bu skin 피부
p'i-gon-ha-da(*hae-yo*) to be tired 피곤하다(해요)
p'i-im-gi-gu contraceptive 피임기구
p'i-ja pizza 피자
p'il-leum film (photography) 필름
P'il-li-p'in Philippines 필리핀
p'in pin 핀
p'i-ryo-ha-da(*hae-yo*) to need 필요하다(해요)
p'i-u-da(*p'i-weo-yo*) to smoke (tobacco) 피우다(피워요)
p'o-do grapes 포도
p'o-ham-ha-da(*hae-yo*) to include 포함하다(해요)
p'o-jang-ha-da(*hae-yo*) to wrap 포장하다(해요)
p'ok-p'o waterfall 폭포
p'ol-li-e-seu-t'el polyester 폴리에스텔
p'o-k'eu fork 포크
P'o-reu-t'u-gal Portugal 포르투갈
P'o-reu-t'u-gal-eo Portuguese (lang.) 포르투갈어
p'ye-mak-shik closing ceremony 폐막식
p'yeon-do one-way (trip) 편도
p'yeon-do-p'yo one-way ticket 편도표
p'yeon-eui-jeom convenience store 편의점
p'yeong-il weekday 평일
p'yeon-ji letter (mail) 편지

PP

ppa bar 빠
ppae-da(*ppae-yo*) to remove 빼다(빼요)

***ppal-da**(ppa-ra-yo)* to wash (laundry) 빨다(빨아요)
***ppal-gang/ppal-gang-saek** red 빨강/빨간색
***ppal-lae** laundry (clothes) 빨래
***ppa-na-na** banana 바나나
***ppang** bread 빵
***ppang-jjip** bakery 빵집
***ppa-reu-da**(ppal-la-yo) to be fast 빠르다(빨라요)
***ppeo-seu** bus 버스
***ppeo-seu cheong-nyu-jang** bus stop 버스 정류장
***ppi-da**(ppi-eo-sseo-yo) to sprain 삐다(삐었어요)
***ppong** filling (tooth) 뽕
***ppyeo** bone 뼈

R

***ra-di-o** radio 라디오
***ra-i-t'eo** lighter 라이터
***ra-ji** large (size) 라지
***ra-k'et** racket 라켓
***rak-k'a-p'e** rock café 락카페
***rap-ppi** rabbi 랍비
***re-gyul-leo** regular (gasoline) 레귤러
***re-k'o-deu** record 레코드
***ren-jeu** lens 렌즈
***Reo-shi-a/So-ryeon** Russia 러시아/소련
***Reo-shi-a-eo/So-ryeon-eo** Russian (lang.) 러시아어/소련어
***Reo-shi-a sa-ram/So-ryeon sa-ram** Russian (person) 러시아 사람/소련 사람
***reo-shi-a-weo** rush hour 러시아워
***reom** rum 럼
***reon-ning-shyeo-ch'eu** undershirt 런닝셔츠
***re-seul-ling** wrestling 레슬링
***rin-seu** cream rinse 린스
***rip-seu-t'ik** lipstick 립스틱

***ro-k'eun-rol** rock n'roll 로큰롤
***ru-jeu/ip-sul-yeon-ji** rouge/blush 루즈/입술연지
***rum-sal-long** room salon 룸살롱
***rum sseo-bi-seu** room service 룸 서비스

S

***sa-bal/tae-jeop** bowl 사발/대접
***sa-da**(sa-yo) to buy 사다 (사요)
***sae** bird 새
***saek-kkal** color 색깔
***sael-leo-deu** salad 샐러드
***saen-deu-wi-ch'i** sandwich 샌드위치
***saeng-gang** ginger 생강
***saeng-gang-ch'a** ginger tea 생강차
***saeng-su** water (bottled) 생수
***saeng-il** birthday 생일
***saeng-ni-dae** sanitary napkins 생리대
***saeng-seon** fish 생선
***saeng-seon-gu-i** fish (grilled) 생선구이
***sa-eop** business 사업
***sa-eop-kka** businessperson 사업가
***sae-rop-tta**(sae-ro-wa-yo) to be new 새롭다(새로와요)
***sae-u** shrimp 새우
***sa-go** accident 사고
***sa-gwa** apple 사과
***sa-gyeok** shooting (sport) 사격
***sa-i-da** lemon-lime soda 사이다
***sa-i-e** between 사이에
***sa-i-k'eul** cycling 사이클
***sa-jeon** dictionary 사전
***sa-jin** photograph 사진

sa-jin-gwan photography studio 사진관

sa-jin jjik-tta(*jji-geo-yo*) to take a picture 사진 찍다 (찍어요)

sal-da(*sa-ra-yo*) to live 살다 (살아요)

sam-tta(*sal-ma-yo*) to boil 삶다(삶아요)

sam-gye-t'ang ginseng chicken 삼계탕

sam-gye-t'ang-jjip ginseng chicken restaurant 삼계탕집

sa-mu-shil office 사무실

sa-mu-weon office worker 사무원

sam-weol March 삼월

san mountain 산

sang-dae-bang opponent/ counterpart 상대방

sang-yeong showing (movie) 상영

sa-ram person 사람

sa-rang-ha-da(*hae-yo*) to love 사랑하다(해요)

sa-t'ang candy 사탕

sa-u-na sauna 사우나

sa-weol April 사월

se-geum tax 세금

se-gwan shin-go-seo customs declaration form 세관 신고서

seo-bu yeong-hwa western (movie) 서부영화

seo-da(*seo-yo*) to stand 서다 (서요)

seo-jeom bookstore 서점

seo-jjok west 서쪽

seol-myeong-ha-da(*hae-yo*) to explain 설명하다(해요)

seol-sa-na-da(*na-yo*) to have diarrhea 설사나다(나요)

seol-t'ang sugar 설탕

seom island 섬

seo-myeong signature 서명

seon-bak-p'yeon sea mail 선박편

seon-geul-lae-seu sunglasses 선글래스

seon-geum/po-jeung-geum deposit 선금/보증금

seong-ham name (honorific) 성함

seong-hyeong-oe-kkwa eui-sa surgeon (cosmetic) 성형외과 의사

seong-nyang matches 성냥

seon-mul gift 선물

seon-mul ka-ge gift shop/ souvenir shop 선물 가게

seon-mul-p'o-jang-ha-da (*hae-yo*) to gift wrap 선물포장하다(해요)

seon-p'ung-gi electric fan 선풍기

seon-saeng/seon-saeng-nim teacher/teacher (honorific) 선생/선생님

seon-saeng-nim you (sing., honorific) 선생님

seon-seu-k'eu-rin sunscreen 선스크린

seon-t'aen ro-shyeon suntan lotion 선탠 로션

seo-ryu documents 서류

Seo-ul ol-lim-p'ik tae-hoe Seoul Olympic Games 서울 올림픽 대회

seo-ye calligraphy 서예

se-t'ak-so laundry (place) 세탁소

se-u-da(*se-weo-yo*) to stop (v.t.) 세우다(세워요)

seu-k'a-ch'i scotch (whiskey) 스카치

seu-k'a-ch'i t'e-i-p'eu Scotch® tape 스카치테이프

seu-k'aen-ha-da(*hae-yo*) to scan 스캔하다(해요)

seu-k'e-jul itinerary/schedule 스케줄

seu-k'i-t'a-da(*t'a-yo*) to ski 스키타다(타요)

seul-lip/sok-ch'i-ma slip 슬립/속치마

seul-li-p'eo slippers 슬리퍼
seu-mol small (size) 스몰
seung-gaek passenger 승객
seung-ma equestrian 승마
seung-mu monk's dance 승무
seup-kki it-tta(i-sseo-yo) to be humid 습기 있다(있어요)
seu-p'ae-neo/ren-ch'i wrench 스패너/렌치
Seu-p'e-in Spain 스페인
Seu-p'e-in-eo Spanish (lang.) 스페인어
seu-p'eu-re-i spray 스프레이
seu-p'on-ji sponge 스폰지
seu-t'a-il style 스타일
seu-t'en-re-seu stainless steel 스텐레스
seu-we-t'eo sweater 스웨터
sha-weo-jang shower (place) 샤워장
shi-ga cigar 시가
shi-gan hour, time 시간
shi-gan-p'yo timetable 시간표
shi-geum-ch'i-na-mul spinach (seasoned, blanched) 시금치나물
shi-gol countryside 시골
shi-gye clock/watch 시계
shi-gye-ppang watch and clock store 시계방
shi-jak-k'a-da(k'ae-yo) to begin 시작하다(해요)
shi-jang market (traditional) 시장
shik-ch'o vinegar 식초
shik-k'ye rice punch 식혜
shik-ppi meal cost 식비
shik-p'um-jeom grocery store 식품점
shik-sa-ha-da(hae-yo) to have a meal 식사하다(해요)
shik-ssu potable water 식수
shik-ttang-ch'a dining car 식당차
shi-kkeu-reop-tta(shi-kkeu-reo-weo-yo) to be noisy 시끄럽다(시끄러워요)

shil-k'eu silk 실크
Shil-lye-ham-ni-da. Excuse me. 실례합니다.
shim-jang heart 심장
shim-jang-ma-bi heart attack 심장마비
shi-nae downtown 시내
shi-nae cheon-hwa local call 시내 전화
shi-nae chi-do city map 시내 지도
shi-nae-mul stream 시냇물
shin-bal/ku-du shoes 신발/구두
shin-bu/shin-bu-nim priest/priest (honorific) 신부/신부님
Shing-ga-p'o-reu Singapore 싱가포르
shing-geop-tta(shing-geo-weo-yo) to be bland 싱겁다(싱거워요)
shing-shing-ha-da(hae-yo) to be fresh 싱싱하다(해요)
shin-mun newspaper 신문
shin-mun p'an-mae-dae newsstand 신문 판매대
ship-i-rweol November 십일월
ship-i-weol December 십이월
_____-go ship-tta(shi-p'eo-yo) to want to _____고 싶다(싶어요)
shi-reop-eu-ro toen ki-ch'im-yak cough syrup 시럽으로 된 기침약
shi-seol-mul facilities 시설물
shi-weol October 시월
shi-woe cheon-hwa long-distance call 시외 전화
sho-p'ing-ha-da(hae-yo) to shop 쇼핑하다(해요)
shwip-tta(shwi-weo-yo) to be easy 쉽다(쉬워요)
shyam-p'e-in champagne 샴페인

shyam-p'u shampoo 샴푸

shyeo-t'eul-beo-seu shuttle bus 셔틀버스

shyo-p'ing-mol shopping mall 쇼핑몰

so-gae-ha-da(hae-yo) recommend/introduce 소개하다(해요)

so-geum salt 소금

so-got underwear 속옷

so-hwa-pul-lyang indigestion 소화불량

so-ju soju (sweet potato wine) 소주

so-mae retail 소매

son hand 손

song-byeol-hoe farewell party 송별회

son-kka-rak finger 손가락

son-mok wrist 손목

son-mok shi-gye wristwatch 손목 시계

son-su-geon handkerchief 손수건

son-su-re pushcart 손수레

son-t'op nail (finger) 손톱

son-t'op-jjul emery boards 손톱줄

son-t'op ka-wi scissors (nail) 손톱 가위

son-t'op-kka-kki nail clipper 손톱깎기

son-t'op ta-deum-neun chul nail file 손톱 다듬는 줄

so-p'eu-t'eu k'on-t'aek-t'eu ren-jeu soft contact lens 소프트 콘택트 렌즈

so-p'o parcel 소포

so-yeom-je decongestant 소염제

su-bak watermelon 수박

su-ch'eop notebook (pocket) 수첩

su-do capital 수도

su-go-ha-da(hae-yo) to work hard 수고하다(해요)

Su-go-ha-shyeo-sseo-yo. Thank you. 수고하셨어요.

su-gong-ye-p'um handicrafts 수공예품

su-gu water polo 수구

su-ha-mul(shin-go) baggage claim 수하물(신고)

_____-hal su-it-tta(i-sseo-yo) can (be able to) _____ 할 수있다(있어요)

su-jeong-gwa persimmon punch 수정과

su-je-p'um hand made 수제품

suk-ppak-ppi lodging cost 숙박비

su-kka-rak spoon 숟가락

sul-jjip drinking establishment 술집

su-myeon-je sleeping pills 수면제

sup forest 숲

su-p'eo-ma-k'et supermarket 수퍼마켓

su-p'yo check (money) 수표

su-san-mul shi-jang fish market 수산물 시장

su-shin-in chi-bul cheon-hwa collect call 수신인 지불 전화

su-yeom beard 수염

su-yeong-bok swimsuit 수영복

su-yeong-ha-da(hae-yo) to swim 수영하다(해요)

su-yeong-jang swimming pool 수영장

su-yo-il Wednesday 수요일

SS

ssa-da(ssa-yo) to be inexpensive/cheap 싸다 (싸요)

ssa-i-jeu size 싸이즈

ssa-in-ha-da(hae-yo) to sign 싸인하다(해요)

ssal rice (uncooked) 쌀

ssal-ssal-ha-da(hae-yo) to be cool 쌀쌀하다(해요)

sseu-da(*sseo-yo*) to use 쓰다 (써요)

_____**-sshi** Mr./Mrs./Ms./Miss _____ 씨

sshi-di p'eul-le-i-eo CD player 씨디 플레이어

sshing-k'eu-dae sink 씽크대

sshi-reum wrestling (traditional Korean) 씨름

sso-i-da(*sso-yeo-yo*) to receive a sting 쏘이다 (쏘여요)

T

ta-ch'i-da(*ta-ch'yeo-yo*) to be injured 다치다 (다쳐요)

ta-deum-tta(*ta-deu-meo-yo*) to trim 다듬다 (다듬어요)

tae-ch'u-ch'a jujube tea 대추차

tae-dan-hi/a-ju very much 대단히/아주

tae-hak-kkyo university 대학교

Tae-han-min-guk South Korea (Republic of Korea) 대한민국

tae-jung-ga-yo folk songs 대중가요

Tae-man Taiwan 대만

tae-na-mu bamboo 대나무

tae-sa-gwan embassy 대사관

ta-eum next 다음

ta-i-a-mon-deu diamond 다이아몬드

ta-i-bing diving 다이빙

tak-kko-gi chicken 닭고기

takk-tta(*ta-kka-yo*) to polish 닦다 (닦아요)

tal month 달

tal-da(*ta-ra-yo*) to be sweet 달다 (달아요)

tam-bae cigarette 담배

tam-bae-ka-ge tobacco shop 담배가게

tan-ch'u button 단추

tan-gol favorite place (where one is a regular customer) 단골

tan-gol-son-nim regular customer 단골손님

tang-jang immediately 당장

tan-p'ung fall colors 단풍

ta-reu-da(*tal-la-yo*) to be different 다르다 (달라요)

ta-ri bridge 다리

ta-ri leg 다리

ta-ri-da(*ta-ryeo-yo*) to iron 다리다 (다려요)

ta-ri-mi iron 다리미

ta-shi again 다시

tat-tta(*ta-da-yo*) to close 닫다 (닫아요)

teo cho-t'a(*cho-a-yo*) to be better 더 좋다 (좋아요)

teop-tta(*teo-weo-yo*) to be hot 덥다 (더워요)

teo-reop-tta(*teo-reo-weo-yo*) to be dirty 더럽다 (더러워요)

te-seu-k'eu-t'ap k'eom-p'yu-t'eo desktop computer 데스크탑 컴퓨터

teul-da(*teu-reo-yo*) to carry 들다 (들어요)

teul-p'an field 들판

teung back (body) 등

teu-ra-i-beo screwdriver 드라이버

teu-ra-i-k'eul-li-ning dry cleaning 드라이클리닝

teo-reo ka-da(*teu-reo ka-yo*) to go in 들어 가다 (들어 가요)

teu-reo o-da(*teu-reo wa-yo*) to come in 들어 오다 (들어와요)

teu-re-sseu dress 드레스

teu-ri-da(*teu-ryeo-yo*) to give (honorific) 드리다 (드려요)

teut-tta(*teu-reo-yo*) to listen 듣다 (들어요)

ti-bi-di pang DVD room 디비디 방

ti-bi-di p'eul-le-i-eo DVD player 디비디 플레이어

ti-jel/kyeong-yu diesel 디젤/경유

ti-jeo-t'eu dessert 디저트

to also 도

to province 도

to-ch'ak-k'a-da(k'ae-yo) to arrive 도착하다(해요)

to-ch'ak-kku arrival gate 도착구

to-ch'eong so-jae-ji provincial capital 도청 소재지

toe-da(twae-yo) to become/be ready 되다(돼요)

_____ *-do twae-da(toe-yo)* to be all right to _____ 도 되다(되요)

teon-jang-jji-gae stew (soy bean paste and vegetables) 된장찌개

To-gil Germany 독일

To-gil sa-ram German (person) 독일 사람

To-gi-reo German (lang.) 독일어

to-gu tool 도구

to-ja-gi ceramics/porcelain 도자기

tok-ppang single room 독방

to-mae wholesale 도매

ton money 돈

tong-an during 동안

tong-jjok east 동쪽

tong-mul-weon zoo 동물원

to-ra ka-shi-da(to-ra ka-shyeo-yo) to die (honorific) 돌아 가시다(돌아 가셔요)

to-ra-ji bellflower root 도라지

to-ra o-da(to-ra wa-yo) to return (v.i.) 돌아 오다 (돌아와요)

to-ro street 도로

to-ro chi-do road map 도로 지도

to-seo-gwan library 도서관

to-shi city 도시

to-shi-rak box lunch (Korean-style) 도시락

tot-jja-ri mat(straw) 돗자리

to-u-mi hostess/helper 도우미

to-wa chu-da(to-wa chweo-yo) to help 도와 주다

tu-bu bean curd 두부

tu-da(tu-eo-yo) to play (board games) 두다(두어요)

tu-t'ong headache 두통

tu-t'ong kam-gi head cold 두통 감기

twae-ji-go-gi pork 돼지고기

twi-ch'uk heel 뒤축

twi-e behind 뒤에

T'

t'a-bak-ssang bruise 타박상

t'a-da(t'a-yo) to take (as in transportation) 타다(타요)

T'ae-guk Thailand 태국

t'aek-shi taxi 택시

t'ae-kkweon-do martial arts (Korean) 태권도

t'ae-p'ung typhoon 태풍

T'ae-p'yeong-yang Pacific ocean 태평양

t'a-i-eo tire 타이어

T'a-i-mal Thai (lang.) 타이말

t'a-ip/seu-t'a-il type/style 타입/스타일

t'ak-kku table tennis 탁구

t'al-ch'um mask dance 탈춤

t'al-jji-myeon cotton 탈지면

t'am-p'on tampon 탐폰

t'a-ol/su-geon towel 타올/ 수건

t'ap-seung su-sok check-in (flight) 탑승 수속

t'e-i-beul table 테이블

t'em-p'eul seu-t'e-i p'eu-ro-geu-raem temple stay program 템플 스테이 프로그램

t'e-ni-seu tennis 테니스
t'e-ni-seu-hwa tennis shoes
테니스화
t'el-le-bi-jeon television
텔레비전
t'eul-li-da(t'eul-lyeo-yo) to be
wrong 틀리다 (틀려요)
t'im team 팀
t'i-nun-yak corn plasters
티눈약
t'ip/pong-sa-ryo tip/service
charge 팁/봉사료
t'i-shyeo-ch'eu tee shirt
티셔츠
t'i-shyu tissue 티슈
t'o-ma-t'o tomato 토마토
t'o-ma-t'o chyu-seu tomato
juice 토마토 쥬스
t'ong-gwan customs
inspection 통관
t'ong-haeng-geum-ji
curfew 통행금지
t'ong-no aisle 통로
t'ong-yeok-kkwan
interpreter 통역관
t'o-seu-t'eu toast 토스트
t'o-yo-il Saturday 토요일
t'wi-gi-da(t'wi-gyeo-yo) to
fry 튀기다 (튀겨요)

TT

ttal daughter 딸
ttal-gi strawberry 딸기
ttal-leo dollar 달러
ttam-bok sweat suit 땀복
ttang-k'ong peanuts 땅콩
tta-tteut-t'a-da(t'ae-yo) to be
warm 따뜻하다 (해요)
tteok rice cake 떡
tteo-reo-ji-da(tteo-reo-jyeo-yo) to fall off 떨어지다
(떨어져요)
tteo-reo-tteu-ri-da(tteo-reo-tteu-ryeo-yo) to drop
떨어뜨리다 (떨어뜨려요)
tteul courtyard 뜰

ttok-ppa-ro straight
(direction) 똑바로

U

u-bi raincoat 우비
u-ch'e-guk post office 우체국
u-ch'e-t'ong mailbox 우체통
um-ji-gi-da(um-ji-gyeo-yo)
to move 움직이다 (움직여요)
un-dong sports 운동
un-dong-jang stadium
운동장
un-dong seon-su athlete 운동
선수
un-jeon myeon-heo-jeung
driver's license 운전 면허증
un-jeon-su driver 운전수
u-p'yo stamp 우표
u-ri we 우리
u-san umbrella 우산
u-seung-ja champion 우승자
u-yu milk 우유

W

wa/gwa and 와/과
wae why 왜
wa-in wine (western) 와인
wa-i-shyeo-ch'eu shirt
와이셔츠
wang king 왕
wang-bok round-trip 왕복
wan-ha-je/pyeon-bi-yak
laxative 완하제/변비약
we-i-beu-ji-da(jyeo-yo) to
be wavy (hair) 웨이브지다
(져요)
weon won (Korean currency)
원
weon-ha-da(hae-yo) to want
원하다 (해요)
weo-ryo-il Monday 월요일
woe-t'u overcoat 외투
wi(-ro) up 위(로)
wi-e on 위에

wi-gwe-yang ulcer (stomach) 위궤양

wi-seu-k'i whiskey 위스키

woe-guk sa-ram foreigner 외국 사람

woen-jjok left 왼쪽

Y

ya-ch'ae/ch'ae-so vegetables 야채/채소

ya-gu baseball 야구

ya-gu-jang baseball stadium 야구장

yak medicine 약

yak-kkuk pharmacy 약국

yak-k'a-da(k'ae-yo) to be weak 약하다 (해요)

yak-ssok/ye-yak appointment 약속/예약

yak-tto map (hand-drawn) 약도

yang-sang-ch'u lettuce 양상추

yang-bok-jjeom tailor 양복점

yang-gung archery 양궁

yang-hwa-jeom shoe store 양화점

yang-mal socks 양말

yang-p'a onion 양파

yang-shik Western-style food 양식

_____*-ya toe-da(twae-yo)* to have to _____ 야 되다 (돼요)

ye-bae religious service 예배

Yeo-bo-se-yo. Hello. (telephone) 여보세요.

yeo-gi here 여기

yeo-gwan inn 여관

yeo-haeng trip 여행

yeo-haeng-ha-da(hae-yo) to travel 여행하다 (해요)

yeo-haeng-ja su-p'yo travelers checks 여행자 수표

yeo-haeng-sa travel agency 여행사

yeo-haeng-yong al-lam-shi-gye travel alarm clock 여행용 알람시계

yeo-ja woman 여자

yeo-ja a-i girl 여자 아이

yeok station 역

yeok-sa history 역사

yeok-tto weightlifting 역도

yeo-kkweon passport 여권

yeol-ch'a/ki-ch'a train 열차/기차

yeol-da(yeo-reo-yo) to open 열다 (열어요)

yeol-lak-k'a-da(k'ae-yo) to contact (communicate) 연락하다 (해요)

yeol-soe key 열쇠

yeom-saek color tint 염색

yeon-eo salmon 연어

Yeong-eo English(lang.) 영어

Yeong-eo-ja-mak English subtitles 영어자막

yeong-eop shi-gan business hours 영업 시간

yeon-geuk play(drama) 연극

Yeong-guk England 영국

Yeong-guk sa-ram British(person) 영국 사람

Yeong-guk tae-sa-gwan British Embassy 영국 대사관

Yeong-han sa-jeon English-Korean dictionary 영한 사전

yeong-hwa movie 영화

Yeong-jja shin-mun newspaper (English language) 영자 신문

yeong-su-jeung receipt 영수증

yeon-ju-ha-da(hae-yo) to play(concert) 연주하다 (해요)

yeon-ju-hoe concert 연주회

yeon-mot pond 연못

yeon-p'il pencil 연필

yeon-se age (honorific) 연세

yeon-sok mu-ni print (pattern) 연속 무늬

yeop-sseo postcard 엽서

yeo-p'e beside 옆에

yeo-reo-bun you (plural, honorific) 여러분

yeo-reum summer 여름

yeo-ri it-tta(i-sseo-yo) to have fever 열이 있다 (있어요)

yeo-wang/wang-bi queen 여왕/왕비

ye-ppeu-da(ye-ppeo-yo) to be pretty 예쁘다(예뻐요)

ye-yak reservation 예약

yo mattress (Korean-style) 요

yo-geum fare/fee 요금

yo-jeu-eum nowadays 요즈음

yong-gu/ki-gu equipment 용구/기구

yo-ri-ha-da(hae-yo) to cook (v.t.) 요리하다(해요)

yo-t'eu-t'a-gi yachting 요트타기

yu-do judo 유도

yuk-ssang track and field 육상

yu-myeong-ha-da(hae-yo) to be famous 유명하다(해요)

yu-ri glass (window) 유리

yu-t'ae-gyo hoe-dang synagogue 유태교 회당

yu-weol June 유월